In Search of the Sacred

Anthropology and the Study
of Religions

Clinton Bennett

CASSELL

Cassell
Wellington House
125 Strand
London
WC2R 0BB

215 Park Avenue South
New York, New York
10003

First published in 1996

British Library Cataloguing in Publication Data
A catalogue record for this book is available from the British Library.

ISBN 0 304 33681 5 (hardback)
    0 304 33682 3 (paperback)

Library of Congress Cataloging-in-Publication Data
Bennett, Clinton.
    In search of the sacred: anthopology and the study of religions
    Clinton Bennett.
        p. cm.
    Includes bibliographical references and index.
    ISBN 0-304-33681-5.—ISBN 0-304-33682-3
    1. Ethnology–Religious aspects. 2. Religion—Study and
teaching. 3. Religions–Study and teaching. I. Title.
BL256.B44 1996
306.6—dc20   95-38602
                                                            CIP

Typeset by BookEns Limited, Royston, Hertfordshire
Printed and bound in Great Britain by Redwood Books, Trowbridge, Wiltshire

Contents

Acknowledgements

Readers of this book will quickly become aware of my admiration for, and academic indebtedness to, the work of two North American scholars, respectively a student of religions and an anthropologist. The first, Wilfred Cantwell Smith, I have met; the second, Clifford Geertz I have not met. I acknowledge with gratitude the influence of both men on my own thought and writing. I hope they will approve of what follows. Geertz's latest book, however, *After the Fact: Two Countries, One Anthropologist* (Harvard University Press, 1995), appearing almost simultaneously with the completion of this text, has not been discussed in this work. Notices in any detail suggest that this book expresses pessimism about the future of anthropology as a 'much reduced science'. Having read the book, however, I think Geertz remains cautiously optimistic. My own book ends on a positive note. My indebtedness to other scholars – perhaps especially to Eric J. Sharpe and Brian Morris – will be obvious from my references to their work, and I would like to express appreciation for their invaluable contributions to this field of enquiry.

Early in the project, several colleagues encouraged me to persevere with my proposal: Dr Frank Whaling of Edinburgh University, Dr Kim Knott of Leeds University, Dr Eleanor Nesbitt of Warwick, Professor Peter Donovan of Massey University, New Zealand and Dr John Berthrong, my North American reader, from Boston University School of Theology (and a friend from various World Council of Churches' consultations). All these more than merit my thanks. Already, these colleagues are combining textual and historical, with ethnographic research, in their work, and have long encouraged their students to do so too. Here at Westminster College in Oxford, fellow members of our study of religions teaching team, who put up with my preoccupation during the writing of this book, have given me their support, advice and friendly criticism. My thanks go to Peggy Morgan, who commented in detail on my penultimate draft, to Dr Laurence Brown, Dr Anne Eyre and to Dr Elizabeth Harris, one of our research fellows, whose doctoral thesis I consulted for its analysis of T.W. Rhys David's scholarship. I must also thank Dr Bernard Farr, our Director of Research, for ensuring that my teaching schedule allowed time to write this book, and our Principal, the Revd Dr Kenneth Wilson, for appointing me to work in such a stimulating academic environment in the first place!

As I am pathologically incapable of proofreading my own work, several friends have scrutinized various drafts for me; I wish especially to thank Jane Barrington and Dr Justin Meggitt. Justin, another of our research fellows, also offered useful comments on my text. In a book about encounter and dialogue, it would be odd if I were to omit any acknowledgement of help from those whose traditions it is my job to study and teach. Naming names can be invidious but among many others I wish to thank Dr Zaki Badawi of the Muslim College, Ealing, Khurram Bashir of Birmingham Central Mosque, and all my friends at the Oxford Centre for Islamic Studies for their encouragement, and for receiving endless visits from my students. I must also express my gratitude to Jane Evans, my former editor at Pinter Publishers, for initially supporting my proposal, and to my current editor at Cassell Publishers, Janet Joyce, for seeing the project through to completion. Cassell are a very efficient and author-friendly publisher and it has been a pleasure to work with them on this project.

Various libraries have, of course, contributed to what follows by allowing me to use their facilities. Much of the initial research was completed whilst I was a visiting scholar at the Henry Martyn Institute of Islamic Studies, Hyderabad, India during Summer 1994. As well as using our own Library at Westminster College, I conducted research in the India Institute Library, Oxford, in the Tylor Library at the Institute of Social and Cultural Anthropology, Oxford, where I tried hard to check primary references to the 'founding fathers' in the classical texts, in the Bodleian Library, Oxford, in the Birmingham Central Library and in the Central Library of the Selly Oak Colleges, Birmingham, where I am an Associate Member of the Centre for the Study of Islam and Christian–Muslim Relations. I am also grateful to Professor Mary Douglas for her willingness to discuss her work with two of my students, and myself. Her Highgate verandah on a warm Spring day was an ideal venue for exploring anthropological themes.

This book's content largely arises from my teaching, and aims to contribute to the future development of our programmes as well as to those of other institutions. Thus, since they have had to endure lectures on which some of this material is based, or have had to read open learning units in which I have tested some of my ideas, I conclude by dedicating this book to my students, past and present, residential and non-residential. What makes academic life such a wonderful privilege is interaction with other enquiring minds, full of questions which demand if not answers, then at least clarification and careful thought.

Clinton Bennett
The Vestry Study
Westminster College
Oxford OX2 9AT

Introduction

This book arises out of my teaching and research interests at Westminster College, Oxford. When I was appointed to my present post (in September, 1992) I joined an increasingly multidisciplinary team within the field of the study of religions. Although primarily trained as an Islamicist, my brief was to contribute an anthropological approach to the study of religions programme. Following current trends in the academic study of religions, Westminster was putting in place staff who would combine specialist knowledge of one or more religion with a distinctive methodological perspective. Our team now comprises a phenomenologist of religion, a sociologist and a psychologist, in addition to myself. Thus, our teaching team aims to fulfil the second task which Gerardus van der Leeuw (1890–1950) set for the study of religions at the Amsterdam Congress for the Study of the History of Religions (1950): to maintain 'contact with other branches of learning, such as philosophy, archaeology, anthropology, psychology and sociology', whilst our location within a school of theology places us in a good position to fulfil his first task: 'a friendly relationship between history of religions and theology' (cited in Kitagawa, 1959: 25). My own first degree was in theology. Ordained in 1978, I remain an accredited minister of my denomination. Similarly, writing more recently about the task of the student of religions, Garry Trompf, who teaches religious studies in the University of Sydney, remarks:

To do it properly requires more skills, or more hermeneutical (= interpretive) tools than most, if not all, other disciplines ... one is encouraged to turn over as many stones as possible to look at religions from as many different angles as possible – the psychological, anthropological,

1

sociological, geographical, ecological, political, economical and the like – with some awareness of current theological debates as well. (1990: 8)

Similarly, Jacob Neusner, in his inaugural lecture at Arizona State University, Tempe: 'I am certain that there is no discipline of the academic curriculum in humanistic or social studies which Religious Studies can afford to neglect' (1979: 6). Ninian Smart, first Professor of Religious Studies in the pioneering Lancaster department (UK), in his sevenfold scheme outlining 'what has been said or implied about the modern study of religions' writes: 'it is polymethodic: it uses many methods drawn from various disciplines – history, art history, philology, archaeology, sociology, anthropology, philosophy and so on' (1983: 16).

My anthropological *bona fides*

Thus, the student of religions calls many 'auxiliary disciplines' into service and, since 'few claim competence in all phases', most choose to 'concentrate on one or two of the auxiliary disciplines' (Kitagawa, 1959: 12). Hence our interdisciplinary team. However, unlike my sociologist and psychologist colleagues, who are trained in their respective disciplines, I am not a trained anthropologist, although I did attend lectures by an anthropologist whilst a student in the Selly Oak Colleges (1978–79) prior to three years service as a field missionary in Bangladesh. During that academic year I took the Certificate in the Study of Islam (University of Birmingham) through the Centre for the Study of Islam and Christian–Muslim Relations at the Selly Oak Colleges. This course placed much stress on encounter and dialogue so I did have some inkling of what it means to be a 'participant observer' (the dominant methodological technique in anthropological fieldwork) before I reached the subcontinent. There, I spent my first year in full-time language study. This is also the first requirement for anthropological fieldwork: 'The modern social anthropologist ... must know the local language sufficiently well to follow what is going on around him and to record it with accuracy and subtlety'. His aim is to 'immerse himself as thoroughly as he can in the life of the community he is trying to understand' (Lewis, 1992: 24). This was, in fact, the task I set myself as I continued to 'try to understand' Bangladeshi Islam, Bengali culture and life in general, first encountered amongst the Bangladeshi community in Birmingham. Unlike the professional anthropologist, though, I was perhaps not very systematic in my observing, nor in my recording (I didn't keep the requisite 'field diary', for example) yet the following description would not too inaccurately describe my own experience:

the anthropological research worker seeks to seize the essence of life around him and to incarnate its animating spirit. He dashes about from place to place and function to function endeavouring to record all aspects of the local scene, trivial as well as tragic. His range of interests is as large as life; births, marriages, animal husbandry, home-crafts, rhetoric, religion, cultivation, all claim his interest. The minimum required of the social anthropologist is that he should write the biography of the people he studies. (Lewis: 25)

I was particularly interested in observing evidence of Hindu influence on Islam in Bangladesh, and, whilst stationed in the north-west district of Rangpur, I also had the opportunity of witnessing how local animist traditions continued within the Christian villages. This intermingling of cultures, or syncretism – 'the combination or blending of different religious (or cultural) traditions' (Seymour-Smith, 1986: 274) – is a common concern of anthropologists. In retrospect, having subsequently studied more anthropological handbooks and texts, I find myself in a good position to reconstruct an albeit impressionistic biography of the people amongst whom I lived. As we shall see in a later chapter, Clifford Geertz, the leading American anthropologist, suggests that:

the ability of anthropologists to get us to take what they say seriously has less to do with either a factual look or an air of conceptual elegance than it has to do with their capacity to convince us that what they say is a result of their having actually penetrated (or, if you prefer, been penetrated by) another form of life, of having, one way or another, truly 'been there'. (1988: 5f.)

Geertz himself, in much of his writing, unashamedly draws on literature, art and history, as well as on the social sciences, to inform his own quite often impressionistic accounts, or sketches. Geertz's initial degree was in literature and philosophy. His *Islam Observed: Religious Development in Morocco and Indonesia*, for example, begins thus: 'bad poets borrow'; T.S. Eliot has said, 'good poets steal' (1968: v). Unlike his earlier books, especially *The Religion of Java* (1960) (his Harvard PhD thesis), *Islam Observed* does not systematically reproduce interview data, fieldwork notes and observations. Rather, as the dust cover says:

Geertz writes with clarity and charm on an immensely complicated and ambitious subject. His work is rooted in the comparative religious view of the fundamental and social theorists and their progenitors, but has a lucidity and persuasiveness that few of them have achieved. (citing Douglas E. Asford, *American Journal of Sociology*)

Later in this book, I shall suggest that the study of religions, too, can gain much from a less prosaic presentation of its subject matter. Travel writers and novelists may actually capture the essence of a belief or practice more poignantly than can an academic, factual description! To penetrate another language world, another world-view, to see through others' eyes, demands imagination. One reason, perhaps, why it is difficult to claim a purely scientific status for any subject in which the imagination plays a crucial role. This demands what Ninian Smart calls 'a process of structured empathy' or the crossing over of 'our own horizons into the worlds of other people' (1983: 16). 'It is', says Geertz, 'persuading us that this off-stage miracle has occurred, where the writing comes in' (1988: 5). Or, as one of my senior colleagues puts it, 'novelists do what phenomenologists and anthropologists think they do!' An excellent example of this genre, which we recommend to our students, is Heather Wood's *Third Class Ticket* (1980) which tells the story of the author's travels in India through the eyes of her fellow passengers. She travelled 15,000 kilometres over a period of seven months. In fact, it was anthropology that took Wood to India – she was working on a BLitt in Bengali anthropology.

After returning to the United Kingdom in 1983 to pursue my doctoral research in Islam and Christian–Muslim Relations at the University of Birmingham, I continued to immerse myself in Bangladeshi society. Again, my encounter was with an expatriate community which enabled me to observe how a culture and a religion copes with transplantation. This is another major concern of contemporary anthropologists. Also, having visited India regularly over recent years I have developed a particular interest in how Christianity in India is 'inculturating' (anthropologists tend to use 'acculturate') itself into Indian forms. I have included, at this stage, this brief resumé of my anthropological exploits, such as they are, to justify my appointment to our multidisciplinary team, and for writing a book on the interaction between anthropology and the study of religions. It may well be, though, that the most I can professionally claim for this book is what Geertz claims for much of his writing, that 'in so far as it is more than archival (a function of anthropology much underrated)' it is at least 'ethnographically informed (or, God knows, misinformed)' (1983: 5).

What is the study of religions?

The poly-methodological approach, which has become character-istic of the study of religions (and which our Westminster team represents), has stimulated debate about whether the study of religions is a discrete discipline in its own right, or a field of studies. As anthropologists, psychologists, sociologists and others may all study religion, are they students of religions, or 'primarily scholars of the discipline concerned, or both' asks Frank Whaling (1984a: 1: 24). On the one hand, some social scientists have questioned the 'integrity of *Religionswissentschaft* ... as an academic discipline' (Kitagawa, 1959: 5) usually by impugning its objectivity; on the other hand, Ninian Smart, who has often addressed methodological issues in his writing, comments that, 'there seems no intrinsic reason why the history of religions and the sociology and anthropology of religion should not be treated as a single, investigatory enterprise' (1984: 372). It becomes difficult, for example, to classify Clifford Geertz as an anthropologist with an interest in religion, and not as a *bona fide* student of religions (even though he holds his chair in social science). However, as Smart observes, whilst the distinction between these various disciplines is 'somewhat artificial', they do 'create one advantage ... the institutionalization of differing approaches leads to effective intellectual lobbies against the neglect of certain areas' (*ibid.*:

373). Frank Whaling concludes that, whilst anthropologists and sociologists usually study 'only one religion, or only one "aspect" of a religion … a specific theme or a specific society', students of religions study religions in their totality. Whaling also describes the study of religions as,

primarily the study of man, rather than the study of nature, or the study of transcendence – even though it retains an interest in man's view of nature, and man's views of transcendence (1984a: 1: 441).

This again highlights the close relationship between the two disciplines. Similarly, Wilfred Cantwell Smith writes: 'In comparative religion, man is studying himself. The fact of religious diversity is a human phenomena, common to us all' (1959: 55). Again, the study of religions is seen to be closely allied with the 'study of man', that is, with anthropology. Incidentally, there is no agreement amongst my own colleagues about whether the study of religions is a field or a discipline in its own right. My own view is that, whilst always drawing on other disciplines, the study of religions does have its own academic integrity – as a discrete discipline. The recent survey, *Religious Studies: The Making of a Discipline* (1995) by Walter H. Capps, shares this view.

What I set out to explore in this book, therefore, is the cross-fertilization which has occurred (and which continues to occur) between these two closely related disciplines. I especially focus on ideological and methodological convergence and divergence between the two, demonstrating how their methodological and philosophical assumptions, research techniques, interests and agendas have critically interacted. A study of this interaction is, I believe, long overdue. Several books examine anthropological approaches to the study of religions, especially its search for the origin of human religiosity. Garry Trompf's *In Search of Origins* (1990), for example, deals mainly with anthropological, or with anthropologically inspired, theories. The often reprinted anthology, *A Reader in Comparative Religion: An Anthropological Approach* (1979) edited by W.A. Lessa and E.Z. Vogt contains numerous monographs dealing mainly with aspects of tribal religion, which – proving Smart's point – have often been neglected by students of religions who tend to focus on the so-called world religions. This anthology includes extracts from the writing of many anthropologists whose contributions we discuss in this book: amongst others Tylor, Frazer, Geertz, Leach. These represent important contributions. From Africa comes *Expressing the Sacred: An Introduction to the Phenomenology of Religion* (1992) by James L. Cox. However, whilst this clearly and usefully focuses on methodology, and refers *en passant* to significant anthropologists, it fails to identify them as anthropologists! Similarly, Sharpe's *Comparative Religion: A History* (second edition 1986) shows, by its frequent references to anthropologists, how anthropology has assisted and influenced the development of the scientific study of religions. Waardenburg's impressive *Classical Approaches to the Study of Religion* (1973) includes biographical sketches of, and extracts from, eminent anthropologists. As a source of primary texts, it makes a good companion to my own survey. The best discussion of anthropological theories of religion is Brian Morris' *Anthropological Studies of Religion* (1987), which has been described as 'an invaluable guide to the writings on religion of all the major figures in anthropology' (back cover). That the book is 'indispensable for all students of anthropology and of the social sciences generally as well as for those interested in comparative religion' is, I think, no exaggeration. However, none of these writers, including Morris, attempt to place the development of the study of religions, its assumptions, agendas, methodological techniques, alongside those of anthropology with a view to systematically examining their interaction as an aid to teaching and studying religions today. This has occupied much of my time at Westminster, and forms the subject matter of this book. Whilst what follows does not even pretend to cover everything that has preoccupied the two disciplines since their inception, it does aim to discuss some of their main themes, issues, problematics, and personalities. Although I have tried, wherever possible, to use primary sources I have also turned to the works of those who have spent more time than I have wrestling with the contributions of my subjects. Where I am more indebted to these scholars than to primary sources will, I hope, be clear from my text. Anyone interested in anthropology *per se*, or in the study of religions *per se*, should also familiarize themselves with some basic introductory texts. It may be invidious to offer a recommendation, but for the former I recommend I.M. Lewis' *Social Anthropology in Perspective* (second edition, 1992), for the latter, Eric J. Sharpe's *Understanding Religion* (1983).

Even though my own preference is to regard the study of religions as a discrete discipline, the fact remains that it is often taught as a sub-branch of theology; debate also continues about whether it properly belongs within the social sciences, within the liberal arts, or within humanities. In fact, departments of religion, of religious studies, of comparative religion or of the study of (or history of) religions will be found located in all these faculties (and sometimes in philosophy as well). It varies from university to university. Of all fields of study, this has perhaps had the greatest difficulty finding a name for itself. Fashions change, and what was once understood as 'comparative religion' is now more commonly known either as religious studies or as the study of religions. As we shall see, this is because some of the presuppositions of the 'comparative method' used in the first phase of scholarship in this field were later discredited. In this book, since my own teaching at Westminster College is within a 'study of religions' strand, I use this designation. However, where I cite from writers who use 'comparative religion' (Wilfred Cantwell Smith prefers this term, for example) or 'religious studies' they are, at least in my reckoning, alternatives to my preferred term. Some of the different implications of the various names by which the field is, or has been, known will be discussed elsewhere in this book. The discipline's academic or faculty location is not a question which will concern us very much in this book, although the premium which I myself place on imagination perhaps suggests that I veer towards placing my subject within the liberal arts. We shall see, too, that anthropology has had a similar debate.

Theology and the study of religions

Generally, the study of religions has been anxious to differentiate itself from theology (albeit also, as we have already noted, keen to maintain close links with theology, even sometimes to broaden the remit of that discipline). Eric J. Sharpe discusses the relationship between theology and religious studies in his *Understanding Religion* (1983). 'Theology', he suggests, is normally able to assume that students hold a secure place within the tradition being studied, while religious studies is able to assume only that the student wishes to grasp something of the role of the religion as an aspect of life, and is prepared in pursuit of this quest to turn to cultural areas remote from his own. (1983: 16)

Earlier, Joachim Wach of Chicago University (1898–1955) suggested that theology is 'a normative discipline ... concerned with the analysis, interpretation, and exposition of one particular faith' whilst 'the general science of religion' is 'essentially descriptive, aiming to understand the nature of all religions' (1944: 1). As we shall see, the pioneers of the academic study of religions (who certainly claimed scientific status) wanted to break away from the polemical, apologetical, or philosophical brief of earlier writers on the religions, whose aim was often to assert the superiority of the Christian religion over and against all others. Description was to take the place of evaluation. More recently, Julius Lipner of Cambridge University, also addressing the distinction between theology and religious studies, writes:

Religious studies I take to be the understanding, and then the expounding of this understanding, of the various kinds of religious phenomena (doctrines, beliefs, texts, institutions, forms of worship, etc.) and their interplay. Here, one does not seek to determine enduring truth and value; one's aim is primarily to explain and classify, one applies the so-called phenomenological epoche in respect of the religious commitment one may (or may not!) have, together with those canons of 'objective' academic inquiry which are generally regarded to be conducive to as faithful an interpretation of the available data as possible. (1983: 200)

In Chapter 5, we shall return to this discussion about the relationship between the study of religions and theology, arguing for a different understanding from the distinction drawn by Lipner.

Our next chapter traces the emergence of the study of religions in the late nineteenth century. It was, as we shall see, very much a product of Romanticism and of the Enlightenment. It claimed to be 'value-free' but actually brought many ideological presuppositions to bear on its subject. This was paralleled by anthropology; also a product of the Enlightenment, and supposedly value free, anthropology applied its own preconceptions to the study of mankind. As

Hendrik Kraemer (1888–1965), for many years Professor of the History of Religion at Leiden, observed:

In its infancy, the Science of Religion operated consciously or unconsciously – the last case is the most difficult to get to terms with – on the assumption that it was purely objective, scientific, an assumption which was pervaded by a sincere longing for truth and at the same time oblivious of the problematics implied in the matter of objective truth. Like all sciences in the human field, the Science of Religion was born out of a very definite life-situation, a fact which is nearly always forgotten, as most people treat it as if it had been born of a neutral vacuum. This life-situation was the emancipation from unquestionable and dogmatic thinking and the confidence that reason would be able to master all the problems and remove all mysteries. (1956: 45)

We visit this 'life-situation' in much more detail in Chapter 1. Another problematic, almost as difficult as finding a name for the discipline, is the question of identifying its subject matter. In the following pages, we shall visit many different definitions of religion, some contradictory. As we shall see, anthropology and the social sciences have often preferred 'reductionist definitions' which explain religion as something other than religion: for example, as the result of human neurosis, or of ignorance, or as a product or creation of society. Whilst aiming to avoid what Lipner describes as 'value judgements in the course of' their work about 'which religious response, or part thereof, is better or worse, more or less adequate, for human living in the light of the transcendent', many students of religions have yet argued that the transcendent and the sacred (or holy) do exist as (*a priori*) categories in themselves, and cannot be explained away as something else. Thus, Mircea Eliade (1907–86) wrote:

To try to grasp the essence of such a phenomenon [religion] by means of physiology, psychology, sociology, economics, linguistics, art or any other study is false; it misses the one unique, and irreducible element in it – the element of the sacred. (cited in Kitagawa, 1959: 21)

Therefore, whilst remaining 'faithful to descriptive principles' the study of religions directs its enquiry to 'the meaning of religious phenomena' (*ibid.*: 21). Of course, terms such as 'reductionist' and 'non-reductionist' definitions of religions are not value-free, so perhaps good social scientists should avoid their use. However, the former does usefully distinguish definitions which religious people, generally, find acceptable from those which they usually consider inadequate, or wrong, so in a book concerned with insiders' perspectives these terms may have their place. Since both students of religions and anthropologists have found the concept of the sacred useful, whether understood as a human concept or as something which exists in and of itself, *In Search of the Sacred* suggested itself as an appropriate title for this comparative survey.

Anthropology's subject matter

For its part, anthropology has had less difficulty distinguishing itself as a discrete social, scientific discipline (although it, too, may be located in various faculties). However, given that the modern sociologist and other social scientists now employ, quite often, the methodological techniques which were pioneered by anthropology, it, too, is not without its identity crisis. As Whitten and Hunter put it, currently, 'the field is struggling with many fundamental questions about its very nature and its future as a social science is not certain' (1993: vii). Despite such debate, and its traditional subdivision into psychological, archaeological, cultural, social (and sometimes also into physical) anthropology, as the science of man, anthropology's subject matter is reasonably self-evident. One useful way of distinguishing between these subdivisions is to regard social anthropology as concerned with human relationships, cultural with what men/women make or produce, psychological with what they think, and archaeological with the study of human remains. Physical anthropology has its roots in nineteenth-century craniology, which measured the head sizes of different racial groups and compared them. An issue which attracted much discussion was whether all people sprang from common progenitors or from many. Many ascribed 'to their own stock superior mental abilities' (1993: 4). Whilst the racist overtones of this are obvious, physical (sometimes called biological) anthropology today remains interested in the variations of appearance between different ethnic groups. The search for the 'missing link' was another quest that has occupied both archaeological and physical anthropologists. Early anthropologists were also much concerned with the classification and distribution of races.

I should protect myself, at this point, from possible criticism; in this survey, I tend to ride roughshod over the distinctions between anthropology's subdivisions. However, since I shall focus on fieldwork methodology, which does not differ overmuch across the social, cultural and psychological sub-branches, which are the three on which we draw, this somewhat cavalier attitude is, I believe, not unjustified. Lewis, in fact, suggests that the distinction between 'social anthropology' and 'cultural anthropology', at least, is nowadays somewhat arbitrary; they are, he says, 'two sides of the same coin' – 'one treats culture as a medium for social relations (or, sometimes, as their content) while the other treats society as a display of culture' (1992: 380–1). I should also mention here the distinction, or lack of it, between anthropology and ethnography. The first refers, technically, to the general science of man (or of humankind), the second to the study of particular groups. Consequently, ethnography is often used as a 'doing word' (what one does in the field), whilst anthropology is used to describe thinking about human life generally. However, both Lewis and Levi-Strauss consider that social anthropology, and what is usually called ethnography in non-English-speaking countries, are actually the same, 'in Anglo-Saxon countries ... the term ethnography has become obsolete – as social and cultural anthropology' (Levi-Strauss: 2, see also pp. 356–9; Lewis: 37n). Levi-Strauss also calls ethnography and anthropology different 'moments in time' in 'the same line of investigation' (*ibid.*: 356). Also, as we shall see in this survey, since anthropologists have, on the whole, expressed caution before moving beyond the study of particular people towards drawing any general scientific principles about human life universally, 'the traditional distinction between ethnography and anthropology' may be 'spurious' (Seymour-Smith: 99). In other words, all ethnography is anthropology and all anthropology is ethnography!

The study of religions' subject matter

As I have already suggested, the subject matter of the study of religions, for its part, is much more difficult to pinpoint. Religion has proved itself remarkably elusive of a definitive definition. Kraemer put it like this: 'religion ... is perhaps the most elusive, intriguing and difficult subject for scientific treatment' (*op. cit.* 37). Geertz writes: 'The comparative study of religion has always been plagued by this peculiar embarrassment; the elusiveness of its subject matter' (1968: 1). Eric Sharpe devoted a chapter of his *Understanding Religion* to 'The Question of Definition'. After addressing some significant attempts to define what religion is (most of which we shall discuss in this book), he concludes:

Definitions of religion, in a sense, remind one of the fable of the blind men attempting to define an elephant. One touches its trunk and describes it as a snake; another touches its ear and describes it as a winnowing-fan; another touches its leg and describes it as a tree; another its tail and describes it as a broom. (1983: 46)

Nevertheless, says Sharpe, most of us can actually recognize a religion when we 'see' one, since, unlike the men in the fable, we are not 'blind'. We know, for example, that religions tend to possess books, to have histories, rituals, buildings, which can be read, studied, observed or visited. We can at least recognize these as products of religiosity when we encounter them. Thus, says Sharpe, 'to define religion is ... far less important than to possess the ability to recognise it when we come across it', whilst 'to impose an inadequate or one-sided definition may well lead to a refusal to acknowledge whatever does not appear to conform to that definition' (*ibid.*: 47). For example, any definition of religion which includes 'belief in God' disqualifies non-theistic traditions, such as Buddhism and Advaita Vedanta Hinduism. I find, for example, that some of my students who hold to this definition are reluctant to concede that Buddhism is a religion, and not a philosophy of life. Given the problematic of identifying a sufficiently inclusive definition, Sharpe and others have instead identified various characteristics, or dimensions, which we might expect to 'recognize' when we 'see' a religion. These also provide useful schemes of ideas to facilitate the systematic study of each religion. The scheme which I find most useful (and often employ in my teaching) is the one proposed by Frank Whaling of Edinburgh University. It is worth quoting this at some length in order to convey the flavour of this framework, or model (we shall discuss other models in Chapter 3):

In the first place, all the major religious traditions of the world contain eight inter-linked elements. The major religions are dynamic organisms within which there are eight interacting dimensions; they are historical chains within which there are eight connecting links. The eight links are those of religious community, ritual, ethics, social involvement, scripture/myth, concepts, aesthetics, and spirituality. All major religions have some sort of religious community, they all engage in different forms of worship, lying behind them all are certain ethical norms, they are all involved in social and political outreach within the wider community, sacred texts and myths are important for them all, they all emphasise particular clusters of doctrines, they all produce religious art and sculpture, and they all infer distinctive modes of spirituality. In other words there are eight common elements within the great world religions and it is a great help to be aware of this for they provide pegs upon which knowledge can be hung. (1986: 38)

Finally, Whaling suggests that behind all major religions lies some apprehension of the transcendent, or of ultimate reality. It will be useful to bear this schema in mind as we pursue our comparative survey. Whilst it does not claim to define religion it does help us identify what anthropologists and students of religion actually do study! At different times, though, different aspects (or elements) of religion have commanded more attention. For example, in the early days of the discipline (if discipline it is – and not a field of study!) scriptures and histories provided the main subject matter. Later, as concern for living religions, for religions as lived and practised today, became of interest, more attention was paid to worship and to rituals. Focusing more on believers as the providers of information about their own beliefs and practices than on texts, this brought the subject matter of study of religions much closer to that of social and cultural anthropology. Later still, as the inner faith, the existential experience of religious believers became an acceptable focus, spirituality (in as much as it can be studied) came under closer scrutiny. This brings us closer to the subject matter of psychological anthropology. This focus on people and on practice also enabled the study of popular, rather than of 'official' expressions of religiosity.

Another possible definition of religion should be mentioned. Richard Gombrich, whose work in Sri Lanka will be discussed in Chapter 4, discussing whether Buddhism is, or is not, a religion, prefers, 'to leave the definition of religion to the practitioners themselves. Sinhalese Buddhists', he says, 'call Buddhism (*Buddhagama*) a religion (*agama*), so I will not gainsay them'. Similarly, he 'would allow that there' is 'a religion wherever a group claimed *bona fide* that it had one' (1971: 9). Gombrich also describes how, when a new school textbook appeared in Colombo (1965) which stated on its first page, 'The Buddhist religion is not a religion' (a result of Western influence), a political storm ensued; Marxists had infiltrated the Ministry of Education and the book 'was part of their campaign to abolish Buddhism' (*ibid.*: 63). I also incline towards the view that what people themselves define as religion qualifies as religion. This definition has the advantage of avoiding the type of value judgement implied by a term such as 'cult', which some scholars apply to some religious groups. Similarly, I prefer to describe different substrands within traditions as 'schools' or 'movements' rather than as 'sects', which also carries a negative (heterodox) connotation. This, as we shall see, can be called a phenomenological approach; it is also a characteristic of the dialogical approach; 'One of the functions of dialogue,' says the World Council of Churches' *Guidelines*, 'is to allow participants to describe and witness to their faith in their own terms' (*Guidelines on Dialogue*, revised 1990: 17). *A priori* value judgements, or self-serving definitions which support preconceived views about a religion's (or religions') origin, must be 'bracketed out' (see Chapter 3 below).

Chapter 1 will explore in much more detail how our two disciplines were born during the post-Enlightenment period, when the widening of Europe's horizons enabled travellers and others to bring back tales of other cultures and faiths, together with texts and artefacts. In classifying and comparing these data collected from afar, and in translating the texts, the trend was to deduce universal theories about the origin of religion, or about the evolution of human civilization. This was known as the 'comparative approach'. This often also evaluated, placing religions and peoples on a higher, or lower, level of development. The European was usually, if not always, at the top of the scale. I shall also explore some of the common philosophical assumptions within our two fields. This phase of our survey is the one which has been most adequately covered by earlier scholars, such as Sharpe (1986), Morris (1987), Tambiah (1990), and I offer no excuse for drawing on their perceptive analyses of the contributions we review. What is new, I think, about my treatment is its emphasis on methodological convergence and divergence.

In Chapter 2 I shall suggest that, in the next phase of its development, anthropology diverged methodologically from the study of religions. Now, the anthropologists left their Victorian armchairs and took to the field, where they largely abandoned the comparative approach, whilst the students of religions remained text-bound. Their first phase lasted longer. Their emphasis was on constructing histories of religions, on identifying origins and on the development of classical dogmas. In contrast, the fieldworking anthropologists were somewhat 'hostile to history' (Evans-Pritchard, 1963: 1). I shall also refer to the two disciplines' struggle for academic recognition – albeit anthropology struggled less. Sir Edward Evan Evans-Pritchard (1902–73), in his *Theories of Primitive Religion* (1965), itself a useful survey, writing about the acknowledged founder of the study of religions, Max Müller (1823–1900), observed:

Müller was battling for the recognition of the languages and religions of India and China as important for an understanding of language and religion in general, a fight which it is true to say has yet to be won (where are the departments of comparative linguistics and comparative religion in this country?). (1965: 2)

Sharpe later commented about the general lack of interest in comparative religion at Manchester, 'its oldest stronghold in the country' ... 'in 1956–7 a "special course" mustered only three students, and before its end one third of the class had fallen by the wayside' (1986: 287). When I was a student there two decades later, special courses I attended in comparative religion only succeeded in mustering half a dozen students. However, they set me on the path which led to my teaching, and studying, religions.

Chapter 3 then argues for convergence in the next common phase of development. Now, the students of religions adopted the phenomenological approach, and also took to the field. Informed by anthropological writing on the religions, they became interested in practice as well as in precept. Scepticism developed about whether 'great traditions' could be studied at all, and students of religions began to share something of the anthropologists' reluctance to extrapolate from the particular to the universal. Certainly, traditions were now studied as independent entities and scholars became very reluctant to draw comparisons with other independent entities. The emphasis shifted from theory to fact. Interest in how faith convictions are translated into social, ethical, political involvement also emerged as major themes. Chapter 4 continues to explore this convergence, both of methodology and of subject matter, as the diversity, complexity and multifacetedness of religions replaced earlier notions of unitary traditions. Anthropological interest in 'small traditions', in local variations, added to the traditionally 'great tradition' subject matter of the study of religions. I shall discuss examples of cross-fertilization and, where appropriate, draw on my own fieldwork experience. Chapter 5 argues that, in their current phase, we can again identify convergence in the emphasis on cross-cultural hermeneutics, on aiding cultures in their understanding of other cultures and of other communities. People, rather than rites, texts and institutions become the main subject of interest and enquiry – as Wilfred Cantwell Smith puts it:

The externals of religion – symbols, institutions, doctrines, practices – can be examined separately ... but these things are not in themselves religion, which lies rather in the area of what these mean to those who are religious. The student is making effective progress when he recognises that he has to do not with religious systems basically but with religious persons; or at least with something interior to persons. (1959: 35)

I call this the 'go-between function'. Significantly, Clifford Geertz, who argues for 'cultural hermeneutics' as the primary anthropological task, interpreting 'them' to 'us' and 'us' to 'them', acknowledges the 'intellectual presence' in his writing of Wilfred Cantwell Smith. Geertz has spoken about the go-between function – anthropologists act as go-betweens ... for the people they study and the people they write for (Johnson, 1992: 150).

This chapter will also address several critiques of the West's scholarship of non-Western cultures. These will include Edward Sa'id on 'Orientalism', which, he says, represents 'a style for dominating, restructuring, and having authority over the Orient' (1978: 3), a feminist critique, and the so-called 'nativist' debate: should we only study, and write about, ourselves? A subtle critique of the social sciences has been offered by Michel Foucault, which we will also address. He saw the 'disciplines of modern social science as *disciplinary* in the literal sense' (Whitten and Hunter, 1993: 13). The social sciences, he says, 'objectify the poor, the alien, the insane' by positing a 'radical separation between observer and observed' (*ibid.*: 13). This, as we shall see, does not resonate at all with Geertz's approach, in which the observer must identify with the observed. Thus, my thesis is that text-based study of religions has yielded to interest in what people themselves think, feel, and do; observation has yielded to conversation, monologue to dialogue.

Chapter 6, by way of a conclusion, suggests that both disciplines, far from being of limited relevance for postmodern humanity, remain relevant (provided that the observers are liberated from their observation towers and rejoin the rest of the human race). As Whitten and Hunter argue for anthropology:

Perhaps the end of anthropology is not far off. But we doubt it ... of all the social sciences anthropology is best equipped to explore the fundamental questions of what it means to be human and what the study of human beings can contribute to solving the problems of our species and the world we inhabit. (*op. cit.* 8)

Similarly, Wilfred Cantwell Smith's understanding of the student's of religions task, to increase 'respect, learning and mutual insight between cultures' is, suggests Edward J. Hughes, essential 'if there is to be a future for our planet' (1986: 163). Perhaps controversially, I shall argue for an approach to scholarship of the religions which resembles the critical paradigm: aiming to 'smash myths and empower people to change society' (Neuman, 1994: 75). However, the main task of my concluding chapter will be to draw out some useful pointers from my comparative survey to assist students of religions today, especially as they pursue further research. I shall do this by outlining some ideas for projects and programmes.

1 Common Roots

In this chapter, we trace the origin of study of religions, and of anthropology, which – although not lacking antecedents – began as we know them today at about the same time. F. Max Müller coined the term 'scientific study of religion' in his *Chips from a German Workshop* (1867, 1884), and elaborated what he meant by this in more detail in his *Lectures on the Science of Religion* (1870) and in *Introduction to the Science of Religion* (1873). He also used the terms 'comparative religion' and 'comparative theology'. Also in 1873, Boston University appointed William Fairfield Warren as its first Professor of Comparative Theology and of the History and Philosophy of Religion. Müller himself never held a post in the study of religions but pursued his pioneering thought in this area as Oxford's Professor of Comparative Philology. It was through philology that Müller began to study religion. Just over a decade later, in 1884, Sir Edward Tylor (1832–1917) was appointed to the first university post in anthropology, at Oxford, although the Anthropological Institute had been established in 1871 (after 1907, the Royal Anthropological Institute). Thus, give or take a year or two, the two embryonic sciences were born at about the same time. Many of the presuppositions and assumptions which influenced the two infant disciplines, however, predate their birth; as Kraemer rightly comments, no 'science of man is born of a neutral vacuum', but rather 'of a very definite life-situation' (1956: 45). Below, we examine post-Enlightenment rationalism, empiricism, Victorian paternalism, the historical dialectic of Hegel, the positivism of Comte, Spencer (and others), and Romanticism as part of this intellectual milieu or life-situation. Perhaps 'strands of thought' might be a good description of these influences. Next, we discuss some of the main theories on religion proposed by the early pioneers, and the means by which they deduced these theories. In doing so, the presence of our strands of thought will be easily discernible. The first half of this chapter thus focuses on the intellectual background behind the work of Müller, Tylor and their colleagues, whilst the second half focuses on how they actually set about their respective tasks, as anthropologists or as students of religions. As already suggested, divergence of methodology will be argued during this initial phase of development. The disciplines were born, however, of similar stock.

Kraemer, in his analysis, identifies at least one 'parent' of the science of religion as 'Reason', our first intellectual strand:

Scientific methodical, critical investigation of religion as known in the last two centuries, its forms, its great manifestations and its frenzies, has in its decisive moments of birth and development always been a child of Reason, and has asserted the primary claim of the ratio to be the arbitrator and judge . . . . (1956: 36)

The age of discovery

Anthropology was born of the same parent. This confidence in reason, in human ability to decipher mysteries and to uncover secrets was itself a child of the Enlightenment, a by-product of the Age of Discovery. From the great discoveries of Columbus (1451–1506), of Magellan, (1440–1521), of the inland explorers and seafarers of the post-Enlightenment period onwards, information about other cultures, other peoples, other religions, began to reach Europe. Travellers, missionaries, sea captains, colonial adminis-trators, adventurers, even pirates and soldiers of fortune, all reported 'their impressions of the peoples they encountered' (Whitten and Hunter, 1993: 3). A vast amount of data was thus accumulated – descriptions of strange ceremonies, dress, deities, totems, exotic rituals and dances. Much of this was actually badly remembered, or misunderstood. Nevertheless, it fell into the hands of scholars who, naturally, began to classify and to categorize the data in 'a more or less systematic manner' (ibid.: 5). It was these sometimes amateur ethnographers, as they were usually called, who formed the Ethnological Society in 1843. The Royal Anthropological Institute, established, as noted above, in 1871 united the Ethnographical Society and its rival, the Anthropological Society (formed in 1863). Perhaps typical of the type of work produced by these pioneers was the *Natural History of the Varieties of Man* (1854) by Robert Gordon Latham (1812–88), an attempt to systematize the mass of anthropological data and reduce them into 'an orderly scheme' (Haddon, 1934: 105). *Natural History of Man* (1868) by John George Wood (1827–89) was an illustrated 'account of the manners and customs of the uncivilized races of man'. One question that concerned these writers was the origin of social organization, which later became the subject matter of the social sciences. For example, writing in 1857, Thomas Buckle (1821–62) asked, 'Are the actions of men, and therefore of societies governed by fixed laws, or are they the result either of chance or supernatural interference?' (*ibid.*: 108). Craniology, the attempt to classify peoples according to their head-sizes, has already been mentioned. Johan Friedrich Blumenbach (1752–1849), a German physician (often described as the father of physical anthropology) considered such divisions 'nothing more than artificial constructions in the service of science' but identified five 'races', Caucasian, Mongolian, Ethiopian (including other Africans), Malayan and American (*ibid.*: 4).

The age of empiricism

The Age of Discovery, though, was much more than a period of geographical exploration and imperial expansion. It was also an age of scientific progress. Isaac Newton (1642–1724) had deduced the laws of motion, whilst the influential philosopher, John Locke (1632–1704), the 'founder of English empiricism' had given people new confidence that human enquiry and investigation could make sense of the world and of life. This identifies our second intellectual strand – empiricism. Ever since the discoveries of Galileo Galilei (1564–1642) and his espousal of the Copernican theory, the authority of the old dogmas and explanations sanctioned by the Church had been called into question. Now, the age of the earth itself seemed to be much older than James Usher (1581–1656) had calculated. The archbishop had dated creation on 23 October 4004 BC, based on the evidence of the Bible. The thickness of geological strata in the earth's crust, and the 'nature of the mineral contents' of these strata demanded a much, much longer developmental process than Usher's dating allowed (Whitten and Hunter: 5). Only by pushing back the date of creation could all this be adequately explained. Also, even before Darwin and Lamarck had published their findings, the sheer variety of races seemed to challenge the biblical story of common progenitors in one man and one woman, Adam and Eve. This was another issue which occupied the minds of the pioneer anthropologists. They asked, was there a single act of creation, or several? Those who argued in favour of multiple creations, with its obvious implication that all people are not descendants of Adam and Eve, included 'many of the period's leading sceptics and intellectuals, such as Voltaire and David Hume' (ibid.: 4). Hume (1711–76) ridiculed belief in miracles, and, on an issue which directly concerns the theme of this book, argued that mankind's original religion had been polytheistic, not mono-theistic. Voltaire (1694–1778), 'the most widely known and read author of the Enlightenment' (Latourette, 1975: 2: 1004) was, of course, a professed secularist. He had no time for God. Humanity had now 'come of age', and no longer had need of a benevolent, but fictitious, divine protector. From now on, science

would not only provide knowledge of all there was in the world and in the mind, and of how it worked, [it] would also tell men what their natures – part of the vast harmonious whole called 'nature' – needed, how to obtain it by the most painless and efficient means, and therefore how to be wise, rational, happy and good. (Berlin, 1956: 114)

Humanity could bid farewell to the Church, to revelation from above, to outmoded dogmas and beliefs. The theological 'age of fiction' had given way to the scientific or positive stage. We shall return to positivism below when we visit the contribution of the first social scientists. Some, the Deists, did not go quite so far as Voltaire. However, their God had merely created the world. After that cataclysmic event, God ceased to interfere. This ruled out revelation and elevated reason, logic and empirical enquiry to the status of free agents.

Before leaving the debate about a single or multiple beginning, attention should be drawn to how some of the polygenists (supporters of the multi-creation theory) applied their theory. Many concluded that, since not all races were of a common stock, some were superior to others. Georg Wilhelm Hegel (1770–1831), whose thought we discuss below, probably never saw an African and certainly never visited Africa, but wrote:

[the negro] exhibits the natural man in his completely wild and untamed state. There is nothing harmonious with humanity in this type of character. At this point we quit Africa, not to mention it again; for Africa is no historical part of the world. What we properly understand by Africa is the unhistorical, undeveloped spirit, still involved in the conditions of mere nature. (cited in Davidson, 1984: 16)

James Hunt (1833–69), in 1863, declared:

that the Negro is a different species from the European; that the analogies are far more numerous between the Negro and the ape than between the European and the ape; that the Negro is inferior intellectually to the European; that the Negro race can only be humanized and civilized by Europeans. (Haddon, 1934 : 45)

In 1900, in a book published in the United States, Charles Carroll argued that black people were beasts, not humans: 'The Negro is a beast, but created with articulate speech and hands, that may be of service to his master – the White man' (*ibid.*). Sadly, there is no shortage of quotes to further illustrate this point. Obviously, what this amounted to was an all too convenient mandate for the slave trade, for the conquest and subjugation of inferior species. The Portuguese in the Americas could even argue that, since the Indians weren't mentioned in the Bible, they didn't have souls. The idea, too, of racial characteristics by which the various groups were distinguished, easily resulted in racial stereotyping – all blacks are strong but backward, all Asians clever but dishonest, all Europeans rational and progressive.

Either such apparently primitive people were inferior, or they had somehow slipped back down the ladder of civilization. The not too complimentary term 'reverts' was coined by some anthropologists to describe such peoples. Some might even be the 'missing link'. Thus, the birth of anthropology in Europe coincided with what seemed to be an age of great technological and scientific progress. In comparison, other cultures and peoples appeared primitive. That, at least, is how they were conveniently perceived. It has, however, been convincingly argued that the technological and intellectual gap between Europe and Africa, when sustained contact first began, was more potential than actual (Davidson: 132). Yet this perception of backwardness all too easily resulted in Europeans believing that they were, indeed, more advanced than others.

Victorian paternalism

Another assumption, which also served to encourage this view, arose from the social and political context, at least in Britain. This was hierarchical. The ruling class were natural leaders, the working class natural workers. This social pattern, which was thought to be almost organic, has been described as Victorian paternalism, and identifies our third intellectual strand – 'the English ruling class's assumption that it was organically superior to the working class' (Bennett, 1992: 105). Given the hierarchical nature of Victorian society, it was easy to argue that, just as the English ruling class were superior to the workers, so European men and women were to the non-Europeans, who were destined to be governed by them. Next, the dominant philosophical motif was a confident belief in human progress, in development. This predates scientific evolutionism, and indeed had already done much to prepare the way for Darwin's thesis.

Historical dialecticism

This intellectual strand, belief in progress, development, in an inevitable historical dialectic, was philosophy's contribution to the life-situation we are here reviewing. Initially, this theory was developed by the German, Georg Wilhelm Friedrich Hegel whose disparaging remark about black people we noted above. 'Ideas', he said – he was addressing the perennial philosophical subject of epistemology – begin with a 'thesis', which is then countered by an 'antithesis' and resolved by a 'synthesis'. This process, for him, represented the human intellectual journey, and 'mirrored the divine mind'. Thus, although he remained a practising Lutheran, Hegel's theology was hardly very orthodox. Rather, he conceived of God as 'a totality that manifested itself in thought (logic) in history (spirit, subjectivity) and in nature (necessity, objectivity)' yet 'ultimate reality for Hegel was nondualistic' ... 'neither spirit (culture) or nature but both: the cosmic process itself' (Morris, 1987: 13). Human history, then, was also 'the history of the divine mind' (Trompf: 32). By the dialectic process of thesis–antithesis–synthesis, humanity journeyed towards higher and higher stages of civilization.

Hegel's concept of historical dialectic directly influenced Karl Marx. Hegel thought that, in its most primitive expression, religion had taken the form of 'magic and fetishism' (and reports of magic and fetishism amongst primitive peoples would have lent credulity to this thesis). This was *die Naturreligion*, a religion of nature in which no duality was perceived between nature and spirit. Compared with many anthropological interpretations of these phenomena, Hegel's view of magic was, therefore, actually quite positive. The religions of India and of China, for him, represented an advanced form of this natural religion – with the Brahman–Atman relationship uniting the natural, and the spiritual. Some religions, such as those of ancient Egypt, however, demonstrated the beginning of a separation of nature and spirit. In these, 'spirit, in contrast to its original unformed self, becomes alienated from itself' (Cunliffe-Jones, 1970: 106). Early Persian dualism represents this conflict between non-dualistic (the thesis) and dualistic religion (the antithesis). Thus, eventually, the spirit became a 'subject' – 'a personal deity independent of the natural world' (Morris: 16). God was now 'ultimate reality' and the finite, created world 'receives no recognition'. This, however, gave way to a final phase, the synthesis of *Aufgehoben* – or of revealed religion, in which 'the alienation is overcome and the Spirit is reconciled to itself' (Cunliffe-Jones: 106).

Hegel equated this stage with Christianity, although not with Christianity as commonly understood. For him, *Aufgehoben* was the reconciliation of dualism and of non-dualism in the transcendent but also immanent God of Christian dogma. However, it also involved 'spirit' as 'the subjective' (man's inner life), spirit as 'objective' (family, society, state) and Absolute Spirit (art, religion, philosophy) existing in a type of esoteric unity. This represents, too, a merging of the divine and of the human (perhaps as in the incarnate Christ) into a single consciousness.

Theologians may recognize here a premonition of the 'process thought' of A.N. Whitehead (1861–1947) and of Teilhard de Chardin (1881–1955) in which God, and God's creation, through a process of mutual responsiveness, move towards a mutual 'perfection'. This concept also emerges in the thought of Sir Muhammad Iqbal (1876–1938), the Muslim poet and philosopher (see Bennett: 1995). It is not our task here to critique the philosophical strengths and weaknesses of Hegel's system. That is the job of philosophers. More relevant for us is his concept of religion as an evolutionary phenomenon, which gave licence to both anthropologists and students of religions to order religious phenomena in a hierarchy of excellence. Hegel's belief in history as a journey towards perfection seemed, to many Europeans, self-evidently true as they celebrated their 'technological and, as they saw them, moral triumphs' ... 'obsessed with the necessity for progress in all fields of human endeavour, they felt a positive obligation to contemplate continually the long, hard road from which man's ascent had commenced, long, long ago' (Lewis: 38). Before leaving Hegel, one of his critics deserves a brief mention – Ludwig Andreas Feuerbach (1804–72). It was as a student under Hegel in Berlin that the young Feuerbach decided to exchange theology for philosophy. He rejected Hegel's concept of the divine–human relationship in favour of outright humanism. In his writing, 'religion' was simply symptomatic of humanity's quest for self-knowledge. In other words, 'consciousness of the infinite is none other than consciousness of man's own infinite nature' (Morris: 20). Obviously, by 'man' Feuerbach doesn't mean individual people – but the human race. In this view, man is God but, unable to admit his own perfection, man projected what he himself essentially is onto an imaginary God. Thus religion is 'the projection of our feelings' and 'anthropology ... the secret of theology'. 'Humans', however, 'are inherently religious because they need answers' and invented religion as a false response to a genuine need. We projected God when we should have projected ourselves (*ibid.*: 47). Like Comte, whose thought I outline below, Feuerbach 'hoped to substitute a religion of humanity' (*ibid.*: 23) for conventional Christianity. His concept of 'essence', too, in his *The Essence of Christianity*, (trans. George Eliot, 1841) would prove influential.

As we have already noted, the apparent developmental gap between themselves, and others, assumed by Hegel, Feuerbach and others, too easily resulted in racial arrogance. Since they saw themselves as at the top of the developmental ladder, those further down, especially at the 'primordial zero-point represented the very antithesis of almost everything' which Europeans 'cherished' – order, morality, rationality (Lewis: 39). Thus could Thomas Hobbes (1588–1679), at quite an early stage, depict 'life in the state of nature [as] solitary, poor, nasty, brutish and short' (1651; 1914 edn: 65). No one, he said, in primitive times had respected either persons or property but all indulged in 'primitive promiscuity'. It was all too easy for some anthropologists, observing their subjects, to read promiscuity and immorality into the practices and customs they saw.

Confidence in progress and development

Auguste Comte (1798–1857)

Our next intellectual strand, positivism, also took its cue from Hegel. Proposed by two writers who are counted as 'fathers of social science', its impact on anthropology has been especially marked. They were the Frenchman, Auguste Comte (1798–1857) and the Englishman, Herbert Spencer (1820–1903). It was Spencer who first used the term 'evolution' rather than 'progress' or 'development' in his writing. But let us begin with Comte, the senior of the two, who initially trained as a mathematician at the École Polytechnique, Paris. Like Hegel, he was interested in the history of human thought, and also posited three stages of intellectual development. Unlike Hegel, though, Comte had no room in his scheme for a 'spirit'. His God was man. His thesis was that 'the progress of human effort moved social evolution forward' (Whitten and Hunter: 6). The first stage was 'theological thought' and, since he was a humanist, this represented the lowest rung on the ladder.

Theological thought was nothing more or less than the projection of human characteristics on a supposed higher being. Lacking a rational explanation for the universe, men and women invented a supernatural one and peopled it with gods, goddesses, demons and devils. Within this stage, evolution also saw animism give way to polytheism, and polytheism to monotheism. Next, theological thought itself gave way to metaphysical thought, to the age of the philosopher. Now, as during the great age of discovery, rational, natural laws are discovered. Man begins to come of age, to shake off the need for a divine protector. He now thinks in abstract terms. Finally, metaphysical thought yields pride of place to positive thought (hence 'positivism') in which empirical methods of scientific investigation will, in time, reach positive truths.

Comte, humanist though he was, was no Voltaire. Perhaps anticipating how social scientists would later explain religion, as the embodiment of society, or as fulfilling a social need, he thought that the positive age would still need a religion, and so saw fit to provide one. This would be the positivist church, or the 'religion of humanity'. For this, he supplied a positivist catechism and produced his treatise on sociology (he was the first to use the term) as its guiding principles. He even drew up a calendar on which eminent scholars and scientists replaced the saints. His church actually attracted a few members. With himself as high priest, it had its own sacraments and services. Only a small number of British scholars and French intelligentsia joined the church but, as bizarre as this aspect of his thought may seem, his intellectual influence was widespread. He also believed that each individual person passes through the same three stages of progress in their own intellectual development. As we shall see, amongst those for whom religious beliefs and practices had become outmoded, or even absurd, Comte's explanation of its human and irrational origin provided one of the earliest reductionist interpretations of religion – as superstition, magic, irrational.

Herbert Spencer (1820–1903)

Herbert Spencer was an English free thinker. Denied a university education because of his dissenting principles (then only members of the Church of England could matriculate at Oxford or Cambridge), his only formal training was at a Midland Dissenting Academy. For a while, he worked as a railway engineer. Later, he began writing in such journals as the *Economist* and the *Westminster Review*. His *Social Statistics* and *The Principles of Psychology* appeared in 1851 and 1855 respectively. He quickly acquired a reputation for his views, a type of positivist agnosticism. Other books followed, including *The Principles of Sociology* (1877). Thus, as Comte fathered the French social sciences, Spencer fathered the English. It was Spencer who, in addition to 'evolution' introduced the phrase 'the survival of the fittest' into our vocabulary. His contribution to nineteenth-century thought, although often over-looked, is considerable. Not surprisingly, his writing influenced Charles Robert Darwin (1809–82) as well as the American anthropologist, Lewis Henry Morgan (1818–81). Evolution, said Spencer, 'is not merely change' but 'change from an indefinite, incoherent homogeneity to a definite, coherent heterogeneity, through continuous differentiations and integration' (Whitten and Hunter: 6).

Thus, human life and human society evolves from the simple to the complex. Spencer did not depend on pure conjecture to construct his theory but used 'hundreds of letters, reports, diaries, articles, monographs ... about the far corners of the globe' (Trompf: 23). He read about Andaman Islanders, Australian Aborigines, Melanesian and Polynesian islanders. He was amongst the first to use anthropological evidence to deduce, or support, a universal historiography. Unlike many scholars, he was not really very interested in the question of human origins although, as we see below, he did discuss the origin of religion. What did interest him was evidence of progress, which for him was the supreme law of the universe. Just as social organization had progressed, from the simple to the complex, so had religion; from the primitive to 'the complexities of modern theological systems and of ceremonies which sustain the most highly complex societies' (*ibid.*). A premonition here, perhaps, of the 'functionist' viewpoint. His approach, however, was far from value-free; he assumed always the superiority of the higher over the lower – of the human over the animal, of trees over weeds. Thus, primitive or early religion must be inferior. In his *Principles of Sociology*, though, he did assign rationality to primitive peoples. Drawing on his anthropological evidence, he argued that the earliest notions of the supernatural began with a belief in ghosts, or in ancestral spirits.

Although rational, primitive men and women were (he surmised) intellectually undeveloped. Thus, observing such natural phenomena as the wind, sun, moon, rain, which came and went, and requiring some explanation of their movement, they saw the answer in their dreams since these actually appeared real to them. Quite how Spencer knew this is beyond conjecture, or why he assumed that early humankind was incapable of 'natural explanation' but, he concluded, it was

dreams ... which chiefly gave man the idea of his own duality, and he identified the dream-self which wanders at night with the shadow-self which appears by day. This idea of reality [was] fortified by experiences of various forms of temporary insensibility, sleeping, swooning, catalepsy, and the like, so that death itself comes to be thought of as only a prolonged form of insensibility. And if man has a double, a soul, by the same reasoning so must animals have one and also plants and material objects. (Evans-Pritchard, 1965: 23–24)

Later, the ghosts of ancestors, especially the more important of them, were divinized – accompanied by the development of priestly classes to protect their interests. Food left on the tombs of dead ancestor-spirits to sustain them, or perhaps to appease them, became the sacrifices of the religious cultus. Spencer's theory was both evolutionary and psychological. Religion as a product of dreams anticipated the work of Sigmund Freud (1856–1939). For Freud, though, religion owed its origin to sexual neurosis; also, differing from Spencer, to primitive irrationality. As we shall see, like Spencer, Freud made free use of anthropological evidence to support his thesis. Both may be criticized for leaping to conclusions which cannot be justified by the evidence they used. Later, F. Max Müller would profoundly disagree with Spencer's evolutionary understanding of human progress – and especially criticized his use of anthropological material. He thought Spencer something of an academic upstart!

What all this confidence in human progress meant was that by the time Darwin's *On the Origin of the Species* (1858) was published, which seemed to abolish the notion of a creator once and for all, the way had long been prepared by the empiricists and the positivists for his ideas to receive a surprisingly receptive hearing. Response to Darwin's book is easily exaggerated; it generated much less controversy than many accounts suggest. Even some theologians found it relatively easy to accommodate his thought:

Before Progress there was Providence, and before Evolution, Development and Advancement so that the European mind was hardly taken by complete surprise when the Darwinian paradigm of organic improvement was launched amongst the intelligentsia. (Trompf: 32)

A brief note on Karl Marx (1818–83)

Marx's theory of an 'historical dialectic' by which all human societies will eventually arrive, through successive stages of social and political development, at the communist state, if at different times, drew on anthropological thought. He was especially influenced by Lewis Henry Morgan (1818–81), whose 1851 book about the Iroquois Indians has been called 'the first modern ethnographic study of a native people' (Seymour-Smith: 201). Morgan, who derived his ideas from Spencer, proposed progress through savagery, barbarism, to civilization, and identified each stage with particular technological and political advances. Built into Marxist theory, however, is a conflict view of society; progress results from a power struggle between those who control, and those who work. Eventually, when those who work also own and control the means of production, the communist society will emerge, in which the means of production is commonly owned and controlled. When class and power distinctions cease, so will conflict. As we shall see, anthropologists later questioned the unilinear view of social evolution on which Marx based his theory. However, they have also continued to interest themselves in the relationship between different social groups, in whether ownership and control of the means of production determines who exercises power, and in how power is exercised in various contexts.

Romanticism

Finally, before turning to the development of our two disciplines in more detail, especially to their methodologies and pioneer theories, a word about our last intellectual stream – Romanticism. European interest in primitive peoples during this period was not only as objects of exploitation. Rather, looking with confidence to the future, nineteenth-century men and women also became fascinated with their own history. Where had they come from? Perhaps, by studying people who seemed, for whatever reason, lower down the ladder of progress, they might shed light on their own origins, or on why people act and behave as they do today. Thus, primitive peoples were 'living fossils' whose study might reveal not only the origin of mankind, but also of human religiosity. Adam Kuper comments that what men like Robertson Smith and Frazer did was to 'extend back in time the Enlightenment account of intellectual progress, by which was meant the development of reason and high culture' (1994: 539). The debunking, too, as some saw it, of a transcendent God busy supervising human affairs, enabled them to posit instead an immanent God present in nature and in creation itself – a view not dissimilar to Hegel's. Often called Romanticism, this

gave fresh impetus to the study of the nature, origin and development of religion in terms of immanentism, nature-worship and nature-mythology and poetry. (James, 1968: 18)

Romanticism represents yet another aspect of the life-situation of our two infant disciplines. It could inform a positive view of other religions, not as devoid of any truth, but as participating in the truth which inheres in all creation. It was into this particular intellectual tradition that F. Max Müller was born, so we shall have more to say, later, about its significance. Certainly, those anthropologists and students of religions who were influenced by this strand were less inclined towards racist attitudes. For them, the savage was less the Hobbesian 'brute' than the yet unspoiled 'noble' popularized in the writings of Jean Jacques Rousseau (1712–78), for whom 'man was born free', and was only later enslaved (it was actually John Dryden, 1631–1700, who first coined the term). The image of the noble savage symbolized innate goodness, untouched by the corrupting influences of civilization. The positivists presumed progression from the amoral to the moral – the Romanticists, sometimes, reversed this. Malinowski later pointed out that we have two anthropological inspirations in the writings of Rousseau, 'the use of primitive man as a model for civilized man, as well as a criticism of civilization with parallels from savagery' (1944: 15). The Romantics, through their music and poetry, despaired of the mechanistic universe of the rationalists. It was this tradition which produced modern theology's father, Friedrich Daniel Ernest Schleiermacher (1778–1834). In his *Religion, Speeches to its Cultured Despisers* (1799) and other writing, he reinstated 'feeling' and 'piety' to theological thought. Religion, he said, is the 'feeling of absolute dependence' and all religions owe their origin to charismatic, or God-intoxicated, leaders. Amongst them, however, Christianity shines most brightly because in Christ this God-consciousness reached the point of absolute identity with God. His student, Arthur Schopenhauer (1789–1860), whose interest in Buddhism and Hinduism did much to encourage their serious study, went further. There was, he said, no Absolute Spirit, no God to deliver us from *dukkha* (suffering), only art, music, poetry could 'bring a measure of serenity' (Armstrong, 1993: 405). Rudolf Otto (1869–1937) influenced by Schleiermacher, would also value the place of art and music in the religious life.

Having already identified early anthropology's contribution to racist stereotyping and colonial domination, before we leave this aspect of our survey mention should be made of two pioneers who tended towards the more Romantic approach. Lewis points out that

some of the most eminent of the first anthropologists were really 'philanthropologists', men of the moral calibre of Thomas F. Buxton (1786–1845) and Thomas Hodgkin (1798–1866). (1992: 36)

By persuasion Quakers, and therefore open to the spirit of Romanticism, they supported the anti-slave movement and 'founded the Aborigines Protection Society in the early 1830s' which 'sought to protect the rights of the newly colonised' and provided 'much of the intellectual and moral impetus which ultimately led to the formation of the Royal Anthropological Institute' (*ibid.*: 37).

Sir Edward Burnett Tylor (1832–1917)

As we noted at the start of this chapter, the honour of occupying the first university post in anthropology went to Sir Edward Tylor. Indeed Tylor is often described as the founder of the science of man – for example, in Waardenburg: 'The actual founder of anthropology as the science of man and his culture was Edward B. Tylor' (1973: 29). He is, says Eric Sharpe, 'equally important in the history of comparative religion' (1986: 53). Therefore, appropriately, this initial survey of anthropology's contribution to and interaction with the study of religions will begin with Tylor's life and work. It will quickly become apparent how our several intellectual strands, consciously or unconsciously, influenced his work. Next, we visit the work of the first Briton who occupied a chair, albeit it honorary, in social anthropology, Sir James George Frazer (1854–1951). Next, by way of a bridge into our discussion of F. Max Müller and the methodology of the pioneer students of religions, we visit the work of William Robertson Smith (1846–94). This, as we shall see, represents an example of cross-fertilization between our two disciplines – Smith has some claim to be both an anthropologist and a student of religions. His conclusions, however, differed from Müller's.

Tylor was born into a Quaker family, and attended a Quaker school until the age of 16 when he joined his father's business. Ill health soon forced him to leave, and to travel to a warmer climate. Befriending the ethnologist, Henry Christy (1810–65) he accompanied him on an expedition to Mexico. His first book, *Anahuc, or Mexico and the Mexicans, Ancient and Modern,* an account of his travels, followed in 1861. His *Researches into the Early History of Mankind* was published in 1865, and his classic *Primitive Culture* in 1871. Although self-taught, academic recognition came in 1875 when Oxford awarded him the DCL, and in 1884 the readership in anthropology. Between 1896 and 1909 he was the university's first Professor of Anthropology. In 1888 he presented the first Gifford lectures at Edinburgh, and in 1912 received his knighthood.

Tylor regarded himself as a value-free scientist. Of course, he was by no means free of presuppositions, but he set himself the task of sifting through the mass of anthropological data at his disposal.

Like most of the pioneers, he was, apart from his early travels in Mexico, an armchair, or rather a desk-bound, scholar. (Although often dubbed an 'armchair scholar' I doubt very much if he did work sitting comfortably in an armchair!) He did, however, send students into the field, thus anticipating the later emphasis on fieldwork 'as to anthropology ... what the blood of the martyrs is to the church' (Charles Gabriel Seligman, 1873–1940, cited in Lewis: 27). His aim was to allow the materials to speak for themselves by suggesting categories which could help unravel the story they might tell about human origins. Tylor saw the anthropological task as the reconstruction of prehistory by examining contemporary primitives who, in his view, had somehow 'survived', by-passed by the progress of civilization. He wrote in *Primitive Culture* (1871):

Survivals are processes, customs, opinions, and so forth, which have been carried on by force of habit into a new state of society different from that in which they had their original home, and they thus remain as proofs and examples of an older condition of culture out of which the newer has been evolved. (6th edn, 1929: 1: 16)

An obvious way of classifying data was to group examples of similar customs or beliefs together, thus forming a picture of various types of social organization, government, kinship patterns, or religious practice. To illustrate how Tylor went about this, attempting to allow the data to speak for itself, one example may suffice. This method of interrogating the material, as we shall see, resembles the comparative approach which students of religions would also adopt. Lewis identifies Tylor's work in the field of 'statistical correlations' as one of his most significant contributions to methodology. First, Tylor noted that some cultures went to great lengths to prevent contact between men and their in-laws, whilst others 'were more concerned to keep daughters and parents-in-law from each others' throats' (Lewis: 44). Others didn't seem to care.

This suggested a research question – were such 'variations arbitrary, or could they be explained in any logically consistent fashion?' (*ibid.*). Surveying 350 cases, Tylor found that whenever newly married couples established themselves in the wife's family home, 'avoidance between the latter and the husband' frequently occurred. On the other hand, when newly weds set up home with the husband's family, 'she was obliged to avoid them'. If couples lived elsewhere entirely, avoidance or contact didn't seem to matter. Next, Tylor used this discovery to shed light on other social phenomena. He noted that some societies customarily call fathers not by their own name, but by that of their children, and that more often than not these fathers were living in their in-laws households! Obviously, this example of an early anthropologist applying the comparative approach doesn't shed any light on religion, but it does usefully illustrate anthropological analysis at its most scientific. Positively, this comparative method often identified similarities and differences, patterns of human behaviour, for which rational reasons could then be deduced. Negatively, as we shall see, too much could be made of too little. Data which inconveniently suggested another explanation, or which didn't fit the scheme, could too easily be disregarded.

Tylor's work on religion is much more widely known. Here, he found it less easy to free himself from his intellectual heritage. His view of history was profoundly influenced by evolutionary thought, by Spencer and Comte amongst those already discussed in this chapter. As Malinowski comments, anthropology 'was born under the star of enthusiastic evolutionism' (1944: 4). Tylor assumed *a priori* that human culture progressed, from primitive to advanced. As Sharpe points out, though, on one issue he was more flexible than some of his contemporaries – whether evolution had proceeded from a single source of civilization, or from many (similar to the debate about progenitors). His theory of religion owes something to Spencer's, but instead of 'ghosts' he saw 'belief in the soul' as the beginning of 'belief in spirits'. True, he did not begin with this particular notion in mind. He began with 'a careful arrangement of an immense number of data of all kinds' (Waardenburg, 1973: 30), but he was predisposed to suppose an unsophisticated explanation of religion. Like Spencer, he thought primitive people rational, but mentally undeveloped (although not necessarily unintelligent). Lacking a 'sensible' explanation for such life-crises as death, dreams, illness, disease, primitive man concluded 'that they are to be accounted for by the presence, or absence, of some immaterial entity, the soul' (Evans-Pritchard: 25). Next, souls were projected onto other objects or animals as well, for if people possess them, why shouldn't they? Thus, Tylor's much quoted minimum definition of religion, 'belief in spiritual beings' (1929: 1:424). To describe this process, Tylor coined the word 'animism' – 'belief ... that not only creatures but also inanimate objects have life, and personality ... and ... souls' (*ibid.*: 25).

However, as Evans–Pritchard points out, Tylor's conclusion may be critiqued by his own assumptions, that is, that humanity becomes more and more intelligent and sophisticated. If belief in the soul arose from 'such fallacious reasoning about clouds and butterflies and dreams and trances', why has belief in the soul 'persisted throughout millennia'? Indeed, why is it still 'held by millions of civilized people in his day and ours' (*ibid.*: 24). Anthropological evidence, too, exists aplenty of quite sophisticated belief in supreme beings, and not only of a belief in 'anima' amongst so-called primitive peoples (the term 'primal' is arguably more accurate). Indeed, one of Tylor's own disciples, the Scottish man of letters, Andrew Lang (1844–1912) argued this very point. Originally trained in classics at Merton College, Oxford, Lang – who also criticized some of Müller's conclusions – refuted Tylor's thesis that animism was the mother of all religion. In his *The Making of Religion* (1898) he ventured to suggest

that the savage theory of the soul may be based, at least in part, on experiences which cannot, at present, be made to fit into any purely materialistic system of the universe. We shall also [he continued] bring evidence tending to prove that the idea of God, in its earliest shape, need not logically be deduced from the idea of spirit, however that idea itself may have been attained or evolved. The conception of God, then, need not be evolved out of reflections on dreams and 'ghosts'. (1898: 2)

In an undated letter, he expressed his own surprise that 'alongside their magic, ghosts, totems, worshipful stones' many primitive peoples 'have a very much better God than most races a good deal higher in civilization' (cited in Sharpe, 1986: 63). Anthropological evidence, then, would seem to demolish Tylor's theory of religion as untenable. Nevertheless, his *magnum opus, Primitive Culture* (1871) remains a valuable source of information about the beliefs and practices of numerous peoples and tribes, and still merits reading. As we shall see, where students of religions tended to part company from the anthropologists was over their explanation of religion as denying the reality of the sacred. Perhaps not surprisingly, Lang's refusal to accept that gods could have developed from out of ghosts or spirits commended his work to some avowedly Christian scholars. Amongst them was the Divine Word Missionary, Father Wilhelm Schmidt, (1868–1954) who found evidence of monotheism amongst the 'most archaic people', Tasmanian Aborigines and the Andaman islanders (Morris: 102). In passing, and given my own missionary background, it is interesting to note that whilst the relationship between anthropologists and missionaries has been described as 'one of sibling rivalry', there have been recent calls for the two parties to 'get over this as much as they can'. Schmidt can be cited as an example of someone who 'personally combined the two vocations', and who did so successfully (see Benthall, 1995 and Pickering, 1992). As I shall later point out, several major contributors to the academic study of religions have also had missionary backgrounds.

Sir James George Frazer (1854–1941)

Frazer was an armchair anthropologist. He read classics and philosophy at Glasgow then moved to a Fellowship at Trinity, Cambridge, where he remained. In 1908 he was appointed Professor of Social Anthropology at Liverpool; he only lectured there for a year before returning to Cambridge 'disgruntled by lack of emolument' (Fraser, 1994: xlviii), although he remained Honorary Professor. A recent editor of Frazer's work has commented that he was equally 'disheartened by [life in a] large industrial city', and thus fled 'back to Cambridge' (*ibid.*). In 1911–12 and 1924–25 he presented the Gifford lectures at St Andrew's and at Edinburgh respectively. He was knighted in 1914, and appointed to the prestigious Order of Merit in 1925. A man of great erudition and scholarship, his classic *The Golden Bough* (1890f.) – despite its theoretical weaknesses – represents a fascinating compendium of interesting data and an outstanding contribution to English literature. Something in Frazer, perhaps, of the anthropologist as author. Still of value, suggests Sharpe, are his definition of 'magic', his work on 'divine kingship' and 'his concept of the dying and rising god or goddess of vegetation' (1986: 90). However, we shall focus on his understanding of religion. Like Tylor, he set out to interrogate the vast amount of data to which he had access, mainly by using the comparative method. Much of this data was amassed as a result of a questionnaire which he sent (1887) 'to missionaries, doctors and administrators throughout the empire requesting information on the customs and beliefs of the local inhabitants' (Fraser, 1994: xlvi). He also directed the fieldwork enquiries of Sir W. Baldwin Spencer, whom we shall meet below. Perhaps he was one of the first social scientists to use the questionnaire as a research instrument. In his analyses of anthropological data and of classical literature (he twice travelled in Greece, which provided some data for his interest in classical mythology), his aim was to understand why people did what they did; like Tylor, he was interested in the history of human development. A child of his time, he presupposed progress and, after Comte, adopted a threefold scheme. Picturing primitive people trying to make sense of their world, he attempted to reconstruct the development of social organization, and of religion. His three stages were magic, religion and science. The first stage was an attempt to control, or to manipulate, the forces of nature – wind, rain, sunshine, by magic; the magician, says Frazer, 'supplicates no higher power, ... sues the favour of no fickle and wayward being ... abases himself before no awful deity' (1994: 45). Frazer distinguished between two types of magic: sympathetic (the idea that like influences like) and contagious (the idea that things which have been in contact may continue influencing each other even when separated) (Seymour-Smith: 175; see 1994: chapter three).

Magic gave way to religion when people realized their inability to control, or to explain, the world about them, that they 'had been pulling at strings to which nothing had been attached' (1994: 55). Frazer's rustic philosopher, 'cut adrift from his ancient moorings' then pondered his inability to control nature, and decided that

If the great world went on its way without the help of his fellows, it must surely be because there were other beings, like himself, but far stronger, who, unseen themselves, directed its course and brought about all the varied series of events which he had hitherto believed to be dependent on his own magic. (1994: 56)

Gradually, the human imagination invested 'every nook and hill, every tree and flower, every brook and river, every breeze that blew, and every cloud that flecked with silvery white the blue expanse of heaven' (an example of Frazer's literary finesse) with a multiplicity of spiritual beings (1926: 9f.). This, following inexorable, dialectical, Hegelian laws, resulted in religion, which Frazer defined as, 'a propitiation or conciliation of powers superior to man which are believed to direct and control the course of nature and of human life' (1994: 46). Later, belief in the many deities yielded to belief in 'one supreme creator and controller of all things' (1926: 9). Religion, however, says Frazer, is fundamentally opposed both to magic, and to science; whilst Magic was an 'attempt at science' since it assumed that man could exert control over his circumstances, and that a cause–effect relationship exists, religion abrogates control. Magic was thus, 'the bastard sister of science' (1994: 46). Finally, scientific empiricism and technological progress would indeed liberate men and women from the stages of magic and religion. Religion then becomes redundant. Again, it was anthropology itself which would reveal the weakness of Frazer's argument – it simply is not true that magic yields to religion. There are, as Lang (1901) pointed out, examples aplenty of magic and religion existing side by side. The great Bronislaw Malinowski, too, an admirer of Frazer, would later write about magic as working:

magic, including sorcery, has its practical ... characteristics, which allow us to explain its persistence. Psychologically, magic in all its forms implies the optimistic attitude that through rite and spell something is being achieved in taming chance and restoring luck. (Malinowski, 1944: 199)

In the light of our 'modern anthropological knowledge', Malinowski pointed out, Frazer's

theory of magic, which is also a theory of the primitive outlook on the world, is untenable. We now know that primitive humanity was aware of the scientific laws of natural process. (*ibid.*)

Primitives knew, for example, the cause and effect relationship between kindling and fire. Frazer assumed that 'primitive man' could not differentiate between 'his own subjective associations and external objective reality' and thus 'stumbled' onto magic in the misapprehension that 'words and signs could be used as intruments' to control 'the departure of winter or stay the flight of summer' (Douglas, 1991: 24). Thus, Mary Douglas finds it 'hard to forgive Frazer for his ... undisguised contempt of primitive society' (*ibid..*).

Frazer's own theory possibly represents an early functionalist viewpoint; functionalism, which – as we shall see in Chapter 2 – Emile Durkheim (1858–1917) developed and Malinowski adopted, explains the existence of any belief, practice or institution in terms of its function. His explanation of religion, then, was functional – to propitiate the supreme God. Religion was substituted for magic (which in his view failed) as a means to control one's circumstances.

William Robertson Smith (1846–94)

Smith was something of a polyglot, a scholar of Arabic and Hebrew, he was also a biblical scholar, a philologist, a theologian (he was ordained in 1870) and an encyclopaedist who used anthropological evidence in his writing. Indeed, Mary Douglas credits him rather than Tylor as the 'founder of social anthropology'; 'Tylor', she remarks, 'founded folk-lore' (Douglas, 1991:14). Visiting North Africa, Egypt and Arabia, Robertson Smith combined textual scholarship with some nascent fieldwork experience. Several scholars who stood in his debt, including Emile Durkheim and his own close friend, Frazer, failed to gather firsthand data to support their theories.

Educated at the Free Church College, Aberdeen, he first taught Oriental languages and biblical exegesis there but soon came under criticism for undermining the authority of the Bible. He advocated what was then called the 'higher criticism' of the Bible – source, form and redaction analyses. In 1881 he was removed from his chair. His use of non-biblical material to shed light on the Bible seemed to afford materials such as Babylonian and Phoenician legends the same status as the Bible, thus questioning its uniqueness and inspiration. In fact, Smith retained belief in biblical inspiration but thought that an understanding of the wider social context would further illuminate the biblical record. He stated 'ancient faiths must be looked on as matters of institution rather than of dogma or formulated belief' and 'the system of an antique religion was part of the social order under which its adherents lived'. (1927 ed: 28).

His interest in myth and legend was not in order to find out about 'the past' but to discover 'common elements in the modern and primitive experience' (Douglas: 14). Already editor and chief contributor to the ninth edition of the *Encyclopaedia Britannica*, he had done much to popularize this new trend in biblical scholarship before he lost his Aberdeen chair. In 1883 he became reader in Arabic at Cambridge, where he held the chair from 1889. It was at Cambridge, says Kuper, that Smith 'acquired his most important apostle, another fellow of Trinity, and another Scot, James George Frazer' (1988: 85). Frazer dedicated *The Golden Bough* to 'My Friend, William Robertson Smith, in gratitude and admiration'.

Smith is best remembered for his theory that behind the sacrifices mentioned in the Bible, originally, lay not the concept of propitiation but of communion with God, or with gods. He drew on material provided by anthropology which suggested that 'totemism' (a term which has meant different things to different writers – he meant the worship of sacred animals) had existed amongst the early Semites, and amongst the bedouin whom he visited in Africa. 'In the totem stage of society', he wrote, 'each kinship or stock of savages believes itself to be physically akin to some natural kind of animate or inanimate thing, most generally to some kind of animal' (1927 ed: 124). When such 'sacred animals' were sacrificed, their flesh and blood, if consumed, created a bond between the worshippers and the worshipped: 'the god and the worshipper unite by partaking together of the flesh and blood of the sacrificial victim' (Smith, 1927: 227). Smith also argued that this lay behind the Christian rite of Holy Communion. He addressed another anthropological theme in his *Kinship and Marriage in Early Arabia* (1885). Smith's work represents an early attempt to reconstruct the social and cultural milieux in which scriptural records were produced, and to link historical with ethnographic evidence.

He has been criticized for seeing totemism everywhere, and for building his theory without any real evidence that totemism did lie behind biblical sacrifices. Müller commented that it was nonsense to suppose that totemism lay behind all animal sacrifice (1892: 122).

Nevertheless, what we have here is a pioneer example of how evidence external to scripture can be used to shed light on its interpretation. As Malinowski commented, Smith 'was perhaps the first clearly to insist on the sociological context in all discussions which refer not merely to organization of groups but also to belief, ritual and to myth' (1944: 19). As we shall see, this differed from Müller's approach – for him, the study of the scriptures themselves would provide the most reliable and authentic information (1892: 152).

Friedrich Max Müller – The founder of the scientific study of religion

Müller was born in Germany and was influenced early in his life by Romanticism and the German idealistic tradition through his father's poetry, set to music by Schubert. At Leipzig he read classics and philosophy and gained his doctorate in 1843 for a thesis on Spinoza. Moving to Berlin, acquaintance with Schopenhauer increasingly interested him in the study of Sanskrit and other Oriental languages. This took him to Paris, then (at the invitation of the East India Company) to London to supervise the translation of the Rig Veda, and finally to Oxford to oversee the printing by the University Press. University appointments followed, deputy, then full Taylorian Professor of Eastern Languages, Fellow of All Souls, and from 1868 the Chair of Comparative Philology. From time to time he was consulted by the Government, and was created a Privy Councillor. Throughout his life, Müller remained a communicant Christian, in England joining the Established Church in which he felt, as a former Lutheran, the most comfortable. He disliked both what he called the 'biblio-idolatry' of the Evangelicals, and the dogmatism of the Tractarians.

Whilst Müller shared many of the positivists' assumptions about progress, indeed he believed that humanity's future would be more glorious than its past, his romantic idealism also predisposed him to see early man as fully rational and open to the divine, to the sacred. Müller's view of the origin of religion differed profoundly from that of the anthropologists. For him, it lay neither in ancestor worship, dreams, magic, totemic projection or in an animistic deifying of objects, but in an inherent human ability to apprehend the sacred. This ability to 'apprehend the divine' – to arrive at 'belief in God, in the immortality of the soul, and in a future retribution, can be gained', he wrote, 'and not only can be, but has been gained by the right assertion of human reason alone, and without the assistance of what has been called a special revelation' (1892: 1). Possibly, Müller posited a primal revelation but, for him, religion's origin lay in a rational comprehension of a reality, not in some sort of neurotic behaviour. Thus, he criticized the anthropologists:

anthropologists mostly contented themselves with collecting facts, more or less carefully, observed and comprehended under the ill-defined name of fetishism, Comte went further still, and claimed fetishism as a necessary plan in the universal growth of religion. (*ibid*.: 118)

The popular use of totemism to explain the origin of all sacrifices was, he said, patently untrue. There were many alternative explanations. Anthropologists' evidence, and their methodology, said Müller, were flawed. They collected as much information as they could from travellers, missionaries or traders, 'copied, classified and tabulated' it without any attempt to test the credibility of their witness. He had questioned Hindu students at Oxford about their beliefs and had been 'startled at their ignorance of their own religion' (*ibid*.: 152). On reflection, he commented that perhaps he shouldn't have been quite so startled; he also marked Divinity papers! He continued, 'A traveller or missionary may misapprehend and misunderstand what he sees and hears' (*ibid*.: 180) and 'some natives, particularly those who have been brought into contact with Europeans, are very apt to give the answers which they are expected to give' (*ibid*.: 157). Only eye-witness evidence, he said, should be used. Müller, perceptively, identified a problem which does all too often dog the anthropologists' footsteps. Anthropologists were also mistaken, he said, to suppose that when they studied modern savages, they were studying representatives 'of what the primitive state of mankind might have been thousands of years ago' (*ibid*.: 15) since all societies – evidence oral traditions – have their histories. Müller was right to make this criticism of the work of the early anthropologists. As Adam Kuper demonstrates in his *The Invention of Primitive Society* (1988), the notion of the primitive man has, more often than not, served an ideological political function; 'imperialists and nationalists, anarchists and Marxists' have each used their own versions to justify different social and political views (1988: 239–40). The next generation would recognize that no culture remains static. Thus we have an early critique of anthropological evidence, suggesting that in their early phases the two disciples adopted different methodologies. For Müller, the key lay in language, and therefore in texts. It was through philology, his translation of the Vedas and his editing of the *Sacred Books of the East*, that he became interested in religion *qua* religion, and in its scientific study. Rationality, thought and speech, for him, went hand in hand. He couldn't, in his wide linguistic research into written and unwritten languages, find a single half-developed language, nor could he concede the existence of 'partly rational, partly developed men'. Thus the history of language was the history of thought. He told Darwin so, and the two parted company agreeing to differ. Müller's estimate of primitive man, then, was different from Frazer's credulous infant.

For Müller, language and textual study of such ancient scriptures as the Vedas could take us back further, to a 'lower, more ancient stratum of religious thought' than anthropology ever could. Indeed, 'no student should venture to write on any religion, unless he has acquired some knowledge of the language of the sacred writings' (1892: 157). Thus could one who had 'never been in India', who lacked fieldwork experience, yet speak with authority on matters religious. Travellers, he said, told different tales – the Vedas, even with variant readings and textual flaws, could more easily be made to tell one story. Also, for Müller, since all religious writings reflect some valid apprehension of the divine, no one could claim to understand religion if they possessed knowledge of only one, hence his oft-cited 'he who knows one, knows none' (1873: 16), and

However imperfect, however childish a religion may be, it always places the human soul in the presence of God; and however imperfect and however childish the conception of God may be, it always represents the highest ideal of perfection which the human soul, for the time being, can reach and grasp. (1873; 1882 ed: 192: 263)

His identification of a common root for Aryan, Latin, Greek, Celtic and Slavonic languages (which may or may not be a sustainable thesis) also supported his view that common, rational progenitors have fathered these peoples. He spent much time analysing these vocabularies, and noted, amongst other interesting comparisons (thus he used a comparative method) that words for deities seemed related to words for the sun, or for the sky. This, though, for him represented not humanity's original apprehension of the *numina*, but *nomina*, 'names without beings' (1881: 31). This was, he argued, the result of a 'disease of language' probably brought about by the dispersal of peoples and languages, by a 'pathological condition of the human mind arising from its inability to express abstract ideas except in metaphor' (James: 17). Spencer and company had mistakenly identified not the first, but the second stage of religious development, for Müller's romantic idealism did not preclude for him confidence in human evolution. He also posited three stages, the henotheistic, the mythological and the psychological. Henotheism, a word he probably coined, means worship of one God without necessarily denying the existence of others (some Bible scholars think that Abraham may have been a henotheist). At this stage, people employed physical objects, rocks, fire, and so on, to express (as metaphors for) their consciousness of God. Next, according to Müller's scheme, the diffusion of peoples referred to above resulted in polytheism, or in what he also called 'anthropological religion' by which he really meant 'anthropomorphic religion'. Now, people thought of God in human terms. Finally, this gives way to 'psychological religion' in which people employ abstract thought, metaphysics, to express their religiosity. Nor was Muller's scheme devoid of some evaluation, for all that he claimed to be an objective scholar. His ladder of religions placed Christianity at the top, above the Semitic and Indian religions. He expressed the view that

History seems to teach us that the whole human race requires a gradual education before, in the fullness of time, it could be admitted to the truths of Christianity .... The ancient religions of the world were but the milk of nature, which in due time were to be superseded by the bread of life ... (1860: 32)

Whilst he deemed a 'large number of Vedic hymns ... childish and commonplace' (1884: 1 : 26) and much contemporary Hinduism debased, he welcomed the reforming Brahmo Samaj's 'attempt to bring the modern corrupt forms of worship back to the purity and simplicity of the Vedas' (Shourie, 1994: 135). The Vedas, for Müller, represented not only the Hindu ideal, but (because of their antiquity) also religion's most ancient expression:

We see in the Vedic hymns the first revelation of deity, the first expressions of surprise, the first discovery that behind the visible and perishable world there must be something invisible, eternal or divine ... (cited in Morris: 93)

Contemporary Hinduism, however, in Müller's estimate was a far cry from the Vedic ideal. In his controversial sermon, 'On Missions', preached in Westminster Abbey, December 1873, Müller endorsed Christian missions; Hinduism was 'dying or dead'. This was just the sort of language beloved by missionary writers. The Baptist missionary John Drew Bate (1836–1923), for example, a member of the Royal Asiatic Society and author of the popular *Hindi Dictionary* (1875) (which the government of India placed in all schools) declared:

Hinduism, Buddhism, Mohammedanism and all the other systems which frighten 'Little Faith' are dying, not of old age (for the Gospel is as old as Adam, and therefore older than all) but of inanition ... (BMS Report: 1884: 7)

Yet there is some evidence that Müller deliberately set out to present what he perceived to be positive aspects of Eastern religions, since in his view 'these ... same religions have so often been drawn from their dark and hideous side' so that he thought there 'little danger of people at large forming too favourable an opinion of them, if now and then' he 'should have spoken too well of them' (1892: 78). Against the criticism that he dwelt 'too much on the bright side', he replied:

if other religions do after all appear not so infinitely inferior to our own, not altogether of a different stuff, should we really be poorer, because others are richer than we expected. (1892: 2)

To an extent, Müller saw his reconstruction of Hinduism as a counterbalance to the work of those scholars, mainly Christian apologists, who saw nothing but 'darkness' in the Indian tradition.

Elsewhere, too, he seems to suggest that conventional Christianity will not be the final religion of man, but that a 'new form ... derived ... from all the repositories of truth that are to be found scattered over the face of the earth' will evolve (Sharpe, 1986: 44). 'The true religion of the future', he said, 'would be the fulfilment of all the religions of the past' (1902: 2: 135). Something here of what would later be called a fulfilment theology of religions, a view classically associated with John Nicol Farquhar (1861–1929) from 1923 Professor of Comparative Religion at my own *alma mater,* Manchester University. For Farquhar, though, the religions would find their fulfilment in the Christian religion, whilst Müller's final religion, despite his sermon cited above, would seem to lie in a yet to be realized religion of the future. As we shall see in a later chapter, the study of religions may itself demand a theology of religion. Certainly, Müller, who expressed enthusiasm over the 1893 Parliament of the World's Religions at Chicago, hoped that the science of religion would lead to 'true tolerance and co-operation in behalf of mankind' (Heiler, 1959: 160). Friedrich Heiler (1892–1967), Professor of the History of Religions at Marburg, whose contribution we shall discuss in Chapter 3, himself advocated a similar role for his discipline. In 'The History of Religions as a Preparation for the Co-operation of Religions', his contribution to the important volume, *The History of Religions: Essays in Methodology* (1959) he wrote, 'if the religions ... learn to understand one another and co-operate, they will contribute more to the realization of humanity and thereby to world peace than all the noteworthy efforts of politics' (Kitagawa and Eliade,: 158).

This concludes our comparative survey of the initial phases of anthropology and the study of religions. The first, we leave still influenced by evolutionary theory, still inclined to see the modern primitive as a living representative of our own past, still inclined towards definitions of religions which explain religion as something other than religion, still tending towards universal theories of origins, and still accumulating data from a distance. The second, we leave sceptical of anthropological evidence, critical of reductionist understandings of religiosity and inclined towards belief in the reality of the sacred; and with a marked preference for textual scholarship, since texts cannot lie. The value of Müller's own contribution, though, lies more in the legacy of his translations and in his placing the study of religions firmly on the academic agenda than in any lasting theoretical significance of his work. Andrew Lang, who is generally said to have successfully refuted his more theoretical ideas, criticized Müller for relying overmuch on myths, which were, he said, too confused a blend of the rational and the irrational to unlock primitive thought, about religion or anything else. He also rejected Müller's notion that a time had ever existed, before the 'disease of language', when humankind did not possess any myths. However, we now turn to the next developmental stage. Here, I suggest: anthropology became much more rigorous in its methodology, placing a premium on self-collected data, less inclined towards the theoretical, whilst for a longer period study of religions remained text, and therefore in the main, desk-bound, although also less inclined to theorize about origins. Its relationship with theology, however, remained problematical.

2 Divergence: Armchair Scholarship versus Going Native

As we noted at the beginning of Chapter 1, F. Max Müller never occupied a chair in the study of religions. This honour went to the Pali scholar and Buddhologist, T.W. Rhys Davids, appointed by Manchester University in 1904. Frazer had also given serious consideration to accepting the post, but preferred to stay at Cambridge (presumably Manchester's appeal was no greater than Liverpool's!). Oxford University has never had a chair explicitly in world religions – although occupants of the Spalding Chair in Eastern Religions and Ethics have often ranged outside this regional brief. Once coined, however, the phrase 'comparative religion' became common property; some who used it referred not to the objective, impartial study of religions but to a comparison of their various strengths and weaknesses in order to demonstrate Christian superiority. See, for example, William St-Clair Tisdall's *Comparative Religion*, published in 1909. Distinguishing themselves from those who 'study other religions much as a commander of an invading army investigates enemy territory, and much with the same motivation' (Kitagawa, 1959: 15) has always been a difficult task for the scientific students of religions. Especially in the United States, where religious or theological education is often private, state institutions regarded the new field with suspicion (teaching religion was not within their brief and was it really a *bona fide* science, anyway?), whilst seminaries and church-sponsored universities saw the 'the only legitimate discipline' as a 'theology of religions, or *Missionwissenschaft*'. In their view, religio-scientific study is ruled out because each 'investigator is incurably conditioned by his own religious and cultural backgrounds' (Kitagawa,

1959: 6). In the USA, it is not unusual for chairs in world religions to be combined with missiology.

Some of those who wrote with an apologetic brief, though, did make significant contributions to scholarship. They made information, or texts, available. Some occupants of the Boden Chair of Sanskrit at Oxford, founded in 1811, for example, 'to promote the translation of Scriptures into Sanksrit so as to enable ... the conversion of the natives of India to the Christian religion' (from Colonel Boden's will, cited in Shourie, 1994: 157), also laboured on dictionaries and on translations of scriptures from the Sanskrit. Yet, as its second occupant, Sir Monier Monier-Williams (1819–99) said, his reason for engaging in this work was to aid the missionary enterprise. Monier-Williams was elected to the chair in 1860 over his main competitor, F. Max Müller. Some comparative religionists attempted to classify religions according to an hierarchical scale, or according to their 'truth value'; higher, lower, even lower, for example, usually with Christianity at the top. This, as we saw, was not quite absent in Müller's writing. Thus, an apologetic intent still lay behind much work in this field. Increasingly, those who chose to write about the religions as objective scholars, without an apologetic brief, concentrated, as had Müller, on philology and on history. Wanting to take their place alongside other historians, they saw their task as one of reconstructing what could be known about the development of religious ideas and institutions without any evaluation of them. Lacking, as they saw it, any objective, impartial criterion with which to evaluate religion, they increasingly left that to the theologians. Their discipline would be descriptive. One did not need to hold any particular opinion about religion's origin, or authenticity, to investigate the role it plays in society and in history.

Thus, the study of religions would be the history of religions, 'a branch of the humanities, not of theology' (Sharpe, 1986: 278). Wilfred Cantwell Smith identifies this phase as characterized by a quest for facts, 'the accumulation, organisation and analysis of facts' which, he suggests, reached its climax in the *Encyclopaedia of Religion and Ethics*, 1908–21. This was 'comparative' in that it catalogued rites, beliefs, practices and phenomena under thematic headings (Smith in Eliade and Kitagawa, 1959: 31). In Britain, according to Sharpe's analysis, this historical and descriptive approach dominated until the 1950s. It continued well into the 1970s. Perhaps, too, the field's difficulty establishing its intellectual *bona fides* is reflected in the lack of established teaching posts, at least in Britain, during most of this period.

Mention, in passing, should be made of the positive stimulus which the embryonic discipline received from the 1893 Parliament of the World's Religions, Chicago. Although the delegates attended as members of their religious traditions, or denominations, not as scholars (which many were), in the minds of many Americans especially, 'comparative religion, and the cause of the World Parliament of Religions, became inseparable'. Delegates were instructed that, 'All controversy is prohibited. No attack will be made on any person or organization. Each participating body will affirm its own achievements, and will not pass judgement on any other religious body or system of faith or worship' (Kitagawa, 1959: 4). Although not all those who spoke found it easy to keep to this neutral, non-polemical brief, the idea that religions could be discussed and studied from a neutral point of view became a more widely accepted notion. For the wider significance of the Parliament, see Marcus Braybrooke's *Pilgrimage of Hope: One Hundred Years of Global Interfaith Dialogue* (1992). Oddly enough, the Parliament did not change the focus of study away from texts, towards people, even though it did stimulate exchange and encounter between practitioners of the different religions.

The historical approach

Strictly speaking, study of religions means the study of a number of religions, not of one. However, by examining briefly the work of some historians of single traditions we can assess the quality and characteristics of the historical approach. Firstly, the materials were texts – historical documents and records. Primarily, these should be original, but the evidence of travellers and of explorers was used to verify or to critique these sources. History at this stage was, as a field of study, not very self-critical; in the main, it was written from the top down. The history of the church, for example, was the history of orthodoxy. Heretics were discussed, of course, as an aspect of intellectual debate or dogmatic development, but they were on the sideline. The stories, or perceptions, of marginalized people – the poor, women, radical dissenters – were secondary, if much notice was paid to them at all. Thus, the historians of religions set out to tell the story of what were generally perceived to be unitary traditions. Their sources – official court chronicles, canonical *ahadīth* (traditions of the Prophet in Islam), the writings of major religious figures, the journals of kings and princes – tended to tell a common story. As P.H. Vrijhof commented, writing in 1979, 'scientific study and research have been mainly occupied with official religion' – with those beliefs and practices which are prescribed by specialized religious institutions (Vrijhof and Waardenburg, 1979: 694). Reconstruction of non-elite history, often called 'history from below' was not part of the historian of religions' agenda.

However, whilst earlier writers had, always and everywhere, found cause to highlight European, or Christian, superiority over non-European peoples, cultures and religions, this was no part of the historians of religions' brief. Writing about Islam, for example, they could recognize, not denigrate, technological and scientific, medical and philosophical achievement. Of the prophet Muhammad, they felt no need to adjudge his morality, or sincerity. Thus, if we put alongside each other the work of a nineteenth-century historian of the Caliphate, such as the writing of Sir William Muir (1819–1905), and a twentieth-century work on Islam, such as David Margoliouth's modestly sized *Mohammedanism* (1911), we shall see significant differences. Both scholars were linguists, the second referenced Muir's *The Life of Mahomet* (1858–60) and his *The Caliphate: Its Rise, Decline and Fall* (1891) in his bibliography. Both men served terms as President of the Royal Asiatic Society, and were recipients of its Gold Medal. In *The Life of Mahomet*, Muir had written:

Throughout every country where Mahometanism is professed, the same deep pause is made in philosophy, and ... in the east, under the influence of Mahometan belief, the natural progress of mankind, whether in government, or in science, has been retarded ... over the vast nations of the Mahometan world some universal but baneful influences seem to have operated, so as to counterfeit every diversity of national character and restrain every principle exertion. (1858–60: 2: 376f.)

In the later book, Muir, then Principal of Edinburgh University, and showered with academic honours from Glasgow, Oxford, and Bologna, wrote:

The Islam of today is substantially the Islam we have seen throughout history. Swathed in the bands of the Coran, the Moslem faith, unlike the Christian, is powerless to adapt ... to varying time and place, keep pace the march of humanity, direct and purify the social life and elevate mankind. (1891: 598)

(For a more detailed assessment of Muir's scholarship, see chapter five of my *Victorian Images of Islam* (1992)). Margoliouth, Oxford's Laudian Professor of Arabic, held no apologetic brief. His work still bears the mark of the Orientalist scholar, for example, he hints at epilepsy as the cause of Muhammad's trances, and more than hints that the Qur'an was composed by the Prophet, yet in the main he saw no need to evaluate, only to describe. In the Introduction to his *Mohammed and the Rise of Islam* (1905) he had high praise for Muir's *Life* ('not withstanding the fact that' it was 'written with a confessedly Christian bias') but he also expressed the hope that his own book would be 'absolutely free' of any 'endeavour to show the superiority or inferiority of Mohammed's religion' (1905: iv). Thus, he was quite willing to recognize achievement when he saw it:

Artistic prose takes us into the area of the novel, and it is here that Islam has furnished us with one of its classics ... the Arabian Nights .... From fiction we proceed to history, and this is undoubtedly the department of literature which may well constitute the boast of all the Islamic peoples, but especially the Arabs ... near to the study of history is geography, and ... we have a whole series of geographical treatises, dating from the third century of Islam ... (1911: 238f.)

The son of a missionary, Margoliouth (1858–1940) visited India several times, lecturing there at a number of Indian universities. Other scholars found it less easy to escape the view that Orientals were somehow inherently inferior to Europeans. We may not be too surprised to read a statement, such as the following, when made by a colonial administrator, Lord Cromer (1841–1917), whose *Modern Egypt* appeared in 1908:

Accuracy is abhorrent to the Oriental mind ... want of accuracy, which easily degenerates into untruthfulness, is in fact the main characteristic of the Oriental mind ... (1908: 2: 146.)

However, in the supposedly impartial, objective work of Reynold Alleyne Nicholson (1868–1945), a Cambridge professor, and a professor of Arabic at that, we might not expect what follows:

To the Moslem, who has no sense of natural law, all these 'violations of custom' as he calls them, seem equally credible. We, on the other hand, feel ourselves obliged to distinguish phenomena which we regard as irrational and impossible from those for which we can find some sort of 'natural' explanation. (Nicholson, 1975: 139)

Nicholson's book, though, first published in 1914 and still in print, remains a useful introduction to Islamic mysticism, whilst his translations of the Persian mystics also leaves us in his debt.

T.W. Rhys Davids (1843–1922)

Thomas William Rhys Davids, Britain's first Professor of Comparative Religion, stands in the Müller mould as linguist, translator and classical historian. In other respects, though, he differed from Müller; unlike Müller, he spent almost a decade (1866–74) outside Europe – as a civil servant in Sri Lanka, where he also studied Pali and early Buddhism; unlike Müller, he did not receive a formal university education. As the son of a Welsh nonconformist clergyman, this was virtually denied him. However, before sailing for Sri Lanka he did spend some time studying Sanskrit at Breslau University (now in Poland). After leaving Sri Lanka 'in a cloud of misunderstanding and bitterness' (Harris, 1993: 278), apparently caused by personality clashes with his superior officers, he qualified as a barrister at Middle Temple, but chose not to practice. Instead, he embarked on a lifelong 'campaign for the recognition of the worth of Pali and Buddhist studies' (*ibid.*: 279). His *Buddhism* appeared in 1878, *Buddhist Birth Stories* in 1880, followed by several volumes of translation for the Clarendon Press. Founding the Pali Text Society in 1881, more volumes followed, including the *Digha Nikaya* (1899–1910), and *Dialogues of the Buddha* (1899, 1910, 1921). Between 1882 and 1912 he held an honorary chair in Pali and Buddhist Literature at University College, London, in 1904 he became Britain's first Professor of Comparative Religion (at Manchester).

Theological evaluation formed little, if any, part of his brief. Although he knew contemporary Buddhists, and studied under a Buddhist *bhikkhu* in Sri Lanka, his focus was on Buddhism's classical texts. After returning to England, he did not maintain regular 'correspondence with Buddhist monks' (Harris, 1993: 281) but, like Müller, thought that textual scholarship could recover a religion's most original form. 'The Buddhism of the Pali texts' was, he believed, closer 'to the teachings of the Buddha' (*ibid.*: 312) than what he had observed in Sri Lanka. Gombrich (1971: 52) describes Rhys Davids as an 'excellent scholar' but suggests that he tended to stress 'the rationalist elements in Buddhism'. His biographical work on the Buddha suggests some frustration with what he considered 'irrational' about the early Buddhist accounts; he wanted to 'create a narrative appealing to the nineteenth century's sense of historicity and realism' (Harris: 283). He wrote that what the early Buddhist biographers had thought 'highly edifying is often miraculous, and not seldom absurd or childish' (1894: 16). Thus, Orientalist assumptions were not absent in his work and, as Almond (who describes him as the 'eirenic Rhys Davids') comments, he 'thought miraculous incidents in the life of the Buddha to be due "entirely to the love of exaggeration and of mystery amongst rude peoples" ' (1988: 46). He aimed, though, at objective scholarship, and, as Harris observes, his attitude towards the value of the early sources became progressively more positive. Throughout, he stressed the ethical and psychological aspects of Buddhism, which in his view represented its 'essence': 'a positive moral path of self-culture, ethical discipline and intellectual activity' (Harris: 287). Harris comments that 'Rhys Davids found within Buddhism something which he felt had a vital message to the West' (*ibid.*: 289). It was to help to spread this message in the West that he founded the Pali Text Society. Here, we see an early example of a student of religions who saw his task in moral, or spiritual terms, not only as the academic accumulation of knowledge. This anticipates the approach of several more recent scholars, such as Mircea Eliade and Karl Jung, both of whom believed that the Western world could benefit from exposure to Eastern spirituality. Such a view is not altogether absent in Müller, who thought that 'serious study of the great religions of the world may prove a great help and a most efficient remedy against intolerance' (1892: 78).

It is perhaps not insignificant that Rhys Davids' name is still revered in parts of the Buddhist world; an eminent Western scholar comments that he remains one of the 'most influential Pali scholars of modern times' (Gombrich, 1971: 51–2). The 'editions and translations of the Pali Text Society', he says, 'are more used than any indigenous materials by Sinhalese scholars' (*ibid.*: 55). Incidentally, Müller's work, too, remains popular in India, which he never visited. Hyderabad, a city where I have spent much time over the years has, for example, an impressive Max Müller library.

More British contributors

The objective, descriptive approach can also be seen in the writing of some who did attempt more universal histories of religions, not by offering an all embracing theory of religion, but by constructing parallel histories. These scholars used the comparative method to treat religions under similar themes, such as beginnings, development, schism, reform, institutions, and so on. Given that this historical approach lasted longer in Britain than elsewhere, we can cite as recent an example as Geoffrey Parrinder's *The World's Living Religions* (1966). This book was written for a popular readership, but was scholarly and objective, it 'gives a short, impartial account of the major religions ... through a brief history, a summary of the principal teachings, and estimates of movements of reform and revival' (Foreword). Parrinder was Reader (1958–70) and Professor of Comparative Religion (1970–78) in London, and here we see the comparative approach, or method, used not to evaluate, but to treat religions side by side in a systematic way. Of course, such a comparison does reveal similarities – such as the role played by reformers – which might well tell us something about the nature of religion itself, but to treat the material in this parallel way requires no comparative evaluation of their truth or falsehood. This approach can also be seen in Trevor Ling's more academic *A History of Religions East and West* (1968). The title echoes attempts to categorize religions according to their Eastern, or Western origin, or as mystical as opposed to prophetic traditions (a distinction proposed by R.C. Zaehner), but the text sets out to offer an 'impartial study of religious traditions ... of their actual historical records in terms of the ideas they teach, the types of personality they have produced' (1986: xviii). An echo here, perhaps, of psychological analysis. Ling also comments that, in its earlier period, comparative religion had

relied to a considerable extent on the work of anthropologists, indeed it was often difficult to draw any clear line of demarcation between comparative religion and anthropology.

However, he suggests, it is to sociology that students of religion should now look. He writes:

Certainly, it is the sociologists today who are active in studying and reporting on the religious behaviour of men, on the effect which this has upon economic and social structures, and, conversely, the ways in which religious behaviour is affected by social and economic structures.

This moves us some way towards what we shall suggest characterizes the next developmental phase in the discipline, an understanding of religions as complex amd multidimensional, together with the poly-methodological approach, but Ling's tools are predominantly still textual and historical. He gives us 464 pages, including index, of facts, historical analysis, all descriptive of the 'parallel developments or significant divergences' of the world's major religions. It remains a very useful text. Yet, although not unaware of different strands, or of the voice of dissent, it tells the evolutionary, developmental story, of classic, or of 'great traditions'. This suggests, perhaps, that religions are in the grip of some dialectical process. Even objective historians find it difficult to shed ideological presuppositions. Later, after discussing methodological and theoretical development in anthropology, I shall suggest that this comparative, text-biased and largely historical approach, concentrating in the main on classical traditions, yielded to interest in the multiplicity of small traditions. As subject matter changed, so did the materials and the scholarly techniques. For the record, we should note that although these scholars have been book-biased, they have not been book-bound. Ling (1920–95) has worked in Asia; Parrinder was for twenty years a Methodist missionary in

Africa. His interest in African religion and his own fieldwork experience in Africa, too, makes him more an heir of Robertson Smith than of Müller. When he discusses texts, he is not only concerned with their academic study but with doing justice to the believers' point of view (see for example his classic *Jesus in the Qur'an*, 1965 republished 1995).

The work of my own former teacher, John Hinnells, previously Professor of Comparative Religion at Manchester, now a professor in the School of Oriental and African Studies, London, also represents this historical and comparative approach. *A Handbook of Living Religions* (1984), which Hinnells edited, a basic teaching text for several of our courses at Westminster College, 'sets out to challenge many commonly held assumptions: that India is changeless, that Christianity is single; that religions are monolithic wholes' (p. 13). It also seeks to avoid placing religions in a literary 'straitjacket', which all begins to move us away from the focus on the classical towards the approach which characterizes our next phase. Nevertheless, it outlines each religion in a similar, historical-descriptive style, and 'in order to give some unity and coherence to this multi-author work, authors were asked to lay out their material under' the same 'headings, in as far as they are appropriate' (1984: 13). Nor is the encyclopaedic approach absent in Hinnells' very useful *The Penguin Dictionary of Religions* (1984) or in the much larger *Encyclopedia of Religion* (1987), edited by Mircea Eliade. Its articles on methodology, amongst others, belong more properly to our next phase of development, but in its conception the *Dictionary* belongs to this phase: systematic, comparative description of religious beliefs, practices, both historical and contemporary. Hinnells, though, is also extensively travelled; he used to entertain us with amusing anecdotes (as we read our seminar papers over a pub lunch and pint!).

Bronislaw Malinowksi (1884–1942)

In this survey of the second phase in the development of anthropology, we see how those who succeeded Tylor and the pioneers made fieldwork their life-blood. Responding to criticism about the reliability and validity of their data, they became rigorous in their collecting and observing techniques. Two men did outstanding work in the first half of this century, Bronislaw Malinowski (1884–1942), and Franz Boas (1858–1945), so we shall begin with their work. Next, we turn to a social scientist, Emile Durkheim, who, like his predecessor, Spencer, used anthropological evidence to support his functionalist theory of religion. We shall then briefly see how the Englishman, Radcliffe-Brown, developed this framework into a structural functionalism before visiting a sometimes neglected aspect of Durkheim's approach, his semiotics, which also influenced later anthropologists. Amongst these, we discuss the contributions of Claude Levi-Strauss, Sir Edmund Leach and Mary Douglas, another heir of Robertson Smith. In our next chapter, we shall note the close similarity between their view of signs and symbols and the work of a whole generation of students of religions, best represented by Mircea Eliade (hence the presence of this approach in his *Encyclopedia*) and the psychologist, Jung. Jung, as we shall see, combined use of anthropological evidence with a profound and informed interest in Eastern religion. In all this, we note the background influence of linguistics, always closely related to both anthropology and to the study of religions; both work with languages. Finally, before leaving this chapter, we shall add a brief comment on the theologian and Indologist, Rudolf Otto, whose 'Idea of the Holy' anticipated the work of the later symbolists (Eliade and his disciples). For him, as for them, 'Religion can be understood only in its own terms, and its essence can be ascertained only by intuition' (Morris: 175). This led to renewed criticism that this view 'confused *Religionswissenschaft* with theology' (Sharpe, 1986: 275). The problematic of the study of religions in its relationship with theology continues to this day; we return to this problematic in Chapter 5.

One reason why I find Adam Kuper's book, *Anthropology and Anthropologists: The Modern British School* (1973 revised 1987) so insightful is that, in evaluating the work of 'the godlike founding fathers of' anthropology, it 'presents them as human beings, warts and all', or 'desacralizes' them (Willis, 1975: 490). To empathize with the human in the anthropologist seems, to me, eminently appropriate. His analysis of Bronislaw Malinowki's towering contribution to British social anthropology loses nothing by way of critical appreciation for its exposure of his 'overpowering personality' and 'intolerance and rudeness' (Kuper, 1991: 23). Rather, this enables us to see something of the flesh and blood man. Malinowski was born in Cracow, Poland, and later claimed that his parents were members of the lesser nobility. At Jagellonian University, where his father taught Slavic philology, he read mathematics and physics (and later said that he had graduated with the highest honours in the Austrian Empire). Increasingly, however, he turned towards philosophy. He also read, and admired, *The Golden Bough*, later commenting that he had known 'Frazer for the last thirty-one years of his life' and that his death had 'symbolised the end of an epoch' (1944: 179f.). Moving to Leipzig, his father's *alma mater* he added experimental psychology to his interests, especially Wilhelm Wundt's work on the interrelatedness of language, myth (*Volkerpsychologie*) and culture. Next, anthropology beckoned. He had already read English and German anthropological monographs but now went to the London School of Economics 'in search of anthropological inspiration' (Lewis: 53). There, he studied under Charles Gabriel Seligman (1873–1940) and encountered a new emphasis on the need for the anthropologist to be the collector and not merely the collator of data. In fact, he presented his Doctor of Science thesis on 'The Family Among the Australian Aborigines' before going to Australia, but fieldwork soon followed, and in 'the two years he spent on the Trobriand Islands, 1915–17 and 1917–18' ... 'he really did invent modern fieldwork methods' (Kuper: 13). His subsequent monographs on aspects of Trobriand life made him, and the islanders ('Trobriand man'), immortal.

Participant observation

In the Trobriands, Malinowski pioneered 'participant observation'. He was, says Lewis, 'the pioneer, bush-whacking anthropologist, the originator of the doctrine that until you have lived cheek by jowl with an exotic tribe and spoken their language fluently you cannot claim full professional status' (1992: 54). Certainly, after Malinowski, no anthropologist who aspires to academic or to professional recognition can afford to reply as Frazer reputedly did 'God forbid', to the question, 'have you ever lived amongst savages?' The first requisite, said Malinowski, is language. Next, the anthropologist must 'immerse himself' (or herself – several of his early students were women) 'as thoroughly as he [or she] can in the life of the community he [or she] is trying to understand' (Lewis: 24). Observation, and data gathering (for example, by interview) must be systematic. Malinowski himself favoured concentrating, successively, on single topics, whilst retaining as a long-term goal the construction of a total picture. Thus, his monographs discussed such single themes as trading, procreation, family life, myth. In fact, due to 'poor health', he never did deliver a 'statement of Trobriand "culture" as a whole'. He also attributed this failure to his perceived need of quickly presenting 'the theoretical point of view which we now label "functional", and which I could only do by presenting some fragments of my stuff, well placed in an extensive theoretical setting' (cited in Kuper: 25).

Perhaps aware of the type of criticism made by Müller, that anthropologists failed to verify their evidence, verification became a major concern in his work. 'Measure, weigh and count everything', he said (Cheater, 1986: 40). He used synoptic charts to record his data, indicating 'observed' descriptions and interview material, and discrepancies and connections between different aspects of an activity. He also stressed the importance of keeping a diary – to record his own impressions, as well as his 'psychological reactions to the work situation' (ibid.: 40). I shall say more about his *Diary* a little later in this chapter. Not all the technical vocabulary now associated with the verification of data derives from Malinowski, but he used, or anticipated, most of the techniques. For example, he stressed the importance of acquiring information from different informants, recognizing that different people have different perceptions, often influenced by the roles they play. This helps to provide a multidimensional view of the belief, rite, or custom. Evidence should always be checked for accuracy. Does the informant say the same thing twice. If revisited after a few days, does he still say the same thing. The technical term 'triangulation' refers to this process of verification, either time triangulation (asking the same person on several occasions), source triangulation (asking several people), or sometimes method triangulation. If engaged in team work, or aided by an assistant, does a different researcher elicit the same response? Or observing what a person does may be set alongside what they say they do. The social sciences borrowed the term triangulation from surveyors, who 'look at something from angles or viewpoints to get a fix on its true position' (Neuman, 1994: 141).

Thus, Malinowski's chief legacy was a bias towards the empirical, together with the need to verify data. This emphasis on firsthand observation, on data collected by fieldwork techniques, together with the tendency to work in societies which do not possess written records of their own (and, where possible, where few other anthropologists have worked) resulted in 'extreme hostility to history', and to the use of literary sources generally (see Evans-Pritchard, 1961: 1). This contrasts with the historical approach of students of religions during this phase of our survey. Anthropology was to be a scientific discipline. It continued to be positivist in its approach to knowledge; in other words, social reality, like physics, 'is patterned and has order'. These reflect 'preexisting regularities which can be observed' (Neuman: 59). Social theory, then, is a 'logical, deductive system of interconnected definitions, axioms and laws' based on 'facts' which others can verify by repeated observation (*ibid.*: 75). Positivist science also regards itself as 'value-free' – you deduce theory from observed facts, rather than interpret what you observe according to a preconceived theoretical framework. In Chapter 5, we shall discuss whether a 'value-free' science is actually achievable, or even a human possibility.

Malinowski was reluctant to move too hastily from what he could observe locally, and therefore know, towards universal theory, or the comparative approach which had characterized the earlier work of the armchair anthropologists. This was amongst his criticism of Frazer, whose 'theoretical position, ... evolutionism, ... comparative treatment of cultures, and ... explanations by survival' were, he said, 'at times not acceptable' (1944: 211). Only after researching several societies, and establishing similarities, could general theories be made. His brilliant student, Sir Edward Evan Evans-Pritchard (1902–73), expressed reluctance to theorize even after this type of serial research, it 'promised little beyond a rather elementary classification of types' (cited in Kuper: 200). Every culture is a discrete yet complex structure – and they should not be torn apart 'for the purposes of comparative study' (Kuper: 26). Malinowski's work in the Trobriands also established the parameters, or the field, in which anthropologists would work – small, fairly rigidly defined and 'boundaried' societies. Appointed reader at the London School of Economics and Social Sciences in 1924, and professor in 1927, Malinowski chose 'social anthropology' as his title (he remained at the London School of Economics until 1938, when he went on leave to the USA, became stranded there when World War II broke out, and stayed on to teach at Yale). Partly, this was because Frazer at Liverpool and Tylor at Cambridge had taught 'social anthropology', partly because he wanted to identify his discipline as a social science, whilst at the same time *distinguishing* it *from* sociology. In part, too, the distinction lay in subject matter – sociologists concentrated on large social groups, anthropology on small groups. Methodology also differentiated between the two social sciences – sociology used quantitative data, statistics, large-scale questionnaires; anthropology used participant observation and in-depth interviews. Of course, these differences are now much less marked, as contemporary sociologists also study smaller, rigidly defined groups (often using participant observation) and collect and use qualitative data. This blurs the distinction between them. Also, anthropologists now find their subjects living amongst 'us' (Western, industrialist society) as migrant, or minority, communities. Another distinction might be made; anthropologists study 'them', alien societies, sociologists study 'us'. To some degree, this was, and remains, a valid distinction. However, if participant observation works, the 'them' of the anthropologist may (arguably should) become the 'us' of sociology. So again, the distinction blurs, as Lewis comments:

If our frontiers with psychiatry and psychology (including social psychology) are problematic and ill-defined, the situation is even more confused with sociology (and in some respects history). Some authorities even hold that social anthropology is really a sub-division of sociology, a broadly-based comparative 'trans-cultural' or cross-cultural sociology. (1992: 24)

Malinowski's functionalism

Malinowski's theoretical contribution in the field of religious studies stemmed from his overall functionalist approach. For him, every custom, practice, tradition, 'however strange and bizarre, served some contemporary purpose' (Lewis: 55). Savages aren't half-rational or irrational, but do things because they work. Customs survive not as throw-backs but because they fulfil some function. Although he preferred the term 'social anthropology' Malinowski tended to concentrate on the individual; individuals do what they do because it works *for them*. Thus

'human nature' has to be assessed in terms of human needs; of those needs which permanently have to be answered if man is to survive ... the primary necessities of mankind are satisfied through inventions, tools, weapons, and other material contrivances which ... have to be managed by groups, who co-operate and work and live in common, and where tradition is handed down from one generation to another. (Malinowski, 1944: 212)

The reference here to the role of the group indicates that Malinowski by no means ignored the societal altogether. Marriage, for example, works because it fulfils a function for individuals, but also for society: it controls sex by outlawing illicit sex. As we saw earlier, Malinowski suggested that magic works because it fulfils a psychological need. It performs a function. Religion, he said, stemmed not from some ancient neurosis, or irrational belief in spirits, but is 'pragmatically ... necessary to the average individual to overcome the shattering disruptive anticipation of death, of disaster, and of destiny' (1944: 200). Durkheim also thought religion useful in restoring normality after any disruption has caused what he called *anomie*, a sense of normlessness, to social, or group life. Religion fulfils, like magic, a socio-psychological function; by establishing a system of rites and practices, it offers a mechanism to relieve this *angst*. Like Durkheim, (whom we discuss below) Malinowski distinguished between 'profane' and 'sacred' realms, although his view of these differed from Durkheim's. For Malinowski, the former belong to the realm of 'rational mastery' of one's surroundings, whilst magic and religion belong to the realm of metaphysical explanation (Tambiah, 1990: 70).

Such a functionalist view of religion is actually more positive about religion's role, or value, than a view which sees its origin in the totally irrational. Religious belief, too, especially ethical codes, helps maintain moral standards, to regulate behaviour. Whether such beliefs are true or false (whether what is morally condemned is right or wrong), or whether religion has any real connection with some divine, absolute being, or reality, is not for the functionalist to say. Whilst this is a reductionist view of religion, it does not necessarily adjudge religion false, silly or misguided. Unlike the eminent French philosopher, Lucien Levy-Bruhl (1857–1939), who, using anthropological data, argued that primitive peoples' thought was qualitatively different from modern thought, being pre-logical (it did not, for example, separate cause from effect), Malinowski did not think that pre-literate people were any more, or less, superstitious or irrational than any other people. On the 'first page of his most important theoretical work, *Magic, Science and Religion*' (Geertz, 1968: 91) he wrote:

A moment's reflection is sufficient to show that no art or craft, however primitive, could have been invented or maintained, no organized form of hunting, fishing, tilling, or search for food, could be carried out without the careful observation of natural processes and a firm belief in its regularity, and without confidence in the power of reason. (1948: 1)

'A diary in the strict sense of the term'

Malinowski, like his predecessors, thought that savages represented our own past still living in the present. By studying them, we could better understand that past. This is why he bemoaned the disappearance of his subject matter, as European influence changed, or destroyed, traditional cultures. 'Just as we have reached a certain academic status', he complained, 'and developed our methods and theories, our subject matter threatens to disappear' (1938: xii). Earlier, in 1906, Frazer and seventy-six other anthropologists had written to the government of Victoria urging that as much data on the Aborigines as possible be collected before they died out. However, Malinowski also suggested new areas and themes for research: what happens when cultures meet? Here, three subjects emerge, the encroaching cultural influences, the original culture, and the *'tertium quid*, in which a new syncretic culture' emerged (Kuper: 33). Here we have material, too, for students of religions: what happens to religions in their encounter with each other? (we explore this area in Chapter 4).

Although Malinowski still thought that study of 'savages' could inform us about our past, as he penetrated deeper into Trobriand life, attempting to see the islanders in their humanity, he perceived that, through them, he saw himself: 'What is the deepest essence of my investigations?', he wrote in his *Diary* in 1917, 'To discover what are his [Trobriand man's] main passions, the motives for his conduct, his aims ... His essential, deepest way of thinking. At this point we are confronted with our own problems: What is essential in ourselves?' (1967: 115). He became less interested in the reconstruction of the past, more in understanding the 'why' of the present. The savage becomes a man alongside ourselves, not an exotic remnant or survivor (albeit a notion Malinowski did not reject). Although, as we have noted, he criticized Frazer, he also admired him. One reason for this admiration was that he saw, in Frazer's writing, belief 'in the essential similarity of the human mind and of human nature' (1944: 212). We may note how this appraisal of Frazer differs from Mary Douglas', cited above!

Malinowski's *Diary* (published in 1967) also reveals the frustrations, boredom, and difficulties of the lonely anthropologist. Published posthumously, it reveals how hard it is, even for a master of his craft, to become fully immersed in another culture. 'To put it delicately', says Geertz, Malinowski 'was not an unmitigated nice guy. He had rude things to say about the natives' and 'spent a great deal of his time wishing he were elsewhere' (1983: 56). More recently, several anthropologists have published amusing and witty accounts of their own mistakes and bumblings. Do they really ever understand what they see? Geertz's famous, if borrowed, illustration of the wink demonstrates how easy it is to misunderstand. There is, he says, a world of difference between a wink as a conspiratorial sign, and a physical, involuntary reaction to a gust of wind! To learn language, let alone to correctly interpret non-verbal modes of communication, requires assistance, and often more time than the anthropologist's research grant will allow. See Nigel Barley's outrageously funny *The Innocent Anthropologist: Notes from a Mud Hut* (1983), for example: 'The anthropologist's assistant is a figure who seems suspiciously absent from ethnographical accounts. The conventional myth seeks to depict the battle-scarred anthropologist as a lone figure wandering to a village, settling in, and picking up the language in a couple of months'. It isn't that easy. Barley continues, 'In England, a man may have studied French at school for six years and with the help of language-learning devices, visits France and exposure to the literature and yet finds himself hardly able to stammer out a few words of French in an emergency. Once in the field, he transforms himself into a linguistic wonder worker, ... without qualified teachers, and often without grammars' he becomes 'fluent in a language much more difficult for a Westerner than French' (1983: 44). Barley also writes about the difficulty of acquiring the information you want:

Dowayo explanations always ended up in a circle I came to know well. 'Why do you do this?' I would ask.
   'Because it is good.'
   'Why is it good?'
   'Because the ancestors told us to.'
   (Slyly) 'Why did the ancestors tell you to?'
   'Because it is good.'
   I could never find a way round 'the ancestors' with whom all explanation began and ended. (*ibid.*: 82–3)

Or, as Richard Gombrich points out, informants, from sheer politeness, may tell you what they think you want to hear:

The Sinhalese are deeply courteous, and do not consider it a virtue to tell unpleasant truths. The answer to any leading question is therefore likely to be 'Ov' (yes). This word, *ov*, which we translate as 'yes', in effect has rather the meaning, 'I have heard'; it must not be taken as an answer to a question without further probing and corroboration. (1970: 37)

Such accounts suggest that the good anthropologist needs to be aware of the difference which his or her own presence makes. Clifford Geertz, in his work, has stressed that anthropologists must be able to 'shift among perspectives', or to engage in what he sometimes calls 'reflexivity'. The danger is, as we shall see when we return to this problematic in Chapter 5, that anthropology will become too preoccupied with its own uncertainties, with what Geertz calls a 'sort of epistemological hypochondria, concerning how one can know that anything one says about other forms of life is as a matter of fact so' (1988: 71). The challenge is to respond creatively, as the authors of the studies in Don Fowler's and Don Hardesty's *Others Knowing Others: Perspectives on Ethnographic Careers* (1994) attempt to do, exploring 'how the field experience changes one as an observer and as an interpreter of another culture' and asking 'What new perspectives on oneself as a scholar, and on the peoples one studies, are gained?' (p 4). Barley's book, although written for a popular readership, is a good example of reflexivity.

Years after Malinowski's own pioneering work in the Trobriands, a missionary gave us this unflattering description: 'It was a surprise to me to find Malinowski was mostly remembered by the natives as the champion ass at asking damnfool questions' (Kuper: 18). Perhaps it is easier to totally 'go native', to blend anonymously into your surroundings, within a larger cultural context than it is in a rigidly defined community. In Bangladesh, in my third year, I had passed Junior and Senior Language Examinations, was tanned, bearded, wore locally manufactured clothes, and, when travelling, found that I was not automatically taken for a foreigner. Had I tried to blend in within a small, rigidly defined community, possibly speaking its own dialect, I would immediately have been identified as an outsider. Whether we are regarded as an insider or as an outsider, too, may influence how our questions are answered, or how others treat us. We are treated differently when we are thought to be members, or insiders, than when we're thought to be outsiders. When I first went to register at the Bodleian, the University of Oxford's central library, I arrived at 4.30 pm expecting the Admissions Office to remain open until 5.00 pm. It had just closed. The porter was rather impatiently explaining that I would have to come back another day, when the door opened and a colleague (who works both at the Bodleian and at Westminster College although I did not then know that she worked at the former!) came out, saw me, greeted me by name (and with the title 'Doctor') and proceeded to enrol me. We then went off together for a cup of coffee and, as I passed him, I observed a new look, of respect, on the porter's face. I was clearly an insider. Had I been about to interview him for some purpose of inquiry, I may have elicited a different story to any story I might have heard if I'd interviewed him before encountering my colleague!

Franz Boas (1858–1942)

What Malinowski is to British anthropology, Franz Boas is to American. After Malinowski and Boas, in both countries, fieldwork became mandatory for the would-be professional anthropologist, almost an anthropological rite of passage (as it is often now called). Boas was born into a middle class, German Jewish family. At university, he oscillated between the hard sciences (physics) and the humanities (geography), taking his doctorate at Kiel in 1881. He was, he said, interested in understanding 'the relation between the objective and subjective worlds' (cited in Kuper, 1988: 132). After a scientific expedition to Baffin Island (1883–4) where he lived amongst the Eskimos, he began teaching at Berlin, but interest in the American Indians soon took him back to North America, where he settled, eventually becoming Professor of Anthropology at Columbia and a curator at the American Museum of Natural History, New York. Earlier, whilst working at Clark University, he gained 'the first American PhD in anthropology' (*ibid..*). Boas' contribution resembles Malinowski's: methodical fieldwork, cautious analyses, and a reluctance to make comparisons. He warned against attempts to construct speculative histories, favouring instead the meticulous collection of data, and aiming at the total recovery of data from each individual culture. Between 1888 and 1894, Boas made 'five visits, each lasting several months' to the Kwakiutl peoples; he was interested in relationships between the Eskimos, and the American Indians (Kuper, 1988: 133). His aim was to 'capture their worldview' (*ibid.*: 134). Only after total recovery of a people's worldview, he said, could generalizations be made. Each culture should be treated as an entity in and of itself, the product of its own special, or divergent, history. In Boas' view, all cultures have histories, and no custom, or indeed people, can be understood without attempting to construct their particular cultural history. To intelligently understand complex phenomena, he said, 'we have to know not only what it is, but also how it came into being' (cited by Evans-Pritchard, 1961: 6). Boas was thus more interested than Malinowski in historical reconstruction, in what Levi-Strauss, referring to Boas, calls 'microhistory' (see Levi-Strauss, 1963: 9). Boas used his reconstruction of Kwakiutl history to attack the 'dogma that all societies progressed from a matrilineal to a patrilineal form of organization' and to criticize 'the orthodox theory of totemism' (Kuper, 1988: 135). This, we shall see in our next chapter, would have its impact on the scientific study of religions. To impose an overall (or unilinear) evolutionary scheme, suggested Boas, does violence to the particularity of each individual religion or culture. He wrote:

serious objections may be made against the assumption of the occurrence of a general sequence of cultural stages among all the races of man; ... rather we recognize both a tendency of diverse customs and beliefs to converge towards similar forms, and a development of customs in divergent direction. (1938: 173)

Culture provided Boas and his successors with their main subject matter, hence 'cultural anthropology' dominates in the USA. American trained anthropologists have sometimes regarded British social anthropology, 'with its emphasis on social relationships and social structures' with a degree of suspicion (Ottenberg, 1994: 101). Boas' tool, then, like Malinowski's, was empirical fieldwork, in contrast to our book-biased historians of religions during this phase of our review. Unlike Malinowski, though, Boas mainly used 'local experts who were bilingual, literate and of mixed ancestry' who, he thought, could collect data more easily than he could himself. They worked under his close control, and systematically – rather like 'technicians in laboratory research' (Kuper, 1994: 547).

Boas rejected the idea of genetic superiority; cultural diversity stems from cultural relativity:

Culture is ... the result of innumerable interacting factors and there is no evidence that the differences between human races, particularly not between the members of the white race have any directive influence upon the course of development of culture. (1938: 179)

He equally disliked 'the racial interpretation of history' and the embryonic science of 'eugenics' – both were 'irremediably dangerous' . This, suggests Derek Freeman, explains his bias away

71

from biological towards cultural determinism (Freeman, 1983: 5). Boas' *The Mind of Primitive Man* (1911), in its revised edition (1938) provided some intellectual stimulus to the civil rights movement in the USA, with its affirmation that, 'there is every reason to believe that the Negro when given facility and opportunity, will be perfectly able to fulfil the duties of citizenship as well as his white neighbour' (1938: 240). The back cover of my 1963 edition comments: 'Today's defenders of racial segregation in the United States and of apartheid in South Africa still jibe at this measured, objective analysis'. Vehemently opposed to the Nazi movement in his native Germany, where copies of *The Mind of Primitive Man* were burnt, and his PhD rescinded, he equally denounced anti-Semitism, and the concept of 'racial purity': 'Since a remote period there have been no pure races in Europe and it has never been proved that continued intermixture has brought about deterioration' (1938: 231). Boas aided war refugees in New York, and died somewhat dramatically 'at a luncheon given by him for his friend Professor Paul Rivet of Paris, then a refugee from the Nazi oppression' (Herskovits, 1963: 7). Addressing his colleagues on racism, he 'had a sudden heart attack, and fell, dying, into the arms of the man sitting next to him, who was Claude Levi-Strauss' (Kuper, 1988: 151). It has been said that no one, this century, has done more than Boas to combat racist attitudes.

The ethical, or moral, consequence of anthropological work, is one of the themes we shall consider in Chapter 5. On the one hand, Boas' work has clearly had ethical (anti-racist) consequences; on the other, his understanding of culture, which views every culture as autonomous, tends to preclude anthropologists from making moral judgements about the cultures they study. Their aim, to understand a group's values and norms by its own standards, discourages them from measuring these values against their own. Too often, said Boas, anthropological investigators have been conditioned by their own sense of superiority:

the idea is rooted in the minds of investigators that we should expect to find in the White race the highest type of man. Social conditions are often treated from the same point of view. We value our individual freedom, our code of ethics, our free art so highly that they seem to mark an advancement to which no other race can lay claim. (1938: 21)

Commenting on Boasian anthropology, Adam Kuper writes, 'if there was no necessary course of cultural development, cultures could not be rated higher or lower', and, favouring cultural relativity, if values are also 'culturally variable' ... 'there can be no objective evaluation of cultural traits' (Kuper, 1994: 539). Boas' view of culture also critiques Marx's 'historical dialectic'; if there is no single evolutionary path along which all cultures will inevitably travel, then the emergence of the communist state cannot be a universal norm. Some anthropologists question whether there are any universal norms, since exceptions have even been identified to such possible candidates as the family, and the subordination of women to men. Malinowski, for his part, had taken the family as a universal norm, fulfilling 'a universal human need for the nurturance and care of children' (Moore, 1988: 23). Henrietta Moore, however, is less confident that even the family can be considered a universal category (see Moore: 26–8). The role of nannies, too, in rearing children, whom children understandably love more than their mothers, 'questions the singular relationship between mother-child units' (*ibid.*: 27). Mother–offspring bonding may not be universally experienced. Even gender is differently construed in different societies, and is therefore – in all probability – a social construct (*ibid.*: 13f). The issues of women's subordination to men, which has also been taken as a universal norm, and of gender, will be addressed in Chapter 5. Here, suffice it to say, that anthropologists have sometimes assumed subordination, when the actual power dynamic between the sexes in certain societies is more complex, distinguishing their roles, for example, so that each exercises power in different spheres. To label this as the subordination of either sex to the other may well be to misconstrue the data. Having spent much time discovering that 'what were taken to be natural phenomena' are 'in fact cultural ones', some anthropologists have 'even claimed that there is no such thing as a human nature'. However, comments Dan Sperber, if this is indeed the case, anthropology's subject-matter disappears! (Sperber, 1979: 19).

Fieldwork as the norm

If we find ourselves unable to identify any universal cultural norms, what we can affirm about this phase of anthropology's development is that it ceased to be an armchair discipline and adopted fieldwork and participant observation (sometimes caricatured as 'going native') as its normative research methodology. It was 'us' talking about 'them'; the 'they' were primitive peoples in small, rigidly bounded societies, and research was to be conducted in the field, not in the university study. Research focused on kinship relations, on power structures, on gender roles, and, as we shall see when we turn to the consequences of Durkheim's work especially, on symbols, signs, art, myth and legend, sacred time/space, on mundane time/space, and on the role which these play in traditional societies. Anthropologists were also interested in identifying whether different people (young, old, men, women, priests, laity, rulers, the ruled) had different perceptions, in why this was so, and thus in the relationship between the ideal, and the actual behaviour or practice. They tended to see religion in functionalist terms; as a tool for social control, or as a catalyst to help bind societies together, which suggested human origin. Consequently, some traditional theologians perceived anthropology as an anti-religious science, at odds with theology. On a positive note, though, discovery of oral traditions, and of the role played by myth in pre-literate societies, did contribute to biblical scholarship about how the scriptures had been formed and shaped by oral traditions. In part, this explained the different strands within the Hebrew Bible. Since Robertson Smith, Bible scholarship of the more liberal persuasion has looked to extra-biblical sources of information to help understand the Bible within its historical and social context. The conservative approach, believing that the text of the Bible was composed by God, has little need to identify, or to understand, human influence.

Emile Durkheim (1858–1917)

Functionalism is especially associated with the writing of the French sociologist, Emile Durkheim, whose work did much to develop its theoretical framework. Durkheim held the Chair of

Sociology at the Sorbonne – which from 1913 became the Chair of Education and Sociology. There, he was influenced by anthropology; in turn, he was a profound influence upon anthropology. Early in his life he read the work of Robertson Smith, which he described as a 'revelation'.

In summary, Durkheim saw culture (including religion) as a social construct. Influenced by psychology yet wishing to distinguish sociology as a discrete discipline, he developed a schema to interpret, and to analyse, social phenomena *sociologically*. Social facts existed *sui generis*, not, for example, as the product of Marxist determinism. In his view, religions, legal codes, accepted or normal cultural practices, rules of commerce, all develop in order to create and maintain harmony within society. Deviancy might also serve a positive purpose, if not too rampant; harsh punishment 'symbolically re-affirmed and restored the moral values and common loyalties which' had been desecrated (Lewis: 48). Deviancy can also, if consensus allows, push 'forward the frontiers of morality' (Parkin, 1992: 30). Culture and religion, together with their external signs and symbols, are expressive of a collective consciousness, or identity. Religion is thus the sacralization of society itself, an expression of collective identity. His classic contribution to our field is *The Elementary Forms of the Religious Life* (1912; English translation, 1915) in which he attempted to study religion 'in its most primitive and simple form' . . . 'to account for its nature by examining its genesis'. He kept good company here – Tylor, Frazer, Malinowski, had all theorized about religion's genesis. Even the most barbaric religious practices, he believed, must be responsive to some sort of human need. Durkheim turned to the Australian Aborigines to help identify the origin of religion because he held that:

Every time that we set out to explain something human taken at a given point in time – be it a religious belief, a moral rule, a legal principle . . . or an economic system – we have to begin by going back to its simplest and most primitive form. (1912: 4–5; trans. Parkin)

His conclusion? That religion is:

a unified set of beliefs and practices related to sacred things, that is to say, things set apart and forbidden – beliefs and practices which unite, into one single moral community ... all those who adhere to them. (1915: 47)

Before reaching this conclusion, Durkheim discussed alternative definitions, and found them wanting. He then supported his theory with anthropological data from the Arunta tribe, which used totem animals to identify specialist groups (*shamans*) within the larger group, around which ceremonies 'devoted to the increase of the species' developed. Durkheim 'wondered aloud' why the totem species, its emblem and sometimes its human servants, were regarded as sacred when none of these were 'themselves in any way remarkable' (Parkin, 1992: 47). His solution lies in his view that, unable to grasp the abstract and remote notion of the clan meaningfully, the tribe transfers its collective sentiment and emotion onto a chosen emblem, or totem. This then serves as a concrete symbol of the abstract consciousness. Durkheim knew, however, that tribes also believed in some 'quasi-divine principle' within their totems. Calling this the 'totemic principle' it becomes, he said, identified as a 'great spirit' or as a 'god' but is actually 'nothing else than the clan itself, personified and represented to the imagination under the visible form of the animal or vegetable which serves as totem' (1915: 206). Religion is thus the worship of society itself, a 'system of ideas by means of which people represent to themselves the society of which they are members and the opaque but intimate relations they have in it' (1915: 323). Following Robertson Smith, Durkheim surmised that when the totem animal is eaten during ritual ceremonies, this represents a type of 'communal and sacramental meal' through which the clan members are spiritually rejuvenated (see Morris, 1987: 118). Robertson Smith's influence is easily discernible; he was criticized, as we saw, for seeing totemism everywhere. What neither Smith nor Durkheim, unlike some psychological anthropologists, was prepared to contemplate was that genuine communion might occur between the clan, and their totem. 'An anthropologist evaluating shamanism from a psychological perspective will tend', suggests Nevill Drury, 'to be more interested in the altered states of consciousness accessed through trance, the visionary origins of the shaman's magical and religious beliefs and other factors ... associated with shamanism'

(1989: 5). Durkheim was dependent on the pioneer fieldwork of Sir Walter Baldwin Spencer (1860–1929) and Francis James Gillen (1856–1912) for his anthropological data. Their work, according to Adam Kuper, may have been directed along certain theoretical lines because of the relationship which Spencer enjoyed with Frazer; Spencer 'depended on Frazer ... for ideas and encouragement'. Whilst he thought his job was to check, document, and 'if necessary refute' the theoretician's ideas, the fact that his research was guided by the questions which Frazer posed may have left some relevant areas untouched (Kuper, 1988: 102). Durkheim's own analysis thus represents a 'third order interpretation', which 'assigns general theoretical significance', in this case, to second order material (see Neuman: 324). His lack of firsthand encounter makes Durkheim atypical of this phase. He was, however a sociologist making use of anthropology, rather than an anthropologist theorizing from an armchair.

Durkheim, born Jewish, briefly Catholic, for most of his life an atheist, was uninterested in evaluating whether religious beliefs are good or bad, true or false. However, his view of religion was positive in as much as he saw religion as contributing to social harmony. In fact, Durkheim did not believe in any 'collective untruth'; thus, 'In reality, there are no religions which are false, all answer, though in different ways, to the given conditions of human existence' (1915: 3). What would be taken up especially by our next generation of scientific students of religions, however, was Durkheim's distinction between the sacred and the profane, and the task of interpreting the symbols which demarcate this divide. Durkheim wrote:

All religious beliefs, whether simple or complex, present one character-istic; they presuppose a classification of all things, real or ideal, of which men think into two classes ... generally designated by two distinct terms which are translated well enough by the words profane and sacred. (1915: 37)

Although suspicious of psychological explanation, Durkheim was influenced here by psychological and linguistic theory. This has argued that the human mind, in order to make sense of experience and to cope with the apparent contradictions of life, invariably thinks in terms of binary opposites – life, death; hot, cold; sacred, profane. Some go so far as to say that, like a computer programme, the human mind is built, or designed, to operate in this way. Such distinctions clearly do play a significant role in maintaining religious identity – the Jewish Sabbath evening service, or *havdalah* ritual, which 'involves three symbols – a cup of wine, a box of spices and a twisted candle – and a prayer praising God for "making a distinction between holy and profane" ' (Gollberg and Reyner, 1987: 344), for example. Or Islam's *haram–halal* distinction, and the Qur'anic injunction to 'enjoin right conduct and forbid indecency' (Qur'an, chap. 3: 104). Durkheim explored this linguistic phenomena in his *Primitive Classification* (1903), co-written with his nephew and collaborator, Marcel Mauss (1872–1950). The 'Hopi … who particularly enjoyed Durkheim's and Mauss' attention, classify living creatures and natural phenomena by means of a vast system of correspondences' (Levi-Strauss, 1966: 40). Where some students of religions would part company with Durkheim is in their belief that the sacred–profane distinction has a divine, not a human, or socially controlling, origin.

After Durkheim, psychological anthropology has tended to dominate French anthropology. In the USA, Durkheim's influence has led to the general recognition of linguistics as a sub-branch of anthropology, alongside other branches – such as cultural, biological, archaelogical, and so on. The French philosopher, Levy-Bruhl (to whom reference was made on p. 66), was also much influenced by Durkheim. His view that pre-literate people were illogical can be misunderstood. By this, he did not mean to imply the inherent inferiority of primitive peoples, living or dead, but that they perceive the universe differently from literate peoples. They move, he argued, in a 'mystical reality'; thus, 'stones and trees are never just perceived as natural objects' but as 'receptacles of mystical powers' or as 'possessed of sacred characteristics' (Morris: 184).

Clearly, Durkheim's 'consensus' model of society contrasts with Marxist theory. For Durkheim, culture and religion are products of social consensus; for Marx, both were created by the few, to control the many. Debate between a 'consensus' model and a 'conflict' model continues within the social sciences. In Chapter 5, I shall suggest that anthropologists probably need to oscillate between both theoretical frameworks. If few societies represent a total consensus, few are conflict riddled through and through. Parkin points out another fundamental difference between Durkheim's sociology, and Marx's – Durkheim looked to the past to throw light on the present, Marx reversed this. For him, 'The anatomy of the human being is the key to the anatomy of the ape', not vice versa, thus 'less evolved forms could only be made intelligible in the light of forms at a more advanced stage' (Parkin: 42). According to Marx, suggests Parkin, Durkheim should have examined Islam, or Christianity, not the Arunta 'to penetrate the mysteries of totemism' (*ibid.*).

Durkheim's successors

Durkheim's more socially oriented functionalism was influential on the work of the Englishman, Alfred Reginald Radcliffe-Brown (1881–1955). Educated at Cambridge, Radcliffe-Brown did field-work in the Andaman Isles (1906–8) and in Australia (1910–12) where he was later Professor at Sydney University (1926–31). Although born of lower middle class parents, he later adopted the double-barrelled name and the *persona* of an upper-class don, 'and in his long exile in South Africa, Australia and the United States he played the rather archaic part of an eccentric English nobleman abroad, even affecting a cloak and opera-hat on inappropriate occasions in the egalitarian milieu of Sydney in the 1920s' (Kuper, 1983: 41). After teaching at Chicago, he became Oxford's first established Professor of Social Anthropology (1937). Often referred to as Malinowski's rival, Radcliffe-Brown developed a structural-functionalist understanding of how societies work. This approach distinguishes between *structures* as the social networks which sustain social frameworks, and *function* as the way such networks contribute to a society's peaceful, harmonious functioning. His understanding of religion, which within this structuralist frame-work primarily concerns us, remained close to Durkheim's. He did not think there was much profit speculating about the origin of religion, which possibly (or probably) lies in 'erroneous and delusory beliefs'. However, he said, religious beliefs and observances do form part of 'a complex system by which human beings live together in an orderly fashion' (Morris: 127). What we can examine empirically is the function which religions perform in this maintenance of social harmony: 'To understand a particular religion we must study its effects. The religion must therefore be studied in action' (cited in Waardenburg, 1973: 604).

There was, though, room in his scheme for something very much like Schleiermacher's 'feeling of absolute dependence': 'As a general formula ... it is suggested that what is expressed in all religions is what I have called the sense of dependence in its double effect, and that it is by constantly maintaining this sense of dependence that religions perform their social function' (*ibid.*). In one of his last lectures, he suggested that religious typologies may vary according to social structures. For examples in a 'lineage system we may expect to find ancestor cult' whilst 'the Hebrews and city states of Greece had national religions in conformity with their types of political structures' (Evans-Pritchard, 1965: 75). Here, he was falling into the old trap of forming a speculative theory without due regard to empirical evidence. There are plenty of tribes which worship ancestor-gods who have other than lineal systems of leadership. On magic and religion, however, Radcliffe-Brown made a useful contribution. He thought it doubtful if either could be explained as giving psychological comfort; they are as likely to 'give men fears and anxieties from which they would otherwise be free ... the fear of ... magic ... or of spirits' (1952: 149). Thus, it is necessary to investigate their meaning both in terms of any function they might fulfil, and symbolically.

Claude Levi-Strauss (1908–90)

Claude Levi-Strauss applied linguistic theory to anthropological research, especially to the study of thought and symbolism. Levi-Strauss first studied law and philosophy in Paris, where he was influenced by Jean-Paul Sartre (1905–80), the existentialist writer. Existentialism, with its emphasis on human individualism and freedom is generally said to 'reduce theology to anthropology'; its 'opponents have claimed that Existentialism ... is anti-metaphysical and anti-cosmological in character' (Cross, 1985: 492). Later,

Levi-Strauss taught in Brazil and travelled amongst the Brazilian islanders. In 1959 he became Professor of Social Anthropology at the College of France. His *The Elementary Structures of Kinship* (1945) and *Tristes Tropiques* (1955) (The Sad Tropics) earned him his reputation; as Brian Morris remarks, he has been dubbed 'an "institution", a modern Heraclitus'. (1987: 264). His *Savage Mind* appeared in 1966. Geertz described *Tristes Tropiques* as one of the 'finest books ever written by an anthropologist', even though it is also 'very far from being a great anthropology book' (1973: 347). Similarly, Dan Sperber writes: 'No anthropologist has ever gained greater fame than Levi-Strauss, yet few have been more abstruse' (1979: 26). Building on Durkheim, of whom he calls himself an 'inconstant disciple', Levi-Strauss moved towards psychology; 'ethnology', he said, 'is first of all psychology' (1966: 131). His visit to the 'Sad Tropics' in search of the lost primitive (or perhaps of the Noble Savage – he admired Rousseau) confronted him with just that: 'Alas! They were only too savage ... there they were ... as close to me as a reflection in the mirror; I could touch them, but I could not understand them' (cited by Geertz, 1973: 349). This experience convinced him that empirical observation was not the key to comprehension; rather, this lies in the patterns of human thought and language. 'All problems', he says, 'are linguistic ones' (cited in Pace, 1986: 144).

Levi-Strauss' thesis is that human thought operates, largely, quite independently of the existential realities around us. It can match what we perceive with mental concepts, images, ideas, but when at a loss to make a connection between an observed reality, and any mental idea, it can also invent 'abstractions', or metaphors, 'structural models representing the underlying order of reality as it were analogously', (Geertz, 1973: 352). He also uses the expression 'synecdoche'; when people lack a word to designate an abstract concept, they represent it by some concrete object, such as an animal, which possesses that particular quality, or characteristic.

Drawing on the concept of binary opposites, cultural systems, says Levi-Strauss, are built up by contrasting experiences and concepts, hot–cold, raw–cooked, death–life, sleep–wakefulness, sacred-profane. Systems, whether social institutions or religio-mythical, consist of such binary opposites, and may themselves 'be a manner of commenting on, or resolving contradictions inherent in the other' (Seymour-Smith: 270). They also attempt to reconcile the 'norm' with the 'ideal'. Myths, for example, are to be decoded not by attempting to reconstruct a 'linear story', but by breaking them down into sets of binary opposites. By using such codes, 'myths attempt to provide logical models capable of resolving, at this level at least, some of the insupportable contradictions and problems of' human life (Kuper, 1983: 182). Although clearly influenced by Levy-Bruhl, he rejected his view that the savage mind is illogical: 'the thought of the savage is logical ... contrary to the opinion of Levy-Bruhl, this thought proceeds by way of judgment, not through affectivity, with the help of distinctions and oppositions, not by confusion and participation' (1966: 268). 'When faced with a novel problem', he argued, the primitive mind 'goes back through its collective experience and rearranges existing concrete elements to produce a pattern which expresses the new situation' (Pace: 141). In interview, Levi-Strauss has stated that 'nothing could be more dangerous' for anthropology 'than to build up two categories, the so-called primitive peoples, and ourselves' (Steiner, 1966: 35). He pointed out, for example, that the Hopi Indians could differentiate between 350 different plants and were thus quite capable of handling and categorizing complex data. Whilst Levy-Bruhl's primitive mind is 'mystical', Levi-Strauss' primitive mind is 'mythical'.

To decode cultures, then, we must first decipher their binary-code, since these surface-systems refract the deep processes of human thought. Levi-Strauss' 'structural anthropology' thus refers to the structure of ideas. Since ideas, or thought, 'have nothing to do with empirical reality but with models which are built up after it' (1963: 279) empiricism is not the be-all and end-all of anthropological research. As Geertz says, anthropology for Levi-Strauss is 'fundamentally the study of thought' (1973: 352). Therefore we do not, after Malinowski or Durkheim, understand the meaning of customs by deducing their function, but by decoding language. Here, too, we move away from the empiricism of Boas and Malinowski. Levi-Strauss wrote:

If, as we believe to be the case, the unconscious activity of the mind consists in imposing forms upon content, and if these forms are fundamentally the same for all minds – ancient and modern, primitive and civilized (as the study of the symbolic function expressed in language, so strikingly demonstrates) it is necessary and sufficient to grasp the unconscious structure underlying each institution and each custom, in order to gain a principle of interpretation valid for other institutions and other customs, providing of course that the analysis is carried far enough. (1963: 21; see Pace: 155)

Post-modernist theory (see Chapter 5) is, I think, evident in Levi-Strauss' valuable and thought-provoking contribution (see Pace: 182). His idea that thought can be deciphered by unravelling its internal logic, rather than by empirical observation, resonates with Foucault's theory that there is no necessary connection between internal thought, and external reality. Levi-Strauss wrote in *Tristes Tropiques*:

Phenomenology I found unacceptable, in so far as it postulated a continuity between experience and reality. That one enveloped and explained the other I was quite willing to agree, but I had learnt ... that there is no continuity in the passage between the two and that to reach reality we must first repudiate experience ... (cited in Geertz, 1973: 356)

Although he debated with Sartre over the significance of history, and found existentialism too subjective, his elevation of psychology over empiricism also echoes existentialist theory. Since, in a later chapter, I shall commend historiography as an aid to anthropology, we should perhaps note why Levi-Strauss' approach is said to be ahistorical. Briefly, if linguistic analysis can, single-handedly, decode peoples' meanings and symbols, little if anything is left for the history of ideas, or of cultures, to unravel. As Pace comments, Levi-Strauss 'brought to the study of culture the spatial and multi-dimensional mind of the chemist, not the temporal and linear categories of the historian' (1983: 103). However, following Boas (whose influence is discernible) Levi-Strauss also argued that 'anthropology cannot remain indifferent to historical processes' (1963: 23). Where history differed from anthropology, in his view, was methodologically: 'History organises data in relation to conscious expressions of social life, anthropology proceeds by examining its unconscious foundations' (1963: 18). History and anthropology are 'a true two-faced Janus' (*ibid.*: 24).

Sir Edmund Leach (1910–89)

Sir Edmund Leach, who studied under Malinowski, and won his fieldwork spurs amongst the Kurds, amongst the Kachin in Burma and in Sri Lanka, has helped to interpret Levi-Strauss' often 'ambiguous and esoteric' thought within the English-speaking world (Morris: 265). Leach published his study of Levi-Strauss in 1970. Knighted in 1975, Leach was Cambridge University Reader in Social Anthropology 1957–72, and Professor from 1972 until 1978. There is considerable overlap between his and Levi-Strauss' approach, but Leach has also diverged from Levi-Strauss. Kuper describes him as a 'neo-structuralist'; and, significantly for this survey, as a 'militant atheist' (1983: 155 and 177).

Writing about the role of rites and ritual, however, Leach suggests that these enable people, at least temporarily, to reconcile the actual, with the ideal. In this sense, they do perform a function, and their signs and symbols do bear some relationship with external reality. As we shall see, Geertz advocates a similar understanding of religion. Leach thus links religious symbolism with social custom and behaviour. For example, long hair is often associated with sexual licence, short, tightly bound hair with restricted sexuality, whilst a shaved head is often a sign of celibacy. Leach tends to locate the use and meaning of signs within particular cultural contexts, rather than seeing them as universally valid (as scholars within the study of religions tend to see them). Here, he is close to Boas's view of each culture as *sui generis* unique. There are, he says, common themes, but in order to interpret their meaning we need to search out their opposites within each particular cultural context. Levi-Strauss' work appears to have assumed the universality of such codes; as Geertz comments, he 'went in search not of men, whom he doesn't care much for, but for Man, with whom he is enthralled' (1973: 356). He replaced 'the particular mind of particular savages in particular jungles with the Savage Mind immanent in us all' (1973: 355). Thought, for Levi-Strauss, is 'pan-human'.

Levi-Strauss' structuralism, says Leach, has rightly drawn our attention to 'the semantic patterning of concepts which operate as normative ideas' (Leach, 1988: 131) but these general patterns vary from context to context. For example, to suppose, as Levi-Strauss and others have done, that rules about exogamy ... and about incest ... directly match up, so that one kind of rule can serve as an explanation for the other, is an ethnographical mistake. (1988: 186)

Leach, more interested in 'particular savages in particular jungles', argues that there is more of a cause–effect relationship between particular cultures, with particular social systems, and their signs and symbols, or meanings. What is taboo in one culture may not be in another. One culture may see hunting as man's work, cooking as woman's, others may make no such rigid divide. For Leach, the 'fascination of anthropology lies just here ... there are no laws of social probability. The fundamental characteristic of human culture', he says, 'is its endless diversity' (1988: 52). On the other hand, at least one set of Leach's examples does seem to hold for several cultures with which, personally, I am relatively familiar – the correlation between hairstyles and sexuality. (see Leach: 1958: 147–64). This is true for Christian societies, and for Buddhist. An exception, though; the wondering *Bhakti sadhu* (devotional mendicant) in India very often has long, unkempt hair (a sign that he only cares about God, not about his physical attractiveness). His long hair may even be his only garment. He is, however, revered and respected as a 'holy man'. One colleague reading an earlier draft of this chapter, too, commented that 'George Fox had long hair, and so I do too'. Perhaps these are the exceptions that proved Leach's thesis. We shall have cause, later, to return to this debate; are there any universal archetypes, or norms, or none at all? Is thought always contingent on context, or does a common structure underlie all human thought? Leach was also interested in differing social patterns within a definable society (such as the Kachin); in anomalies and contraditions, and in competition. In Burma, he identified three competing social systems, arguing that 'communities swung from one type to the other'. They 'were represented' by the 'same set of symbols in different combinations' (Kuper, 1983: 158). Anomalies, says Leach, are things which don't easily fit neatly into any of the usual categories, around which taboos may develop. Take for instance the rabbit. Neither quite pet nor wild prey, 'it is the source of ambivalence, and is likely to be tabooed in some contexts' (Kuper, 1983: 182).

Mary Douglas (b. 1921)

Mary Douglas has also explored language as the clue to decoding social systems, and, like Leach, has been especially interested in things which do not fit. Trained at Oxford (after a term working with the Colonial Office) she underwent her early fieldwork amongst the Lele in the Congo, now Zaire, in the early 1950s; she revisited in 1987. Douglas, who presented the prestigious Gifford Lectures in 1989, taught anthropology at London University from 1951 to 1970, and was Professor at University College, London 1970 to 1978. Between 1978 and 1988 she taught in various universities in the USA, where she is now Avalon Foundation Professor Emeritus in the Humanities at Northwestern University. This writer was interested to learn, when he met Douglas quite recently, that in the USA she taught in departments of religious studies and regards her work over the last twenty years as primarily a contribution to the study of religions. Her work certainly represents a merging of our two disciplines. Her initial interest was in rules of purity, stimulated by two of her teachers at Oxford, in whose respective traditions, Judaism and Hinduism, ritual purity plays an important part. More prosaically, she attributes additional inspiration to her husband's low threshold of tolerance for dirt! (1991: viii).

She has also contributed to biblical scholarship by applying her theory to the Leviticus material, which she discusses in chapter three of *Purity and Danger* (1970). More recently, she has brought her anthropological interpretation to bear on the book of Numbers in *In the Wilderness* (1993). 'Why', she asks, 'should the camel, the hare and the rock badger be unclean?' Taboos about 'cleanliness' and 'uncleanliness' often indicate parameters of socially acceptable behaviour, and may help to maintain the privileges of elite groups (such as *Brahmins*) over non-elite groups (*Shudras*).

Elsewhere Douglas is interested in links between 'animal categories' and social relationships, but in her treatment of the biblical material what she established was a system of purity rules designed to emphasize Israel's corporate identity as a people set apart 'to be Holy'. Animals thought purest are also holy, and can be sacrificed, those thought less pure are unwholesome, and cannot be sacrificed although they may be eaten, whilst those thought wholly impure may be neither eaten nor sacrificed. Only people without blemish could become priests. Symbolically, says Douglas, upkeep of these rules reminds all Jews of their relationship with God as, ideally, his wholesome and holy people. All Jews, not only an elite, are 'heirs of the promise'. The subtleties of her argument fall outside the scope of this survey but, for our purposes, what this approach does is to identify religion and religious symbolism as aspects, or categories, of human language and thought, part of the attempt to make sense of the world. Religious symbols reflect social structure. Categories such as clean and unclean impose order; they help regulate social behaviour, which, in the case of Israel's Law actually fulfils a profoundly religious, ethical function; Jews are constantly reminded of the value of purity and of the danger of impurity. As eating an impure animal is wrong, so is murder, theft, and adultery – which the Law also contrasts negatively with the preservation of life, with respect for property rights and with fidelity in marriage. In visiting her 'hoary old puzzle from biblical scholarship' Douglas follows Robertson Smith's example of bringing anthropological theory to bear on biblical exegesis. Like him, she treats the biblical material as part of a wider phenomenon.

Douglas has also worked on how social conventions can be altered. For example, she argues, 'anomalous' behaviour may be a way, sometimes, of extending or changing the parameters; an individual may 'shake his own thought free of the protected habit-grooves of his culture' (1991: 5). Ambiguous, or anomalous conduct may simply be ignored, or deliberately confronted in order to 'create a new pattern of reality in which it has a place' (1991: 38). Douglas has been especially interested in the process of accusation and blame, asking who denounces whom, and why. We see this very clearly in her work on leprosy and on witchcraft: for example, in chapter five of *Risk and Blame* (1992). Here, Durkheim's influence is clearly evident. Douglas' interest in how societies establish, and sometimes change, parameters of acceptable conduct, means that her work has often focused on some issues, such as sex and body matters generally which have perhaps been neglected by students of religions. It may or may not be significant, to anticipate our discussion of feminist anthropology in Chapter 5, to note here that Margaret Mead (1901–78), another woman anthropologist, has also researched 'body matters', asking whether there is any intrinsic link between biological maleness, or femaleness, and how masculinity and femininity are construed and enacted? Mead worked with Boas at Columbia University, and was sent by him to Samoa in 1925 to research *Coming of Age in Samoa* (1928). Her *Sex and Temperament* (1935), which argued that patterns of personality and behaviour were culturally, not biologically, determined, was dedicated to Boas; see also her classic study *Male and Female* (1950). Incidentally, Mead was one of the first anthropologists to attempt to apply her cross-cultural research directly to her own society, arguing for reform and change in the fields of gender, sexuality and marriage (see, for example, part four of *Male and Female,* 'The Two Sexes in Contemporary America'). Douglas is also interested in applying anthropology to modern problematics; her *Risk and Blame* 'applies insights from social anthropology ... to modern industrial society' (back cover).

Returning to Douglas, perhaps the major debate to which her work contributes is the 'primitive versus modern mind' discussion. She has some harsh words for those scholars who posit a radical difference between primitive, and modern thought. We have already noted her criticism of Frazer. She also thinks Frazer, and earlier writers wrong, to polarize magic, science and technology, or to subdivide primitive thought into different compartments. 'Human experience', she says, 'has been wrongly divided' (1966: 29). This, she suggests, characterizes modern, not primitive, thought. For its part, the primitive worldview was (and still is amongst primal societies) more holistic: 'In any primitive culture, the urge to unify experience, to create order and wholeness, has been effectively at work'. 'The movement', she says, in scientific cultures is 'apparently ... the other way', towards compartmentalization, whilst in the primitive worldview, different elements of experience 'are closely integrated; the categories of social structure embrace the universe in a single, symbolic whole' (1975: 57). In some societies, this integrated worldview may be intrinsically religious. She does, however, allow that some societies may 'get along with partial systems of explanation' (1975: 76). In *Implicit Meanings* (1975), from which the last two citations were quoted, she modifies the impression given by *Purity and Danger* – that cultures share universal 'codes' – and suggests that Levi-Strauss' approach can only decipher universal structures, not 'cultural variables'. To decode these, links need to be established between symbolic systems and particular social systems: 'We must look for tendencies and correlations between the character of the symbolic system and that of the social system' (1975: 12). Her present view is that there are no universal symbolic patterns, only culturally specific patterns of meaning. Douglas thus places more importance on fieldwork, on matching thought to social realities, than Levi-Strauss, in whose system the connection between these is less immediate, lying solely within linguistic structure.

In conversation with this writer, Douglas commented that Leach's work may also have assumed that 'anomalies' walk around wearing labels – despite his interest in particularities he may not always have paid enough attention to context. What Douglas does, suggests Geertz, is to place 'meaning systems' in the 'middle, between social structures, which vary, and psychological mechanisms, which do not' (1983: 151). With Leach, she is usually regarded as a neo-structuralist. In one of her more recent books, *How Institutions Think* (1987), she explores how people 'think' differently within different types of institutions, including religious ones. This perhaps moves towards giving social structure a more pro-active role in influencing, or determining, what the 'psychological mechanism' is able to produce, which emotions it allows people to respond to. She acknowledges Durkheim as a major stimulus; in his schema, whilst social rules reflect the consensus of the collective consciousness, society also takes on a thinking function: 'rather as if the common consciousness is too important to be entrusted to the ordinary people and has to be delegated to the "brain" of society' (Parkin, 1992: 39). Douglas, building on Durkheim, surmises whether this 'brain' does not then start to 'think' independently, and, instead of reflecting the common will, imposes its will on society. Do institutions think for themselves?

Taking stock

Theorizing about religion, we noted, whether as the result of mental processes, or as a psychological crutch, was in the main absent from the work of the historians of religions reviewed in the first half of this chapter. However, speculation about the origin of religion did preoccupy many theologians. Strictly speaking, unless they also occupied chairs in religions, these scholars should not concern us here, since this is not a survey of Christian (or of other) theologies of religion. However, many students of religions continued to come to the religions through theology; trained as theologians, they maintained an interest in theology. Ideas and theories about religion inevitably influenced their own work. Indeed, more than a few – amongst others Whaling, Smith, Parrinder and this author have missionary backgrounds. This builds on an interesting heritage, recently surveyed by Kenneth Cracknell, of missionaries who 'brought to the study of religion ideas like justice and fairness, courtesy and empathy' (1995: xiv) instead of attitudes of inherent superiority, or worse. This again highlights the difficulty of clearly demarcating the study of religions from theological discourse. Some of the theological theories of religion, too, build on the concepts of sacred and profane categories which we have discussed above, and so resonate with anthropological theory. To conclude this chapter, I shall briefly mention the important and influential contribution of Schliermacher's interpreter, Rudolf Otto (1869–1937).

Rudolf Otto's 'Idea of the Holy'

In fact, Otto is often included in surveys of the study of religions, although he always regarded himself as a systematic theologian, occupying that chair at Marburg. He was, however, also a Sanskritist and a philologist, and in that sense stood firmly in the Müller tradition, as Heiler comments: 'The founder of the comparative study of religions was a philologist, Max Müller. The greatest scholars of religion in this century were also philologists; Soderblom–Iranist, van der Leeuw–Egyptologist, Hans Jaas–Japanologist, Rudolf Otto–Sanskritist' (in Waardenburg, 1973: 472). Otto, too, helps to bridge this and our next developmental phase, since he did not formulate his theory about religion whilst reading a text, but whilst visiting places of worship; he travelled in Egypt and Palestine, North Africa, India, Burma,

Japan and China. He wrote about Indian religion and, collecting artefacts from around the world, established his Museum of World Religions at Marburg. It was, though, his *The Idea of the Holy* (1917) that made his name.

Sitting in a synagogue in Tunis, listening to the 'kadosh, kadosh, kadosh' ('holy, holy, holy') of the Jewish prayer, he found himself experiencing a profound sense of awe, invoked by a sense of the 'numinous', of the 'holy', which lifted his mind above the mundane reality of day-to-day existence (something here of Leach's view). This left him 'shuddering before the mysterious, and the tremendous, overpowered by the "Wholly Other" yet drawn, fascinated if not transfixed by the sublime' (Trompf: 76). Thus his *mysterium tremendum et fascinans*. Tremendous, because this apprehension of the numinous comes 'as a profound shock ... *fascinans* because paradoxically it exerts an irresistible attraction' (Armstrong: 52). Yet as *mysterium* no fully rational response is possible. Thus, music, art and worship help interweave the non-rational with the rational (see Trompf: 76). The holy can be discussed, but not defined. It is not, however, merely a category of thought, but exists *sui generis*. Humans respond differently, thus the variety of human religiosity – 'wild, bacchanalian excitement; sometimes a deep calm ... dread awe and humility in every aspect of life' (Armstrong: 11).

Otto, however, does not say how we can know whether different religions respond to the same stimuli, or to different stimuli, or, as Evans-Pritchard comments, 'how does one know whether a person experiences awe or thrill or whatever it may be? How does one recognize it and how does one measure it?' (1965: 44). This theory, he says, cannot explain all religious activities, since many 'are not carried out in situations in which there is any possible cause for emotional unrest or feelings of mystery and awe' (*ibid.*). Otto appears to have regarded all religions as responses to the one, archetypical *numina*, and in 1921 inaugurated an Inter-Religious League to help 'save the world out of its common and enormous want and distress'. Otto denied any desire to create an 'esperanto religion'. He wrote: 'Yet despite the great variety that exists amongst religions, one thing binds them together: the religious character and impulse as such and a common antagonism to materialism and irreligion ... a silent sympathy attracts the religious to the religions' (Otto, cited in Braybrooke, 1992: 115). This theory explains religions religiously, avoiding the reductionist explanations considered elsewhere in this book. In this view, religious ideas are more than a mode of thought, they are 'archetypal images' which stem from the 'collective unconsciousness' of the human race. They are *a priori* not the result of a process of thought. As we shall see, psychoanalyst Carl Jung was influenced by Otto's contribution (it was Otto who suggested the name *Eranos* for the Jung-dominated conferences, from 1933 onwards).

In our next chapter, I argue for methodological convergence between anthropology and the study of religions, although we shall also note some theoretical divergence. If, during this phase, the students of religions were, generally, reluctant to offer any theories about religion's origin, we now enter a phase when theorizing became more common, if problematical. This theorizing drew on the contributions of the psychological anthropologists. Methodologically, students of religions now turn to religious practices as well as to religious texts, as their subject matter. Still cautiously (at this stage) they take to the field. They also begin to perceive religions less as unitary, classical traditions, more as multidimensional, multifaceted phenomena demanding more than textual and historical scholarship to understand and to study them. Chapter 3, then, on convergence, concentrates on anthropology's contribution to the what, and to the how, of the scientific study of religions.

3 Convergence: Seeing Through Others' Eyes

In this chapter, we shall see how, as fewer and fewer traditional cultures remain uninfluenced by the dominant industrialist culture of the Northern nations, this, and other factors (such as the colonialization process and urbanization) changed anthropology's agenda. We saw the beginning of this trend in our section on Malinowski, who pointed to the meeting of cultures as a new field of interest. New themes, such as the impact of dominant cultures on subject cultures, how cultures and religions are affected by migration (transplantation, integration, assimilation processes), how study of the local can lead to a better understanding of the global, all emerged as new topics for anthropologists. Meanwhile, informed by anthropological writing on the religions, students of religions became more interested in practice as well as in precept, in the religions as lived and practised rather than only in classical texts. Some, in the earlier tradition of Robertson Smith, also took to the field. Scepticism developed about whether 'great traditions' can be studied at all, and thus religion as manifested locally became of interest to many students of religions. This will be explored more fully in Chapter 4. Building on symbolic anthropology, the interpretation of religious signs and symbols became another significant area of enquiry. This interest in living traditions, rather than primarily in their classical doctrines and historical development, also led to a new focus on how 'faith' convictions translate into social, ethical and political involvement. Thus, emphasis shifted from the study of global systems to the role which religions play in human lives, as anthropology helped to take the study of religions into believers' homes, to observe how theory translates into practice.

This may have resulted in a reductionist concept of religion. However, from this shift in both methodology and focus of study, the concept emerged of religions as multifaceted, multidimensional phenomena requiring the type of polymethodic study noted in the Introduction to this book. Models for the study of religions, such as Frank Whaling's, which we outlined in our Introduction, were developed. Art, architecture and myth all became subject matter as well as scriptures and official creeds. Malinowski's description of the anthropologist's task as 'to enter into the soul of the savage and through his eyes to look at the outer world and feel ourselves what it must feel to him to be himself' (cited in Sass, 1993: 17) translated into Wilfred Cantwell Smith's description of the job of the 'non-Muslim writing about Islam' as 'that of constructing an exposition that will do justice to the faith in men's hearts by commanding their assent once it is formulated. It is', he added, 'a creative task and a challenging one' (Smith, 1959: 44). All of these developments were also profoundly influenced by a new philosophical perspective, a new 'intellectual strand', phenomenology, which impacted both our fields of study. This, to a considerable degree, replaced the evolutionary perspective or assumption which had influenced our first generation of scholars in both fields. We shall therefore visit phenomenology first, before exploring other converging developments in this phase.

Phenomenology

This perspective was developed in Germany by the philosopher, Edmund Husserl (1859–1938) a Göttingen professor from 1901 to 1916 and, for a number of years, a colleague of Otto. Husserl's aim was to 'get back to things', that is, to phenomena, 'in themselves'. To do this, he said, we first need to free ourselves of preconceived theories and interpretive frameworks into which, if we are not careful, we will try to squeeze our data. We can all too easily mould our material, whether textual, or anthropologically observed, to fit our own views. Husserl's method was designed to filter out distortions and prejudices. To do this, he proposed a five-stage process. His first three stages involved what he called *epoche*, the 'bracketing out' of values, presuppositions, judgements and

prejudices in order to suspend our judgement until the phenomenon has manifested its 'own essence'.

First, this process requires us to bracket out our own likes and
dislikes, including our emotions. Next, we must similarly bracket
out our theories and ideas in order to 'get back to things in
themselves'. Third, we must bracket out all philosophical assumptions so that the phenomena in and of itself can be isolated for study
and scrutiny. Whaling explains the next phases thus:

> fourth, having performed this threefold *epoche*, there was the further step
> of getting behind the externals of phenomena in order to get through to
> their inwardness, the technical term for this process being the exercise of
> *Einfuhlung* (empathy); fifthly, there was the final step of getting behind the
> accidents of phenomena in order to unfold their essence (*eidos*), the
> technical term for this process being 'eidetic vision'. (1984a: 1:212)

The consequences of this for the study of religions will concern us
below. It had a similar impact on anthropology, especially when set
alongside the Boasian insistence on treating each culture as an
independent, autonomous entity. This means that each culture,
indeed religion, must be understood in its own terms. An
illustration I use to explain phenomenology to my students goes
like this: I pick up a chair (much to their surprise), and point out
that if we are going to understand a chair in its *chair-ness*, it is no
use treating it, talking about it, as if it were a table. It is no use
applying the language of *table-ness* to a chair. Similarly, if we are
going to understand Islam in its *Islam-ness*, it is no use discussing
Islam as if it were Christianity. If we want to understand Trobriand
men and women in their *Trobriand-ness*, we need, as Malinowski
put it, to enter into their 'soul', and 'through their eyes to look at
the outer world and feel ourselves what it must feel to them to be
themselves'. We need, then, to see with others' eyes, to hear with
others' ears. This process, arguably, demands imagination as well as
scientific description, another reason why both anthropology and
the study of religions veer towards the artistic. Leach, I think,
rightly comments that 'social anthropology is not, and should not
aim to be, a science in the natural science sense. If anything,' he
says, 'it is a form of art' (1988: 51). At the end of his life, Evans-
Pritchard, amongst the first cohort of Malinowski's students at

LSE (Leach was amongst the last), argued that 'social anthropology was a form of historiography and even of art' (Kuper, 1983: 132).

Similarly, Waardenburg comments that, if the phenomenologist of religions' task is to reconstruct the religious universe of the religion or religions studied, then 'at this stage of research the imaginative faculty' will have to be used. Talk of 'the art of interpretation' implies that there is something of 'art' involved. Also, if we entertain the possibility of 'an active self-involvement on the part of the researcher' – the type of involvement demanded by participant observation – 'in the facts and meanings studied, the implication is that the researcher, even if only temporarily – as an actor we might say – takes the role of one of the people he studies' (1978: 110f). Acting, imagination and empathy are all involved here; very different skills from the linguistic and textual analysis of our first generation.

Clearly, such a bracketing out exercise includes the bracketing out of the type of *a priori* sense of cultural, religious and intellectual superiority which earlier scholars had applied to their study of the religions. Sir William Muir, for example, assuming Muslim dishonesty, attached little historical value to early Muslim texts. Similarly, Professor Nicholson had assumed irrationality. Both assumptions influenced what these scholars said about Islam. Christian writers, convinced that other religions were, at best, futile human enterprise, at worst, Satanic, all too easily read this estimate into their scholarship of the religions. Phenomenology attempts to set such assumptions aside, so that the evidence can be examined without any preconceived notions about its worth, reliability or theological status. The fieldworkers' diary can serve as a type of filter, to confront and bracket out emotions and preconceptions as they occur and reoccur.

Gerardus van der Leeuw (1890–1950)

Husserl did not apply phenomenology especially to the study of religions, but other scholars soon did. Perhaps most eminent amongst these was the Dutchman, Gerardus van der Leeuw whose two tasks for the study of religions, mentioned in our Introduction, helped set the agenda for this book. Van der Leeuw studied theology at Leiden, from 1908 to 1913, during which period he was influenced by one of the pioneers in the history of religions, P.D. Chantepie de la Saussaye (1848–1920). According to Waardenburg, it was Saussaye, alongside the Dutch Egyptologist, Cornelius Tielle (1830–1902) who, together with Müller, made the study of religions an 'autonomous discipline' (1973: 14). Egyptology then beckoned van der Leeuw: two semesters in Germany, work on pyramid texts in Berlin and in the history of religions at Göttingen (where Husserl was teaching philosophy). His Leiden doctoral thesis, defended in 1916, was entitled 'Ideas of God in the ancient Egyptian pyramid texts'. Ordination as a Dutch Reformed minister followed, as did two years pastoral work. In 1918 a university post became vacant at Groningen, and van der Leeuw became Professor of the History of Religions, teaching especially Egyptology. Appointed within the theology faculty, he argued, in his inaugural address, that the history of religions was part of the broader theological task. In 1950, he chaired the Amsterdam Congress which founded the International Association for the History of Religions, of which he served as president until his death later that year. Van der Leeuw was multi-talented; he loved art and music, was liturgically innovative within the Dutch Church, and, politically active as a socialist, he served a brief term as Minister of Education (1945–6).

For our purposes, what is most significant about Van der Leeuw's thought is its inter-connection between theology, anthropology and the study of religions. His classic exposition of phenomenology, *Religion in Essence and Manifestation*, appeared in 1933. Ultimately, he argued, the study of religions must penetrate beyond 'description' – 'an inventory and classification of the phenomena as they appear in history' to an attempt to understand 'all the experience born of what can only become reality after it has been admitted into the life of the observer' (1954: 10). This goes beyond 'the description of what is visible from the outside' to the inner experience of religious conviction, to the psychological, existential experience of what might commonly be called 'faith'. He is close here to Wilfred Cantwell Smith, who, in his inaugural lecture at McGill University, described the scholars of the first phase of the study of religions, engaged in their encyclopaedic quest for facts, as resembling flies crawling on the surface of a goldfish bowl, making accurate and complete observations on the fish inside ... and indeed contributing much to our knowledge of the subject; but never asking themselves, and never finding out, how it feels to be a goldfish. (1950: 2)

Rather, says Smith, religion should be understood 'as the faith in men's hearts'. It is 'a personal thing, in the lives of men'. (1969: 42). For van der Leeuw, as for Smith, the subject of study is the religious man and woman, which, for van der Leeuw, made both the study of religions and theology types of anthropology. 'In his view', says Waardenburg, 'phenomenology [of religion] largely remained a Christian anthropology, and anthropology remained essentially Christian theology' (1978: 211). In other words, since the subject of both disciplines is 'the religious man', both are inherently anthropological. Or, as Smith put it, 'the student is making effective progress when he recognizes that he has to do not with religious systems basically but with religious persons; or at least with something interior to persons' (1959: 35). Similarly, another exponent of the phenomenology of religion, Friedrich Heiler, wrote, 'Religion should not be studied in books, but in living people ... One should not remain on the outside, but penetrate everywhere to the heart of religious experience, from the fixed forms (ceremonies, dogmas) we must penetrate to immediate religious life' (cited in Waardenburg, 1973: 473). Or, as Joseph Kitagawa has it, whilst the scientific study of religions 'has to be faithful to descriptive principles' ... 'its inquiry must ... be directed to the meaning of religious phenomena' (1959: 21). Van der Leeuw, though, did distinguish between the respective remits of theology and of the study of religions. The first, he said, concerns the nature of the 'ultimate reality', or of its 'revelation', whilst the latter studies the human response to the sacred.

The 'sacred' as an *a priori* category

Thus, we see a shift in methodology and a change in subject matter. Texts, of course, remain important. The reconstruction of doctrinal developments, of histories of the religions, does not cease to concern the scholars, but many also turned away from texts to the study of religious persons. We shall examine how this actually took place below, but there are still some important implications of phenomenology to consider. Perhaps the most crucial aspect for our survey is the claim made by several phenomenologists, including Heiler but most notably by Mircea Eliade, that in order to study religions, the student must accept the reality of religious feelings. Heiler argued, 'One cannot be engaged in ethics without a moral sense, in philosophy without love of truth, in the study of religion without any religious feeling' (cited in Wardenburg, 1973: 474). Mircea Eliade, similarly, interpreting phenomenolgy as concerned with penetrating to the essence of phenomena, argued that religious phenomena are *sui generis*, and can only be understood in their own terms. Religion is thus not to be explained away as 'projections of the unconscious', or as 'screens raised for social, economic, political or other reasons' (1969: 68), but as human apprehension of the sacred. As we shall see, Eliade adopted the concept of the sacred as an *a priori* category and, in much of his writing, explores how the 'religious man' expresses this symbolically. In this view, empathy or *Einfuhlung* requires that we 'take seriously the believer's standpoint', including their faith (Whaling, 1984a, 1: 212).

Not surprisingly, not everyone accepted this interpretation of phenomenology. For Geo Widengren, for example, Professor of the History of Religion at Uppsala, the study of religions remained primarily descriptive, a classificatory science. To assume the *a priori*, *sui generis* nature of religion as a category does not keep the bracketing out rules of phenomenology. Others argued that the objective scholar must eliminate any such religiously coloured assumption 'from his studies', including whatever 'religious motives and drives' which may 'make him study religion at all' (Werblowsky, 1959: 3). Waardenburg suggests something of a compromise, which, I shall argue, resembles the view of anthropologist Clifford Geertz. First, Waardenburg is critical of scholars who allow their preconceptions about the status of religion to colour their scholarship:

There is a reason to distrust *a priori* the work of those who interpret their material according to preconceived schemes of reference or closed systems of interpretation, sometimes religiously determined or sanctioned, or who – precisely by limiting all truth to one particular ultimate truth which they confess themselves in a particular way – are precluded from grasping the truthful character, the authentic claim, and so the real significance of the phenomena studied. (1978: 83)

He may have been talking about fellow Dutchman, Hendrik Kraemer. I have cited Kraemer appraisingly earlier in this book, and shall have cause to do so again; his contribution to the study of religions in undeniable. However, he believed that study of religions must ultimately give way to a theology of religions which, for him, meant asserting the superiority of the Christian revelation. For more than a decade a missionary of the Dutch Bible Society in Indonesia, Kraemer's scholarship of Islam and of other traditions during this period earned him his appointment, in 1937, as Professor of the History of Religions at his *alma mater,* Leiden. However, his theology was profoundly missiological. Religions could be studied dispassionately, but in the end Christians must recognize them as inadequate 'gropings' after the divine, albeit each may have its particular strengths, or 'apprehension of the totality of existence', as he called it. Whilst all religions represent human striving, only in Christ has the divine–human chasm been bridged from the divine side. Thus, the Christian revelation is unique, and uniquely saving. Invited by the International Missionary Council to prepare the discussion document for its 1938 Conference (at Tambaram, India) on the relationship of the Gospel to the 'non-Christian religions', Kraemer wrote:

The Christian revelation places itself over and against the many efforts to comprehend the totality of existence. It asserts itself as the record of God's self-disclosure and re-creating revelation in Jesus Christ, as an apprehension of everything that revolves around the poles of divine judgement and divine salvation ... (1938: 113)

Kraemer, it must be said, was also anxious to distinguish Christian religion as embedded in culture and in history, and therefore liable to corruption, from the Christian revelation. He shared Karl Barth's horror of the Nazi identification of church, and of Christian culture, with Germany's national socialist aspirations. Kraemer was also reacting against the findings of the famous Layman's Inquiry which, under the chairmanship of William Ernest Hocking, (1873–1966) published the report *Rethinking Missions* (1932). The 'radical replacement' of other religions by the Christian, said the report, needed to yield to a process of mutual enrichment, all of which helps to contextualize Kraemer's missiology. However, for Waardenburg, Kraemer's judgement upon the religions, and his belief in the *sui generis* character of the Christian revelation, clearly represents an unacceptable *a priori* assumption.

'Faith' as a scholarly concept

For Wardenburg, any *a priori* conviction about the status of religious beliefs, one's own or others', is an unacceptable phenomenological assumption. *A priori* belief in authenticity is as partial as an *a priori* belief in inauthenticity. However, says Waardenburg, whilst putting aside such judgements (which, arguably, may be made by a theologian but not by a student of religions, hence the confusion when a scholar operates as both!) the scientific student of religions can still take the inner convictions, or faith of religious people seriously as a scholarly, but not as a religious, concept. He reaches this conclusion by tracing the origin of everything we can call religious – such as religious language, art, expression – to 'the moment when man expresses himself religiously, that is to say, when this expression of his carries a religious meaning for him'. This meaning, or faith, thus 'indicates the origin of the (religious) meanings which are subject to investigation' (Waardenburg, 1978: 88). Similarly, James L. Cox argues that as phenomenology aims to allow 'the phenomena to speak for themselves', if the phenomena do define religion religiously, the scholar can empathize with this view 'without making any judgements on the object of religious faith', or about the status of that faith (Cox, 1992: 54). On the other hand, to impose a different definition onto the phenomena will 'distort the phenomena from the point of view of the believer' (*ibid*.: 43).

Heiler and others, though, still argued that the student of religions should remain open to the truth-claims of all religions:

one cannot properly understand religion if one dismisses it as a superstition, illusion, or as a scarecrow. Religion is about a final reality ... any study of religion is in the last analysis theology, to the extent that is does not concern itself with psychological and historical phenomena only, but also with the experience of transcendental realities. (in Waardenburg, 1973: 474)

Such openness to truth claims again raises the problematic of the relationship between the study of religions and theology. Is it only legitimate for theologians to speculate about the truth or falsehood of religions, or can students of religions legitimately do so too? Heiler (1959: 142ff) considered the promotion of religious tolerance, even the fostering of unity, a legitimate scholarly objective, and identified 'seven principles of unity' manifested by 'the high religions of the earth'. The Indian scholar, Sarvepalli Radhakrishnan, Spalding Professor at Oxford, and later President of India, similarly held 'sharing' and the fostering of 'unity' to be comparative religion's principal aim. Some refer to this as the *philosophia perennis*, the view that through the many, one divine reality manifests itself. For others, whilst improved inter-religious relations and understanding might be a beneficial by-product of a scholar's work, 'it could never become a matter of primary concern' (Sharpe, 1986: 278) without compromising claims to scientific objectivity.

This problematic will probably remain unresolved. However, amongst anthropologists, the emphasis on culture (including religion as culture) as 'meaning systems' – which can be interpreted by decoding their language, symbolism, rites, rituals, customs and traditions – opens up the possibility of taking faith seriously, even if you do not personally believe in its objective reality. Here, Clifford Geertz's position is, as I have suggested above, close to Waardenburg's. First, Geertz offers a definition of 'religion as a cultural system'. It is, he says,

(1) a system of symbols which acts to
(2) establish powerful, pervasive, and long-lasting moods and motivations in men by
(3) formulating conceptions of a general order of existence and
(4) clothing these conceptions with such an aura of factuality that
(5) the moods and motivations seem uniquely realistic. (1973: 90)

Thus, he suggests,

the religious perspective ... is ... not the theory that beyond the visible world there lies an invisible one (though most religious men have indeed held, with differing degrees of sophistication, to some such theory); not the doctrine that a divine presence broods over the world (though, in an extraordinary variety of forms, from animism to monotheism, that too has been a rather popular idea); not even the more difficult opinion that there are things in heaven and earth undreamt of in our philosophies. Rather, it is the conviction that the values one holds are grounded in the inherent structure of reality, that between the way one ought to live and the way things really are there is an unbreakable inner connection. What sacred symbols do for those to whom they are sacred is to formulate an image of the world's construction and a program for human conduct that are mere reflections of one another. (1968: 97)

In other words, whatever the origin of religious beliefs, whether they are by-products of social identity, as viewed by structuralists, or the projection of human aspirations onto an imaginary divine reality, which tends to be the functionalist view, or whether their source is divine, as religions themselves teach, they manifest themselves in signs and symbols which, as far as believers are concerned, express the way the world actually is. Signs and symbols, he says, both sustain religious faith and serve as those metaphors and images which their 'adherents use to characterize reality'. Signs and symbols, then, are to be read, not merely as dependent on social identity, or as derived from social structure, but as meaningful in and of themselves. Sign and symbol, says Geertz, sustain religions; they are their visible manifestation in the world. Geertz's own interest as an interpretive, or symbolic anthropologist, is not merely to codify data about religious acts and institutions but to ask 'how and in what way particular ideas, acts and institutions sustain, fail to sustain, or even inhibit religious faith?' (1968: 2). Arguably, this takes faith seriously, as a scholarly category. Why, he asks, when reality does not seem to reflect religious convictions about what ought to be, do people persist in their religious beliefs? Partly, perhaps, because the 'aura of factuality' with which the symbols have been clothed, gives reassurance that reality can resemble the vision, but also because the vision can inspire believers to 'transform society' so that it does resemble the vision. 'Religious patterns ... have a double aspect; they are frames of perception, symbolic screens through which experience is interpreted; and they are also guides for action, blueprints for conduct' (1968: 98). Religions both express social and psychological convictions, and, because they are invested with authority, also shape them (1973: 118-19).

Religions as distinct traditions

However, how did this new focus on religious faith, on religions as meaning-systems, and on the phenomenological approach, actually impact on the work of the students of religions? Two quite different consequences (arguably contradictory) will be considered. First, phenomenology, as we have seen, discourages comparison, since to talk about different phenomena as if they were the same phenomena may do an injustice to the actuality, or essence of each different phenomena. It is, for example, a mistake to assume that the Qur'an is to Muslims as the Bible is to Christians, since these scriptures are regarded quite differently by Muslims and Christians within their respective religious traditions. Thus, just as Boas warned against treating different cultures as if they were the same, many phenomenologists of religion warn against trying to construct some universal history, or theory, of religion. Kraemer, despite his negative theological evaluation of the ultimate worth of other religions, did much to encourage their study as self-contained entities. He wrote:

The more one penetrates different religions and tries to understand them in their total, peculiar entity, the more one sees that they are worlds in themselves, with their own centres, axes, and structures, not reducible to each other or to a common denominator which expresses their inner core and makes them all translucent. It is certainly possible to classify the religions in groups, bringing them under a common denominator such as, for instance, tribal religions, universal religions, religions of salvation, but these denominators are, in the limited sense of the word, purely classificatory. (1957: 76)

Or, as Sir Hamilton Gibb (1895–1971) Oxford's Professor of Arabic, described Islam, every religion is 'an autonomous expression of religious thought and experience, which must be viewed in and through itself and its own principles and standards' (1949: vi). Boas might have said this about cultures.

For Kraemer, 'comparative religion' means 'contrasting and

elaborating the peculiar character and structure of different religions' (1956: 76f). Nor should the same religion, always and everywhere, be regarded as identical. Local context must be taken into account. Thus, students of religions began to move away from the reconstruction of total histories, towards understanding religions as locally, and as regionally manifested. Interest in history continued, but those scholars who took this view produced different types of history. Wilfred Cantwell Smith, for example, in his *Modern Islam in India: A Social Analysis* (1943) treated Indian Islam as an expression of that religious tradition within a particular social and political matrix. Part of that particularity is that Islam in India is not sealed off from 'Indian-ness' (or from 'Hindu-ness'). His later *Islam in Modern History* (1957), whilst dealing with Islam in its world-setting, attempted to penetrate to the heart of Islam's self-understanding: 'it sets forth the contention that an understanding of current events in the Muslim world involves an understanding of their Islamic quality' (pp. vi–vii). 'Islam', he says 'is a religion' but 'not merely a religion; it is a particular religion' (p. 17). His book, then, is much more than a history; it aimed to go beyond description to empathy. This approach becomes reluctant to assume parallels and similarities, lest 'differences' be overlooked.

Smith also took himself into the field – initially to India, where he taught for eight years at Forman Christian College, Lahore (where, technically, he was a United Church of Canada missionary). Later, whilst Professor at McGill, he established an Institute of Islamic Studies, and wrote into the constitution that half the faculty would be Muslim scholars, half non-Muslim scholars of Islam. This brought, for him, the 'subject of study' into the place of study. 'Westerners professionally concerned with the Orient', he wrote, 'are now expected to visit the communities about which they write, and must keep in frequent and close personal touch.' He wryly added that 'it is coming to be recognised that part of the cost of setting up a department of oriental studies in a Western university is the provision of travel funds and arrangements for what is still unfortunately called "leave" for staff, who must have access to the Orient just as much as a chemistry professor must have access to a chemistry laboratory' (1959: 32). Certainly, unlike our earlier generation of scholars, when a Max Müller could write about

Hinduism without ever having set foot in India, fieldwork, or at least travel, now becomes important (almost a rite of passage) for the serious student of religions. Heiler points out, for example, that Rudolf Otto did not deduce his 'intuitive sense of what is holy' whilst reading a book, but whilst visiting 'mosques and Eastern temples, and above all, ... a small old synagogue in Tunis' (in Waardenburg: 473). As we shall see, Mircea Eliade, for all his tendency towards universal theory (he also made wide use of written sources, in a way not dissimilar to Frazer) developed his interest in religions as a result of travel and encounter.

Phenomenology, as we have already noted, warns against imposing alien concepts and language on the phenomena we are studying. Arguably, the earlier generation of students of religions quite often fell into this trap. As Joseph Kitagawa points out, the discipline began in the West, and, on the whole, despite 'its avowed neutrality and objectivity has been operating with Western categories' (1959: 27). Everything, for example, had to be classed as an 'ism' – that is, as a unitary system. Thus, as Wilfred Cantwell Smith observed, the word 'Hinduism' was coined, whilst in reality 'the mass of religious phenomena that we shelter under that umbrella is not an entity in any theoretical let alone practical sense' (1963: 64). Even a cautious scholar such as Frank Whaling can fall into the trap of applying an alien preconception to Hinduism when he descibes it as 'lacking a founder'! (1986: 43). It only 'lacks' a founder if you presuppose that it ought to have had one, presumably because some other religions do.

Religions as multifaceted phenomena

Anthropology made another contribution to this new awareness of religions as complex entities subject to local variation. Participant observation, ever since Malinowski, made anthropologists aware that religions operate at different levels. The full-time religious functionary may have one understanding, the worshipper who comes to the sacred grove, or temple, may have a different understanding. As anthropologists moved out of rigidly defined groups into other fields of study, they noted that, alongside what they came to call 'great traditions', such as Hinduism as classically formulated in the official Brahmanical texts, there exist numerous 'little traditions', often village-based. These two terms were developed by American anthropologist, Robert Redfield (1897–1958). He helped pioneer the move away from researching primal to peasant societies. Like Boas, he saw each culture, or tradition, as autonomous. Students of religion soon adopted these terms, and, following Redfield, most (although not all) did so without adjudging a 'little tradition' to be any less valid than a 'great tradition' (which also followed Boas). In other words, a little tradition in a given Indian village should not be regarded as a corrupt, or heretical, form of Hinduism alongside a supposed orthodox great tradition, as Weightman explains:

The writings, beliefs and practices of the Brahmans were understood by early observers in contact with the everyday realities of Hinduism to represent the true 'orthodoxy' and they were obliged to relegate much of what they found to the status of folklore and superstition. More recently, ethnographic and anthropological research has gone a long way towards removing this misleading polarization and has partly succeeded in integrating both aspects into a single totality . . . . . (1984: 193)

We shall explore more examples of this approach in Chapter 4. Wilfred Cantwell Smith, arguably, went even further. For him, not only are religions to be studied as practised by people in their variety of expressions, but they also have no existence apart from their existential existence within people, as faiths. He set forth this thesis in his two influential studies, *The Meaning and End of Religion* (1962) and *Questions of Religious Truth* (1967). Building on his earlier argument that religions inhere in religious persons, he distinguishes between 'religion' as noun, and 'faith' as adjective, and also as verb. 'Religion' as noun, he argues, does not exist in the abstract but only within religious behaviour or religious people. Thus, there are Muslims, Buddhists and Christians rather than Islam, Buddhism and Christianity and, as we have already remarked, the study of religions becomes the study of religious persons, acts and behaviour. 'The reality of Islam', he says, 'is a personal, living faith. New every morning in the heart of individual Muslims' (1957: 18). Perhaps, then, no two Muslims, or no two Christians, experience Islam or Christianity in quite the same way.

Again, this suggests new subject matter for the student of religions. Old interest in doctrines and in scriptures begins to give way to a new interest in worship, ritual, liturgy, religious art and symbolism as well as in how faith is 'acted out' (as verb) in society. Thus we have Smith's interest in Islam as a social system, in what being Muslim means for human relationships, which may differ from person to person, and from place to place. I shall return to Smith's contribution in Chapter 5. Here, we once again connect with anthropology. Now, the student of religions can listen to the testimony of different Muslims, in different contexts, relating different experiences and perceptions, and remain free of the need to evaluate these against some preconceived norm. I shall give further examples in Chapter 4 but my own fieldwork experience in Bangladesh may be cited here, to help illustrate the consequences of this approach for research within the study of religions.

As almost every textbook on Islam states, Islam is a total way of life. The Muslim ideal is not only a pattern for individual conduct, distinguishing right personal conduct from wrong conduct, but also a pattern for corporate living. The *ummah*, community, or nation, of Islam is divinely commissioned, as a people, to 'enjoin right conduct and forbid indecency' (Q 3: 104). Or, as I put it in my contribution to *Rites of Passage*:

Muslim societies have as their model the early *ummah* (the community of Islam) under the leadership of the divinely inspired prophet, governed according to God's law. Just as the life of Muhammad provides the ideal for the life of each individual Muslim, so the corporate life of the ummah provides the model for Muslim society. (1994b: 92)

Every standard textbook will also state that Islam makes no distinction between religion and politics; the ideal for all Muslims is a political-economic-social-religious entity, an Islamic State. However, as Muslim writer, Rafiq Zakaria, in his survey *The Struggle within Islam: The Conflict between Religion and Politics* (1988) shows, 'Muslims ... have invariably reconciled themselves to the opposite'. Indeed, he suggests, Islam as a faith which moves men's and women's hearts, has not appeared to suffer very much as a result of this religion–politics divide, rather 'its influence increased worldwide' (p 280). Sufi Islam especially has little interest in the political dimension: 'it stresses the individual rather than society, the eternal rather than the historical, God's love rather than His power, and the state of man's hearts rather than behaviour' (*ibid.*). For many Sufis, the Law becomes 'a private discipline guiding the person towards transcendent fulfilment', not a blueprint for 'ordering society' or for 'marshalling history into a prescribed pattern' (Smith, 1957: 44–5). Although at times at odds with those who held high political office, and often driven underground, Sufism, says Zakaria, 'remains a force to be reckoned with' (1988: 113).

I knew from my research before going to Bangladesh that, historically, Sufism had flourished there. Although it was the Muslim conquest which made Bengal part of the Delhi Sultanate, and its evangelism may not have been altogether peaceful, nevertheless, there is much evidence that Islam in Bengal was mainly spread by the peaceful preaching of Sufi merchants and mendicants. Often, settling near existing holy places – Hindu or Buddhist, they adapted their preaching to local beliefs. Thus,

The Sufis discovered amongst the Hindu and Buddhist people of Bengal great devotion to their Shrines and great respect for the person of the holy man, or Guru. They thus proclaimed – we have a holy man, a Prophet, whose *Sunna*, or tradition, is the best guide to the book given him by God, wherein is to be found His will for humanity. Sufi Islam [therefore] meshed in comfortably with much existing piety – and when the Shaikhs died, they were often buried in shrines already venerated by the local population. These tombs then continued to attract pilgrims, who brought their gifts of prayer and of flowers. Thus did Islam win the hearts of the Bengali people, and when the conquering troops of Qutb-ud-din arrived, much of Bengal was already Muslim. (Bennett, 1994c: 37)

What I observed in Bangladesh was the continued popularity of the Sufi tradition, despite the antipathy of some of the reformist movements. My observations and conversations suggested that under the reformist veneer, Sufi Islam remained popular and much cherished. Certainly, veneration at Sufi shrines was still widely practised. Also, the *Tablighi-i-Islam* movement, with its emphasis on inner renewal is well-represented, both in Bangladesh and amongst expatriate Bangladeshis in Britain. Founded by Muhammad Ilyas (1885–1944) the *Tablighi* forbids members from discussing politics, and seeks to spread Islam by pious example and persuasion, 'abandoning any idea of imposing Islam by political means' (Ruthven, 1990: 62). My experience of community and development work amongst Birmingham's expatriate Bangladeshi community provided me with plenty of evidence of Islam functioning as an important cultural and social meaning system as well as of Islam as an expression of personal piety, and of deep religious faith. However, I have not perceived very much support for the political aspirations of some British Muslims.

This perception is based on my somewhat unsystematic observations and conversations. However, it is also the opinion of U.A.B. Razia Akter Banu in her *International Study in Sociology and Social Anthropology* series contribution, *Islam in Bangladesh* (1992). In one chapter, she examines the various reformist movements of the nineteenth century, most of which tried to rid Bengali Islam of Sufi and, as they saw them, of Hinduized practices. They failed, she says, to 'purify' Bengali Islam of these elements. 'Popular', that is Sufi, 'Islam still commands the allegiance of nearly half of the Muslims of present day Bangladesh' (p. 63). Her analysis draws on substantial fieldwork in three urban, and in twenty rural areas, presented in sixty-seven tables, 'History speaks, literature speaks. So do numbers and tables', she says (p. 1). Dr Banu identifies three current expressions of Islam in Bangladesh, demonstrating that Islam does not mean the same to everybody but operates at different levels and in different ways. To some degree, the three expressions relate to three different socio-economic groups. The urban upper class tend to be modernist (therefore supportive of democratic government with a liberal interpretation of Islamic Law); the urban middle and rural upper and middle class tend to be orthodox (brooking no separation of religion and politics and little, if any, reform of traditional Islamic Law; government would be by the religious scholars); while both urban and rural lower class tend to follow popular Islam. Dr Banu has adopted a Weberian understanding of social stratification: Max Weber (1864–1920), another founding father of the social sciences, held that specific religious traditions could be identified with certain social strata. For example, he argued that the military and aristocratic classes are generally averse to charismatic, or emotional religiosity, whilst the more 'agrarian the cultural pattern, the more likely that the peasant population will follow a "traditional pattern" ' (Morris: 74–5). Weber, of course, is also known for his concept of a Protestant work ethic. His thesis here is that, in certain circumstances, religion can be a decisive factor in economic and social change, and not, as Karl Marx (1818–83) would have it, always and everywhere, an instrument of social control, of the poor by the rich – 'the opium of the people, the sigh of the oppressed creature, the heart of a heartless world' (Bottomore and Rubel, 1963: 26–7).

Within her Weberian framework, Dr Banu then examined levels of religious observance within her three strands of Bangladeshi Islam. It is, she says, the popular which has the highest levels of religious practice (p. 92). Another chapter explores attitudes towards the Hindu minority (10 per cent). Commenting that a very high percentage of the population enjoy friendships with Hindus, she suggests that this generally indicates a preference for a secular rather than Islamic understanding of citizenship. Given that both the modernists and the Sufi popularists tend to separate religious from political authority, she concludes that 'Islamic resurgence' is unlikely to be 'the wave of the future in Bangladesh'. Citing Wilfred Cantwell Smith that 'almost the whole of Islamic history ... has been a deviation from the classical form of union of religious and political leadership' (p. 163) she concludes that 'both the modernists and orthodox ... seem to have developed a political culture favourable to separation of religion and politics'. This research does not imply that any one approach to the religion–politics relationship is more, or less, authentically Islamic, but rather suggests that, as practised and lived, a tradition may be differently interpreted by different people.

Thus, fieldwork may reveal that what the textbooks says 'is so' is not quite so, or is more complex than we thought, when translated into practice. The combination of textual and fieldwork research is the main focus of our next chapter but another example here may help us to understand the interplay between our two converging disciplines which this chapter aims to establish. Technically, this may be referred to as the relationship between precept and practice or between official and popular religion.

The Lindholms in Pakistan

This example of interaction between anthropology and the study of religions briefly visits the work, in the remote Swat valley in the North West Frontier Province of Pakistan, of anthropologists Cherry and Charles Lindholm. They spent 'nine months in one of the most strict *purdah* societies, the Yusufzai', having gained access 'into the community through a Swat friend' whom they had met 'eight years before' (1993: 231). *Purdah* refers to the Muslim custom of secluding women 'inside the domestic compound', and of veiling (wearing the *hijab*, or *chador*) on the rare occasions when they are seen in public. Some Muslims dispute the scriptural origin of both *purdah* and *hijab*, arguing that the Qur'an itself refers only to the seclusion and veiling of Muhammad's wives, and that modesty of dress, which it does enjoin, applies to both sexes equally (see Bennett, 1994d: 119–20). Muslim feminists, too, such as Ahmed (1992) and Mernissi (1987) have argued that many of the misogynist traditions in Islam developed after the time of Muhammad, and were falsely ascribed to him to claim prophetic authority. Nevertheless, seclusion and veiling are widely practised in parts of the Muslim world, many Muslims do believe that they carry Islamic sanction, and they contribute to the generally prevalent Western stereotype of Islam as oppressive of women.

Does this stereotypical picture resemble what the Lindholm's fieldwork discovered? Is precept (the accepted rules and regulations) matched by practice? The Lindholms were especially interested in finding out whether these accepted rules are broken or manipulated – reminiscent of Douglas. Within most societies some rules are broken; within recognized but unwritten parameters. For example, although smoking marijuana remains illegal in most European countries, it is often ignored, even by the police. What the Lindholms discovered was that, whilst *purdah* is rigorously enforced, both women and men also 'break' the rules. For example, whilst Islam strictly prohibits sexual intercourse outside marriage, 'wives do not mind if their husbands have liaisons with prostitutes, or promiscuous poor women' since this leaves their own status intact. Similarly, whilst Islamically prohibited, homosexuality has been traditionally tolerated, although 'with Western influence', its practice is becoming 'less overt' (1993: 232). Wives do not see homosexual liaisons as a threat to their own position.

Women are regarded as both essential for the 'perpetuation of the social order', and as 'simultaneously the greatest threat to it' (1993: 233). Believing women's sexual appetite greater than their own, men aim to contain and to control their women. The Lindholms argue that hostility is 'built into marriage by the very structure' of Swat society 'which pits every lineage against each other in a never-ending contest to maintain an equilibrium of power'. In times of war, wives used to be taken as contraband, indicating the superiority of the victor – thus, when a bride's family gives her away, they are all but admitting inferiority. Nevertheless, in her new home, the bride will fight to 'defend the honor of her family, even though they have partially repudiated her by negotiating the marriage' (1993: 233). Within the domestic compound, too, conflict continues – between the wives of a polygamous marriage, and between daughter and mother-in-law.

Outside the home, women lack power and influence. Traditionally, they play no part whatsoever in public life. However, as the Lindholms discovered, within the home women can become very powerful indeed. Even though 'no shame is attached to wife beating, and men laugh about beatings they have administered' women do have a weapon: they can 'withdraw domestic services at will' (1993: 234). The men then retreat to the men's house, a 'meeting place for the clan ... center for hospitality and refuge', where many spend much of their time. The older a women gets, too, the more power she is able to exercise within the compound; her sons become allies in the 'fight' against her husband, their father, whom they now regard 'as an obstacle to their gaining rights in land' (1993: 234). The result, often, is that the supposedly all-powerful father is 'surrounded by animosity in his own house'. The precept may seem to be stacked in his favour, but the practice is less one-sided. Sadly, as the Lindholms point out, few women live to 'see their triumph'; in Swat, on average, women die before men, who eat the better food. We might briefly pause, here, to ask whether Swat women are, or are not, subordinate to their menfolk? What the Lindholms' research depicts, I suggest, is more a complex power struggle between the sexes, perhaps after a Marxist model, than a simple subordination of women to men. The research, at the least, leads one to wonder whether the husband, forced to eat in the men's house because his wife has refused to cook, sits there contemplating his wife's subordination! We return to the issue of women's subordination below, in Chapter 5.

This detailed, complex and rounded picture of sexual relations in a remote Muslim society, I suggest, could not have been painted by resort only to classical, or to legal, sources, but required fieldwork. Similarly, in order to investigate the precept–practice dynamic, or to explore the parameters within which 'rules are sometimes broken, or more frequently cleverly manipulated' (*ibid.*: 231) some knowledge of the rules, alongside fieldwork, is equally essential. The Lindholms' survey also illustrates the difference between a superficial (thin) and a deep (thick) investigation, or description, of any society. A more cursory glimpse of life in the Swat valley, noticing lack of women in public places, and men appearing to do what they want, might have suggested that women lack any influence whatsoever.

A changing focus

As we have already noted, as fewer traditional societies remained uninfluenced by transnational, industrialist culture, anthropologists had to find new subjects of study. As well as moving into peasant and into semi-literate societies, they also became interested in groups which find themselves between cultural influences. This soon led to research amongst migrant groups within industrial societies. Some good examples of this type of anthropological work can be seen in the volume *Between Two Cultures: Migrants and Minorities in Britain* (1977) which published monographs by researchers with experience 'at both ends of the migration chain, in the migrants' own country of origin and in Britain' (Watson: 2). Differences between religious practices in a minority, and in a majority cultural context, thus provide new subject matter for anthropologists and for students of religions. Almost by definition, such research must be conducted in the field, since little literature yet exists on these minority communities. I shall give an example of this from my own experiecne in our next chapter. Our first consequence of the phenomenological method, then, is this respect for each religion on its own terms, and the recognition that each operates at different levels as well as differently in different contexts. This, in one sense, limits the students of religions' task – no longer to construct parallel histories of the many religions – whilst in another sense, it broadens the task, since each religion is now viewed as a complex phenomenon.

Our second consequence builds on this complex understanding of religion. As we have already noted, anthropologists see religious acts and symbols as meaning systems. These may be broken down into acts associated with particular aspects of religious observance, indeed into acts associated with different aspects of human life. An early anthropological focus was on 'rites of passage', a term coined by Arnold van Gennep (1873–1957). He was more of an armchair anthropolologist, but did good work in helping to interpret the meaning of ritual practices within their social context. He saw initiation rites, practised widely in primal societies, as symbolically marking changes in individual social status. His full interpretative schema is not our concern here, but this focusing on the significance of ritual acts provides another example of how anthropological work can aid the student of religions. Whilst resisting the imposition of any preconceived framework, or interpretive schema, students of religions, faced with complex traditions can, by focusing on rites of passage, begin to treat their subject systematically. Just as the anthropologist begins by focusing on one area, kinship, magic, witchcraft, or ritual, before moving on to the next (aiming eventually at Boas' 'total recovery'), so students of religions began to narrow their field of study. This is also the intent of such models of study as the one proposed by Frank Whaling, or of Ninian Smart's similar scheme. These are not strait-jackets to impose external ideas upon the religions, but frameworks to facilitate their more or less systematic study.

Thus, a thematic approach can still be adopted. Whilst attempting to study various religions at the same time, or more usually in sequence, this also resists treating the religions as anything other than autonomous phenomena. *The Themes in Religious Studies Series* (1994) edited by Jean Holm with John Bowker, represents this thematic approach. The fact that most religions do regard certain buildings, or places, as sacred (even if they also regard all space as sacred), the fact that most religions have ritual practices, scriptures, moral teachings, and so on, provides themes under which the multifaceted and distinctive practices, beliefs and teachings of major religions can be explored. Thus, volumes in the series include *Sacred Place*, *Rites of Passage*, *Sacred Writings*, *Making Moral Decisions*. The authors were briefed, in their instructions, to 'deal with sociological/anthropological aspects of each religion, and its relation to the cultures within which it is practised, as well as with its classical teachings' (Holm with Bowker, n.d.). Thus, the classical, official expressions studied by the earlier generation of scholars are not neglected, nor are classical sources, but these are set alongside other expressions and traditions for which anthropology and personal observation are as likely to provide the scholars with information, as are any written sources.

However, such a thematic approach can run the risk of manipulating data in order to include every tradition within the same parallel framework. The volume in the *Themes in Religious Studies Series* which came closest to doing this was *Picturing God*. As editor Jean Holm commented, 'Does this book have the right title?' (1994: 1). Some religions do picture God visually, some do not. Thus, my chapter began 'Muslims picture God conceptually, not artistically or visually', whilst Norman Solomon's began, 'Judaism allows no visual representation of God, no image, icon, or symbol'. The value of any such *schema* lies in the flexibility of their categories, or rather descriptors. Some are less flexible than others. One scheme which we have used here at Westminster College to teach introductory courses on the religions follows the format of Owen Cole's with Peggy Morgan's *Six Religions in the Twentieth Century* (1984). This treats six traditions under the headings 'Messengers', 'Scriptures', 'Worship', 'Pilgrimage', 'Festivals'. Here, it is the first descriptor which presents the most difficulty. Whilst 'messenger' is an acceptable translation of the Arabic *rasul*, Muhammad's title, is it an accurate descriptor for Jesus? Was he God's messenger, or himself the message, God incarnate? Was Buddha a messenger? If so, who sent him? Did he not choose to proclaim *dharma*, to delay his own entry into *parinibbana* voluntarily, although he was persuaded to do so by the chief of the Hindu pantheon? Were the Hebrew patriarchs messengers? Some schemes use 'founder' as an alternative. Arguably, this runs an even greater risk of misinterpretation. The Buddha may indeed have founded Buddhism, by establishing the *sangha* with its rules and precepts. However, it is less clear that Jesus founded Christianity, or who founded Judaism, or even when Judaism began, whilst no Muslim views Muhammad as Islam's founder, since Allah himself established and named the religion. Perhaps the description 'seminal figures' solves the problem.

Frank Whaling chose to substitute the term 'concept' in his scheme for Ninian Smart's 'doctrine' because it implies, and allows, greater flexibility. For example, it may be that Christian faith can be determined doctrinally, that people are regarded as orthodox because they subscribe to certain prescribed doctrines, but Hinduism has no prescribed beliefs. Most Hindus hold to certain concepts about the nature of human existence, about how the universe operates, including *samsara* (the cycle of creation and recreation) and *karma* (birth and rebirth) but these do not resemble the doctrines of the Christian creed. Nor does Judaism demand any prescribed beliefs, or doctrinal conformity, of Jews. Many define Judaism as 'tradition', as practice; 'Religious belief', says Nicholas de Lange, 'is only one ingredient in the makeup of the Jew, and it may not be the most important ingredient at that. Indeed there are many people in the world who consider themselves to be loyal Jews in every respect and who would deny that they have any religion at all' (1986: 4–5). However, whilst clearly lacking prescribed doctrines, even the conviction that Jewish *praxis* is worth observing may qualify as a concept. Thus, I prefer Whaling's concepts to Smart's doctrines.

Mircea Eliade (1907–86)

However, not everyone influenced by phenomenology, or who adopted a thematic approach, focused on traditions as autonomous, independent entities. Here, we must consider the work of Mircea Eliade. Those who follow the Boas–Malinowski tradition of cultural relativism tend towards studying each tradition in its distinctiveness. Those more influenced by the psychological-linguistic approach tend to see a basic underlying pattern, structure, or thought-system, beneath all cultures. This approach began with Durkheim and, as we saw, was developed by Levi-Strauss. Mircea Eliade's work represents this more universal understanding of culture and, in his view, of human religiosity. As we have already noted, Eliade viewed religion or the sacred as an 'objective reality'. For him, as for Levi-Strauss, the sacred is a universal category of human thought. Eliade, though, went further; for him, the sacred, as expressed in religious symbolism, is not merely a device for making sense of human experience, but is evidence of human response to the sacred. Moreover, 'man becomes aware of the sacred because it manifests itself' (1959: 11).

Eliade was born in Bucharest, Romania; interested in biology, folklore, alchemy, and literature from an early age, he had already published a hundred articles before he entered the university. He wanted to decode the meaning of the universe, in which he believed lay hidden messages. Attracted to India, and by yoga, he spent several years studying at Calcutta University. He thought Indian spirituality might help the West regain this lost dimension to its culture and thought-world. In India, he developed his notion of 'cosmic religion', based on observed similarities between 'all peasant cultures'. By the 1940s and the outbreak of World War II, Eliade was the author of widely acclaimed novels as well as a respected member of the academic community. World War II took him to London, as Cultural Attaché; cessation of violence took him to Paris, to a chair at the Sorbonne. Now convinced that 'the Indian experience alone could not reveal ... the universal man' (Kitagawa, in Eliade, 1987, 5:87) he turned to a much wider exploration of the religions, of ethnography, and of mythology, all of which we see reflected in his classic *Patterns in Comparative Religion* (1958). It was during his Paris period that 'Eliade solidified most of his important concepts and categories, including those of *homo religiosus, homo symbolicus,* archetypes, *coincidentia oppositorum,* hierophany, *axis mundi,* the cosmic rope, the nostalgia for paradise, androgyny, the initiatory scenario, and so on' which all aimed at what he called 'a total hermeneutics' (*ibid.*). Finally, in 1957 he moved to Chicago, where he later became a distinguished professor in the university.

Throughout his work, Eliade wanted to assert a 'planetary humanism' and, for him, the key to doing so lay in research on the meaning of myths, the structure of religious symbols, and especially on the dialectic of the sacred and the profane. Gathering a vast amount of data (observed, literary, mythical – in a style of working somewhat reminiscent of Frazer), Eliade discerned 'certain basic comparative structures and patterns built into religion whereby man perceives the sacred. These', he said, 'take the form of hierophanies, symbols and archetypes, and identifying these comparatively lies at the heart of the student of religions' task' (Whaling, 1984a, 1:214). By placing alongside each other symbols and types of religious experience drawn from many religions, he sought to 'ascertain their fundamental structure and their archetypal significance' (*ibid.*: 216).

His legacy remains impressive, and often persuasive. In my contribution to the volume *Sacred Place* (1994) I used Eliade's 'general perspective', and found that his theory helped to make sense of how 'sacred places' function in Islam. According to Eliade, religious traditions have an archetypal sacred place, or a 'universal centre', where heaven and earth meet. By duplicating the symbolism of their archetypal sacred place, traditions create other sacred places elsewhere. Nor did Eliade view the sacred–profane division rigidly, but was open to its psychological dimension. This applies well to Islam:

Islam is a practical religion whose realistic view of human nature includes a profound awareness of the importance of symbolism. It knows full well that, although in theory the sacred is to be found everywhere, if people lack anything on which they can specifically focus their awareness of the sacred, it will be too diffuse, too general, to fulfil their psychological and spiritual needs for nourishment. (Bennett, 1994a: 89)

Indeed, says Eliade, the sacred may often manifest itself in something profane (1958: 29). In Islamic thought, the very word used to describe the three sacred cities, Makkah, Madinah and Jerusalem is the word *haram*, which usually denotes prohibited food or behaviour.

Eliade welcomed van der Leeuw's *Religion in Essence and Manifestation* and regarded his own concept of religion as an objective category as the result of having penetrated to religion's essence. However, as Whaling comments, Eliade's

way of doing comparative religion is based not so much upon objective empirical criteria but rather upon his own underlying presuppositions ... his concern to renew the desacralised West by enabling it to encounter primal and Eastern religious worldviews, his stress upon primal man as the model of religious man, his emphasis upon the 'sacred' and hierophanies, symbols, myths and rituals whereby it is manifested and apprehended, his assumption that religious phenomena have a *sui generis* character and that they strike a chord in the 'transconsciousness of man'. (Whaling, 1984a: 1: 219)

Carl Jung (1875–1961)

If something of Durkheim's 'collective consciousness' lurks in the background of Eliade's system, alongside his use of linguistic theory, there is even more resonance between his thought and that of Carl Jung. In the Swiss psychoanalyst, Eliade found an ally for his belief in *homo religiosus*. Arguably, Jung gave some scientific credibility to Eliade's approach. Having enjoyed an early period of collaboration with Sigmund Freud, (1856–1939) sharing his interest in dreams, Jung parted company from him in 1913 as his view of religion began to diverge radically from Freud's. Freud interpreted all neurosis as sexually based (the result of childhood sexual experience), including religion. For him, religion's origin lay in some primaeval and irrational Oedipus fantasy. He thought the primaeval mind incapable of rationality. Religion, therefore, is a type of 'projection', a 'psychological malady' which 'keeps its adherents permanently fixed in a state of childish illusion rather than allowing them to grow up into mature adults who face life realistically' (Cox, 1992: 51). Freud's *Totem and Taboo* (1913), which has been described as an 'anthropological fantasy' (Hughes, 1958: 149) made extensive use of anthropological theory and data, drawing especially on Frazer and Robertson Smith, to develop its view of religion. He called Smith's *The Religion of the Semites* an 'excellent book' and commented that he was unable to do justice to 'the lucidity or argumentative force of the original' in his own discussion of its thesis (1913: 220). Freud's book contains much interesting material but rests on the dubious premiss that a single, primaeval event (the slaying of the patriarchal father) had universal psychological significance.

Jung, who also differed from Freud's view of the sexual basis of all neurosis, was himself profoundly interested in religious experience. Like Eliade, he was attracted by the concept of a universal, religious humanism. Discovering that many of his patients shared a 'god-image', Jung, instead of explaining this as the primaeval projection of the slain Father onto an imaginary 'god-figure', interpreted this 'god-image' as response to an archetypal 'numina', or 'god'. Here, he was influenced by Rudolf Otto, whom he met regularly through the gathering known as the Eranos Conference (which started in 1933). Eliade, Heiler, and van der Leeuw were also associated with this group; the 'list of participants takes on the appearance of a roll of honour of comparative religion', observes Sharpe (1986: 211). This god-image, said Jung, passed into the 'collective unconscious', and continues to inform a 'religious dimension' of human life, alongside other dimensions, such as the scientific and the empirical. Jung claimed empirical status for his research on religion (Morris: 167). For him, the religious dimension was a type of biological substratum, or a 'psychic reality', 'as real as the natural world' (*ibid.*: 172). Like Eliade, Jung thought that Western civilization had largely lost touch with this spiritual, or religious dimension, and believed that it needed to be restored for healthy, balanced living. Like Eliade, he also looked to Eastern, especially Chinese, religion, to help this restoration. Jung travelled in Africa, and also visited India. There, he thought people more 'tuned in' to the collective unconsciousness than they are in the West, where modern civilization drowns and obscures it. This was the main agenda of the Eranos group – to identify meeting points between Eastern and Western thought. In his exploration of the religious dimension, Jung, like Eliade, was interested in interpreting symbols and myths; he also drew on anthropological data in his writing. He actually welcomed the 'rise of fascism as a revival of archaic religious forms' (*ibid.*: 172), excited by its use of myth and symbol. Jung has been accused of a certain naivety; he does not appear to have recognized that religion can have negative as well as positive consequences; 'he seems only to see religion in terms of its positive qualities' (*ibid.*).

By way of concluding this chapter, it seems to me that if Freud was predisposed to see religion negatively, Jung, for his part, was predisposed to see religion positively. Believing, personally, in a religious dimension, he interpreted his data as verifying its archetypal, objective reality. Although, like Eliade, Jung regarded his work to be phenomenologically sound, we must question whether he did bracket out all presuppositions. At the end of the day, the issue whether religion is ultimately to be explained as something other than religion, as 'real', probably lies beyond the proper application of phenomenology, perhaps even beyond psychology. I find myself increasingly in sympathy with Waardenburg's proposal that the most we can do is to take religion seriously as a 'scholarly concept'. Indeed, my own fieldwork experience and research begs the question: Can the sacred be adequately explained in purely functionalist terms, even when obviously fulfilling a social function, unless we also take faith in the sacred seriously? In my chapter on 'Sacred Place', I pointed out how, in North Africa, respect for the sanctity of Sufi settlements, located alongside the village market, helps to maintain inter-tribal peace:

The marabout's settlement ... adjacent to the market, sacralises that space so that visitors from outside the tribe must first deposit their arms at the shrine before trading and bartering. Often, they will be accompanied by one of the marabout's representatives as a guarantee of safe passage. These settlements, too, are usually located at significant boundaries between the various tribes, which enables these holy men to serve as arbitrators between them, guaranteeing peace and good relations. (Bennett, 1994a: 90)

My argument is this: whilst the socially beneficial function served by the shrines is clear, what functionalism fails to explain is why people respect them, whilst at other times, and in other places, they happily engage in inter-tribal war. Recently, I visited a Sufi shrine in Hyderabad, India where alongside a mixed group of Hindu and Muslim devotees I took part in the ritual and received my blessing from the *shaikh*. There, the peaceful coming together of Muslims and Hindus around common respect for Holy Place, and for the saint entombed there, represents communal harmony, and thus fulfils a beneficial social function. What this does not explain, however, is why the shrine enables such peaceful Muslim–Hindu interaction, when elsewhere in India violent clashes between the two communities are, sadly, not uncommon? Waardenburg, I think, is right to say that we must take seriously, as a scholarly concept, their faith in the shrines as places where *barakah* is available, where no violent act can be committed. How else can their function be explained? In our next chapter, I return to the focus of the first part of this chapter, which (perhaps more so than Eliade's work) suggested convergence between our two fields of study. I shall give more examples of how the anthropologically informed view of religions as multidimensional, and as complex, continues to stimulate students of religions, especially methodologically.

4 Interaction: Religions as Multidimensional Phenomena

In this chapter, we focus on the interaction between the study of religions as it takes to the field, and anthropology as it combines textual with fieldwork research. Often now working in more complex societies, anthropologists find themselves turning to official histories and to primary sources about the religions to inform their fieldwork research. Clifford Geertz comments that 'except for highland New Guinea, the Amazon, and maybe a few places in Africa (maybe not even there now, because most people are involved in nation states and large-scale civilization), the Malinowskian image of a tribe on an island hardly fits anybody anymore'. Thus, 'ninety percent of anthropologists' now 'work on people in the context of large-scale societies and civilizations' (in Ross, 1992: 153). Anthropological work in such complex societies requires background historical and political information. This is most readily supplied by written sources. We see this blending of fieldwork observation with literary and historical research in much of Clifford Geertz's own writing and work. His *Islam Observed* (1968) makes much use of such extra fieldwork sources, which he lists in a useful 'Bibliographical Note' at the end of the book; one of my own students, in a recent essay, described the book as 'mainly a history of Islam in the two countries'. Sir Raymond Firth thinks it 'the type of book Max Weber might have written had he studied oriental societies at first hand instead of from the literature' (back cover). Elsewhere, Geertz remarks that archival work is a 'function of anthropology much underrated' (1983: 5). As one writer comments:

Geertz has drawn upon a broad range of disciplines – history, philosophy, psychology, and even literary criticism – in order to support his ideas. (Johnson, 1992: 149)

Based on lectures presented at Yale on 'Religion and Science', Geertz also offered the book as a 'general framework for the comparative analysis of religion', thus seeing it as a contribution to the study of religions as well as to anthropology (1968: v). He also comments that, in their work on religion, too few anthropologists have thought to look beyond their own 'narrowly defined intellectual tradition' to 'philosophy, history, law, literature, or the "harder sciences" ... for analytical ideas' (1973: 88). No one could accuse Geertz of drawing on a narrowly defined intellectual tradition; Mary Douglas calls him 'the anthropologist who [has] mediated with unique success between sociologists and political historians' (cited by Johnson: 149).

In my opinion, Geertz's work represents the combination of anthropological fieldwork with historical research for which Evans-Pritchard has called. As early as 1950 (in the Marett Lecture) he commented that anthropology was 'closer to certain kinds of history than to the social sciences', whilst in a 1961 lecture he suggested that 'in turning its back on history' anthropology had also turned its back on 'the builders of our science', whose primary aim had been 'to discover the principles of developmental trends in social evolution, an aim which can only be attained if the facts of history are used' (1961: 9–10). Malinowski and Radcliffe-Brown may have been 'both extremely hostile to history' (*ibid.*: 1) but, he concluded, negative consequences had followed, amongst them: the tendency to depict 'primitive peoples' ... 'prior to European domination' ... 'as more or less static' (*ibid.*: 6); an 'uncritical use of documentary sources' (*ibid.*: 5) and the failure to distinguish between 'history, myth, legend, anecdote and folklore' (*ibid.*: 8). Diachronic study is also impossible for anthropologists who restrict their methodology to fieldwork; they cannot study social change diachronically, said Evans-Pritchard, without searching 'the past of a society ... to discover whether what' they 'are inquiring into in the present has been a constant feature over a long period of time' (*ibid.*: 17).

Anthropological interest in the encounter of cultures began during Malinowski's lifetime. Later, this interest brought anthropology home: as migrant groups settled in Britain (and elsewhere in Europe), anthropologists asked, 'How do migrant groups maintain their traditions? How does minority status impact traditional practices? What happens when religions and cultures encounter other religions and cultures?'. For their part, now interested in practitioners as well as in texts, in the synchronic as well as in the diachronic, students of religions have found themselves exploring such phenomena as acculturation, continuity, change, unity, diversity within faiths and between geographically dispersed representatives of the same faith. In this phase of development, all these emerge as major themes. A tendency of earlier generations of scholars had been to regard, say, Islam as the same everywhere, adopting what has been described as an 'essentialist' attitude:

Western scholarship has tended to be 'essentialist', to explain all the phenomena of Muslim societies and cultures in terms of the concept of a single, unchanging nature of Islam and what it is to be Muslim. (Hourani, 1991: 57)

Sir William Muir's caricature of Islam as 'counteracting every diversity of national character' (1858: 2: 376–7); as substantially the same throughout history, and as 'powerless to adapt ... to varying time and place' (1899: 598), cited more fully in Chapter 2, is typical of this essentialist approach. Islam, in his view, was always (diachronically) and everywhere (synchronically) the same.

Now, however, with access to fieldwork research as well as to texts, few contemporary students share Muir's view that Islam is, always and everywhere, the same. Today's students of Islam will no longer content themselves with studying the Qur'an and the *Sunna* (tradition) of the Prophet, with classical texts, while constructing a linear history of Islamic civilization, but will also want to observe how Muslims practise their faith in different contexts, and how different people within the same society have different perceptions and experiences. We noted an example of this approach above, in the work of U.A.B. Razia Akter Banu, who, within a Weberian framework, identified three different strands of Bangladeshi Islam, each associated with different social strata, characterized by different degrees of religiosity and by different attitudes towards the religion–state dynamic. Operating at different levels, religion is regarded as multidimensional and multifaceted rather than as unitary and monodimensional. This chapter notes several examples of thematic and methodological interaction between anthropology, and the study of religions. First, I shall use some examples from my own experience to illustrate how context and migration influence religious practice. Second, we shall discuss Clifford Geertz's work in Indonesia as a case study of what may happen when encounter occurs between religions, and his work in Morocco as an example of how the same religion develops differently in different contexts. Third, we discuss Richard Gombrich's work in Sri Lanka to further illustrate critical interaction between anthropology and textual scholarship. As a Sanskrit scholar working with primary Buddhist sources, Gombrich is heir to Max Müller, Monier-Williams, Rhys Davids, and others philologists, whilst two years in a Sri Lankan village adds anthropological observation to this textual scholarship, creating a conversation between these modes of study.

Some sketches of my own: Hinduism in Britain and India: Continuity and change

Before specializing in Islamics, as an undergraduate at Manchester it was Hinduism and the religious traditions of India which fascinated and interested me. I greatly enjoyed attending lectures – on Hinduism and Buddhism especially – although the focus was mainly textual, and visits from Hindus or to Hindu temples formed no part of the curriculum. It was whilst studying in the Selly Oak Colleges as a graduate student that I first visited a Hindu temple – the Heathfield Road Temple, Birmingham, which occupies a former church. Since then, I have visited several other temples in Britain – Leicester, Bradford, Coventry, the Bhakti Vedanta Manor outside Watford – as well as numerous temples in India. Whilst working for a community development and education charity in Birmingham, 1983–6, I befriended Bengali-speaking Hindus, and was often invited as a guest to festivals, cultural events as well as into private homes (including domestic *pujas* in honour of Saytha Sai Baba, a popular Indian *guru*). This gave me many opportunities to encounter Hinduism, also to soak up something of its ethos in the British context. My several visits to India have enabled me to compare this experience of encounter with my encounter of Hinduism in that context. How has the process of 'transplantation' affected Hindu faith and practice? How does this interact with my study of the classical tradition?

Migration has long taken Hinduism outside India – to Indonesia, where a Hindu king established a dynasty in the eighth century CE and, during the nineteenth and twentieth centuries, further afield, to West and Southern Africa, Europe, North America, as well as to islands in the Pacific. Some aspects of Hindu faith and practice transfer themselves more easily than others – rituals based in the home, or in the temple, for example. Others, to do with sacred places, are less transportable; new places may acquire sanctity, but the old ones back in India will remain significant for many Hindus, wherever they settle around the globe. In India itself, much Hindu practice is peculiar to quite narrowly defined geographical areas, or social groups. Arguably, Hinduism is really an amalgamation of myriad little traditions rather than a singular great tradition. The appropriateness of the term 'Hinduism' (as we have already noted), itself a Western invention, has been questioned by several scholars.

However, others point out that whilst it is 'impossible to identify any universal belief or practice that is common to all Hindus ... what ... makes Hinduism a single religious tradition' is a sense of 'shared heritage and a family relationship'. In other words, Hindus who 'have almost nothing in common with each other' will 'accept somebody as a fellow Hindu, in spite of what may be radical differences of faith and practice' (Weightman, 1984: 192).

In the Indian context, individuals are free to opt for particular viewpoints (*Darshanas*), paths (*margas*) or for devotion to a particular God within the *bhakti* (devotional) tradition, although these are usually determined by geographical location, or by being born into a particular social group. For example, if you are born in Vrindaban, you will most likely be a devotee of Krishna, since Vrindaban is a pilgrimage site associated with this *Avatar* of Vishnu. If you are born in Varanasi, a centre of Hindu scholarship and a major pilgrim centre, you may follow one of the philosophical paths, though you are highly likely to practise a strict form of Brahmanism. On the whole, wherever you are, you will be surrounded by people who share your philosophy, or devotional tradition. Temples (*mandira*) in India are usually dedicated to a single deity. This, though, will be plurally manifested, so visitors to a temple will see a plurality of images (of the deity's various manifestations, and of associated deities).

However, once settled outside India, you are likely to find yourself part of a much more eclectic Hindu community. It is unlikely that any single devotional tradition, or one philosophical path, will dominate or attract exclusive allegiance amongst, say, all the Hindus who happen to have settled in Wolverhampton. Thus, visitors to Hindu temples in Britain will also observe a plurality of images (*murtis*) but these will be of different deities – to Vishnu and to Shiva, for example. The Shree Sanatan Mandir, Leicester (housed in a former Baptist church), has shrines dedicated to RadhaKrishna, SitaRama (from the Vaisnavite tradition), to Shiva and to Shakti (from the Shaivite tradition). Tolerance of diversity is said to be deeply embedded in Indian culture. It would be bold indeed to deny this commonly accepted and widely publicized characteristic of Indian culture. However, I will argue that, whilst pluralism is undeniably a feature of Indian culture, its limits are also carefully prescribed. Religious affiliation is not generally regarded as a matter for private, or individual choice, but is deeply embedded in community identity. This is why Gandhi was so opposed to the efforts of Christian missionaries to convert Hindus, and called conversion, 'the deadliest poison that has ever sapped the fountain of truth' (cited in Shourie: 11). To change one's affiliation is to desert one's community. Anthropologist McKim Marriott (1977) has argued that, in Hindu society, there is no concept of the individual as a free social agent. There are, he suggests, *dividuals* rather than *individuals*. Plurality of devotion, too, is rarely encountered within the same temple. Nor is it uncommon for devotees of one tradition to regard devotees of another with scorn. During my most recent visit to India, Hindus in the South told me that they resented the emphasis on Ram by some Hindu nationalists (who want India to be a Hindu state) saying, 'What's Ram to us! He belongs to the Northerners'. At the level of theory, all paths are viewed as equally valid but in practice you may view your own path as superior, others as inferior or even misguided.

Visitors to Hindu temples in Britain will usually be told that it is the house of the one god who manifests him/herself plurally, and that all are welcome. Hindus belonging to the various devotional traditions mingle in this new context. Non-Hindus feel equally welcome; indeed visitors are usually impressed by the warm hospitality they experience when visiting temples in Britain. This contrasts sharply with my experience in India, where signs reading 'non-Hindus not allowed' often adorn temples, and where visitors are frequently restricted to the outer square, or courtyard. Nor have I always felt at all welcome in Indian temples. Priests have hustled me for donations, and I have literally been forced to pay for garlands to be placed on my behalf in the *garbha-grha* (sanctuary) despite not being allowed to enter myself, and my own theological reservations about personal participation in other traditions' worship. On the other hand, I have also been warmly welcomed, and engaged in discussion, once my interest in Hinduism became known to the priest-in-charge.

Nevertheless, to me as an outsider, Hinduism has a very different 'feel' in the British, compared with its Indian, context. Other significant differences can also be identified. Amongst these, a blurring both of class/caste (*varna/jati*) distinctions, and of roles. Marriage outside traditional social groupings is more common in Britain than it is in India. A senior member of the temple committee at Leicester, whose own daughters had married non-Hindus (white men) said that he had no objection at all to his children marrying whoever they wanted to. I was told in the Leicester temple, too, that any Hindu knowledgable in the Vedic rituals could function as a priest. Traditionally, in India, the priestly function is restricted to the Brahmins. Shudras could be punished for accidentally hearing the Vedas, let alone for daring to study them, whilst some Hindu movements active in the West, such as the International Society for Krishna Consciousness, extend priesthood to non-Brahmins and also to non-Indians. Traditionally, membership of the Hindu community is hereditary, 'a person is a Hindu because he is born to Hindu parents' (Weightman, 1984: 209). Nevertheless, in Britain, the Hare Krishna movement, with its non-Indian members (in other words, converts to Hinduism), and even priests, is widely accepted by the Hindu community as 'an authentic strand within their tradition' (Barker, 1989: 185). This inclusiveness, it can be argued, sharply contrasts with a tendency in some contemporary branches of Hinduism in India to exclude – for example, by defining Hinduism in terms of Brahminism and so disqualifying as Hindus all but the highest castes/classes.

Another interesting development is a much more participatory, almost congregational style of worhip – the traditional *arti* ceremony will often incorporate the singing of *bhajjans*, for example. Whilst this is by no means unknown in India, in Britain it has taken on a much more structured and formal pattern. Thus, in Indian temples, one generally sees lone individuals praying or chanting; in Britain I have observed seated rows of devotees chanting from printed texts whilst the priest performs the *arti* (light ceremony) before the images. Kim Knott gives a detailed description of a typical *arti* ceremony, such as I have observed, in Wolffe (1993: 79–84). Outside India, temples also serve as community and educational centres. Another difference between India and Britain is the popularity of *Holi* in the former, which in Britain is hardly celebrated at all. In his *Worlds of Faith* (1983), based on a series of interviews and meetings with members of faith communities in Britain, John Bowker points out that this is mainly due to the difference between the British, and the Indian climate, so that a festival which has 'been described as combining erotic games, comic operas, and folk dancing' isn't 'so easy to stage without the Indian sun' (*ibid*: 13). For the same reason, not many Hindus in Britain observe, at least in a traditional way, the fourth *ashrama*, or stage in life – the *sanyasin*, or 'world renouncer', who gives 'up everything, except a cup for water, a bowl for begging food and a loincloth'. Remarking that 'sometimes you don't even keep the loincloth', a Hindu interviewee added that this 'just isn't possible in Britain' ... 'for obvious reasons' (*ibid.*: 14).

Developments partly stem from the experience of being a minority but they are also influenced by the ethos of the majority community, even, as we have noted, by climactic differences. It could be argued that British society is itself relatively open to, and receptive of, diverse cultures. Whilst this statement will almost certainly attract criticism, I would argue that, although racism is a serious problem, and discrimination of opportunity a statistically verifiable fact, it has not proved too difficult for minority religious groups to acquire (and to legally register) places of worship, or to take a part in the wider social and civic life of British towns and cities. Civic services following the election of Hindu or of Muslim Lord Mayors have taken place in temples and mosques, and religious leaders from minority communities are now routinely invited to attend significant ceremonial occasions alongside church leaders. In different circumstances, in a less open ethos, the Hindu community might have turned in on itself.

Contextual adaptation

My first exposure to Sikhism was also during my 1978 to 1979 period of study in the Selly Oak Colleges, when I visited a Birmingham Gurdwara. I was much impressed by the hospitality – impressed further by how Sikhism's commitment to hospitality, to social service, and to equality, are embedded in its foundation documents. Subsequently, even when my visits to Gurdwaras in Britain have been unexpected, I have experienced the same warm welcome and offer of food in the *langar*. Some Gurdwaras now attract a regular clientele of people who are unable to feed themselves, or who appreciate the friendly atmosphere of the 'anchor' (the literal meaning of *langar*, the common kitchen). A group of my students recently went on a field trip to the Reading Gurdwara and reported how its *langar* operates a type of meals-on-wheels service for local housebound residents, regardless of their cultural or religious background.

However, shortly after my first visit to a Gurdwara I passed through Singapore on my way to Australia, and briefly visited Johore Bahru, the southernmost town of Malaysia. I was delighted to find a variety of temples there, and decided to try to visit as many of them as I could in the short time available. Attempting to enter the Gurdwara, prepared for a warm and hospitable welcome, I was taken by complete surprise when what I received was the very opposite. Although I could not understand the angry barrage of words which greeted me, the look of suspicion on the faces and their physical aggressiveness (barring my entry) communicated well enough that I was not welcome. Rather frightened, I made a rapid retreat. I well remember thinking 'so much for all that rhetoric about hospitality!' I have later reflected, however, that the position of minority religious groups in Malaysia is very different from their position in Britain. In Malaysia, there has been increasing pressure from Muslims to make Malaysia an Islamic state. The Malays, too, see the success of the Chinese and Indian communities as taking away what should rightly be theirs! Consequently, something of a siege mentality has emerged within some of the minority communities. They do not feel wanted, and are, therefore, unused to much contact with outsiders, least of all in their places of worship. Zakaria (1988) comments:

Under the British, the relationship between the various groups, though strained, was under control; but since attaining independence in 1953, Malaysia has been bedevilled by racial, ethnic and even religious conflict. The original Malay inhabitants, all Muslim, are supporters of the 'sons of the soil' theory and press for privileges in every sphere of national life. (1988: 244–5)

This contextualization sheds new light on my unhappy experience. Were that my only experience of Sikhism, I would understandably adjudge Sikhs paranoid and inhospitable. Only by visiting more than one context, and by attempting to understand what factors influence a religion's local, or particular, manifestation, can we begin to construct an accurate picture. In parts of India, too, it is highly unlikely that non-Sikhs regularly enter Gurdwaras. The presence there of people whom you may regard as ritually impure, the possibility of eating food from the *langar* prepared by someone of a lower caste, for example, will deter many. Sikhs in such contexts may not be used to the presence of outsiders in their Gurdwaras, and are, therefore, unsure how to receive them. However, where their presence is more common, they are able to rediscover the tradition of universal hospitality embedded in their own heritage. Thus, movement from one context to another may also lead to a rediscovery of aspects of a tradition which have been forgotten, fallen into disuse, or obscured by cultural accretions. Sikhism's original commitment to absolute equality of the sexes, for example, may be easier to practise in societies where women are able to take a full part in public, as well as in private, life than where their role is restricted to the home. In such contexts, writes

Kanwaljit Kaur-Singh, 'the man thinks himself the breadwinner, hence worthy of occupying a higher position'. Unwilling to 'surrender their dominant role', Sikh men deny women their rightful equality. They happily cook and serve food in the *langar*, 'But at home they think these jobs are for women'. . . 'though if they would turn to their Guru's teachings they would recognise the need to practise equality' (1994: 154–5).

Many Muslim friends, especially English converts to Islam, have spoken to me about the need they feel to distinguish between what is essentially Islamic, and what is culturally Pakistani or Indian, in the practices of the communities which they have joined. Sometimes, they feel they are being expected to become Pakistani, as well as Muslim. Dress traditions, for example, can vary from place to place. Some Muslims will want to imitate the dress of the Prophet, and will regard this as the only authentically Islamic dress, but many regard any modest dress as conforming with the Qur'anic guidelines. Thus, Pakistani Punjabi suits are no more Islamic than a Western suit (depending on the fit – a too tight fitting suit may not be considered sufficiently modest). One Muslim friend, a senior Imam, told me how university students once criticized him, as they put it, for 'not wearing Islamic dress' when he led their Friday prayers wearing suit and tie. They expected him to wear flowing Arab robes. He pointed out that his dress was perfectly Islamic, and that although he had studied in Saudi Arabia, he was not an Arab. Another Muslim friend, Sajdah Currah, writing about her experience of being 'Muslim, young, Pakistani, female . . . and in Britain', comments:

it has seemed as if there is a pecking-order of virtue amongst women, decided by their dress; those in *shalwar kameez* being the most virtuous, those wearing trousers considered respectable but 'modern', and those who wear skirts as beyond the pale! Attitudes have altered somewhat as more people realise that those young Muslim women of Pakistani origin, but born and brought up in Britain, are forming their own identities with their own codes of dress. These are largely based on Islamic principles, not Pakistani ones. (1994: 52)

Returning to their authoritative documents, emigrés and converts may find themselves scrutinizing existing practices to see which are embedded within the tradition, and which may be questioned as later, possibly unacceptable, accretions. Philip Lewis comments:

New Muslims can thus serve to ... remind South Asians that Islam is a universal faith, loosen the link between ethnicity and religious identity, and, where they 'bring an inquisitive mind to their new religion ... may contribute to the continuous evolution of Islam helping to mould it to fit the conditions of contemporary European society'. (1994: 197 citing Gerholm, 1988: 263)

Anthropologists and students of religions observing the development of British Islam, British Hinduism, and so on, have many interesting themes to explore. Philip Lewis' *Islamic Britain: Religion, Politics and Identity among British Muslims* (1994), which Akbar Ahmed has described as an 'insider–outsider account' (flyleaf), for example, explores many of the issues which British Muslims face as 'they give up the myth of return that sustained the first generation immigrants and struggle to define a British Islam' (back cover).

Geertz in Indonesia

We have already noted Geertz's contribution to a theoretical understanding of religion. In this chapter, we discuss other aspects of his contribution to anthropology, and to the academic study of religions; first, his methodology, second, his analysis of Javanese religion, third, his comparison of Indonesian with Moroccan Islam.

Geertz on methodology

Geertz underwent his first period of fieldwork research in Java between 1952 and 1954 whilst a student at Harvard. This work contributed to his doctoral thesis, and was published as *The Religion of Java* (1960). He was based in the village of Modjokuto, which he describes as 'a commercial, educational and administrative center for eighteen surrounding villages' with a 'population of almost 20,000, of whom about 18,000 are Javanese, 1,800 Chinese, and the remainder a handful of Arabs, Indians and other minorities'. Modjokuto, he says, 'marks the point where the flat, fertile countryside begins to tilt toward the cluster of active volcanoes which tower over it to the east and whose periodic eruptions provide much of its fertility' (1960: 1). With his wife, Geertz lived 'during the whole of this period with a railroad worker at the northern edge of the town' (*ibid.*: 383). His second period of fieldwork in Indonesia was between 1957 and 1958, when he lived on the island of Bali. This resulted in several monographs (some co-written with his wife, Hildred), most famous amongst them 'Deep play: Notes on a Balinese cockfight' (1972).

During his first visit, Geertz worked as part of a wider team of six anthropologists, each of whom concentrated on a different aspect of Javanese life. Geertz' focus was religion, but he writes, 'despite the focus ... on religion ... all aspects of Modjokuto culture and society were given some attention in the actual process of research' (1960: 384). All interviews were conducted in Indonesian, and 'no interpreters were ever used'. Geertz did not attempt to interview a 'representative sample in the specific sense' but gathered data from 'every major religious stream, the major occupational groups' and from 'the main political affiliations' (*ibid.*: 385). Most of the time, he says, was 'spent in more informal "participant observation" activities. I attended dozens of public events ... Hours were spent in "idle" conversation, or informal interviewing in coffee shops, in stores and market stalls'(*ibid.*). In his 'Note on methods of work', reflecting on his role as researcher, he comments, 'the overwhelming majority of the people with whom I came in contact seemed willing to accept me as more or less what I said I was', namely, 'a university student come to Java to gather material on the "Javanese way of life" in order to write a dissertation' (*ibid.*: 385).

In his writing, Geertz expresses some discontent with an understanding of the anthropologist's task which overstresses the details of systematic fieldwork: 'anthropology', he writes, 'is not a matter of methods ... selecting informants, transcribing texts ... keeping a diary and so on' (1973: 6). Rather, it has to do with 'interpretation', with 'constructing a reading of what happens' (*ibid.*: 18). 'Anthropological writings', he continues, 'are thus "fictions", fictions in the sense that they are "something made", "something fashioned" – the original meaning of *fictio* – not that they are false' (*ibid.*: 15). Earlier, I have referred to his borrowed illustration of the wink. Geertz uses this to illustrate the difference between what he calls 'thin' and 'thick' description. Thin description describes the wink as a movement of the eye-lid, thick description goes beyond describing the observed phenomenon, to decoding *its* meaning: 'communicating in a quite precise and special way' (*ibid.*: 6). Indeed, as in the case of the wink in Geertz's illustration, there may be several different layers of meaning. The anthropologist's task, then, involves reading cultural sub-texts. Since this requires deep penetration, the wider an anthropologist spreads his study, the less skilled he or she is likely to be at reading sub-texts. 'Tacit knowledge' ... 'the unspoken cultural norms', as well as 'explicit' knowledge, 'what we know and talk about' is required in order to construct 'thick description' (Neuman, 1994: 224). 'Thick description', writes Lawrence Neuman, 'of a three-minute event may go on for pages. It captures the sense of what occurred and the main drama of events, thereby permitting multiple interpretations. It places events in a context so that the reader of an ethnographic report can infer cultural meaning' (*ibid.*).

In his own work, Geertz tends to concentrate on relatively small areas of study, on 'the concrete, the particular, the microscopic' in the hope that he might find in the 'small' what 'eludes' him 'in the large' (1968: 4). His work on the *slametan* ritual (see below) during his first, and on the Balinese cockfight during his second, period in Indonesia, are examples of his approach; to use deep analysis of significant customs to 'get into and understand the soul of a culture' (Ross, 1992: 153). Sometimes, he almost implies that the trick of the anthropologist's trade lies in sudden intuition, rather like a Zen Buddhist intuitively understanding a *koan*; 'Understanding natives' inner lives is more like grasping a proverb, catching an illusion, seeing a joke – or, as I have suggested elsewhere, reading a poem – than it is like achieving communion' (Geertz, 1983: 70). Whilst his aim is to understand 'from the natives' point of view', his method focuses less on what people say and more on what they do. Convinced that the way people think about themselves, and about the world, expresses itself through symbols (rites, myths, art), he has spent much time 'searching out and analyzing' ... 'the symbolic forms – words, images, institutions, behaviours – in terms of which, in each place, people actually' represent 'themselves to themselves and to one another' (1983: 58). We all, he says, (following Weber) occupy 'webs of significance' which we have spun for ourselves; taking these webs as 'culture', the task of analysing culture 'is not an experimental science in search of law, but an interpretive one in search of meaning' (1973: 5). Incidentally, Geertz is careful not to claim that the anthropologist can construct what is called a 'first order' account. He says 'By definition, only a "native" makes first order ones: its *his* culture' (*ibid.*: 15). What he does argue is that a 'second order interpretation', produced by thick description, can authoritatively explicate the webs of significance it has analysed. His interest in symbols has resulted in his identification with the 'symbolic anthropology movement' (associated with Chicago, where he worked between 1960 and 1970) although Geertz prefers the term 'interpretive anthropology'. For him, the anthropological account, or text, is an 'interpretation', yet given empathy, a 'passing over' into the culture studied, such interpretations may carry validity.

Geertz's aim, in his work, is to remove himself from the data, 'to become translucent so that readers can see for' themselves 'something of what the facts look like and so judge the ethnographer's summaries and generalizations in terms of the ethnographer's actual perceptions' (1960: 7). He has written at length about the researcher's role, about 'insider–outsider' perspectives. Despite the problems inherent in any outsider attempting to penetrate other cultures, which Geertz fully recognizes, he more than hints that it is possible, given the right circumstances, for the outsider to break through into insider confidence. In his essay, 'Deep play: Notes on the Balinese cockfight' he describes how, instead of standing their ground and pulling out their 'distinguished visitor' papers, he and Hildred fled with the villagers when the police raided the illegal fight. Whatever their reason for fleeing (cowardice, or to express 'solidarity with what were now our co-villagers') Geertz and his wife found themselves 'on the inside'. Even an old priest, whom other Balinese found 'difficult to approach ... called us into his courtyard to ask us about what had happened'.

In Bali, to be teased is to be accepted. It was the turning point so far as our relationship to the community was concerned, and we were quite literally 'in'. The whole village opened up to us, probably more than it would have otherwise (I might actually never have gotten to that priest, and our accidental host became one of my best informants), and certainly very much faster. Getting caught, or almost caught, in a vice raid is perhaps not a very generalizable recipe for achieving that mysterious necessity of anthropological field work, rapport, but for me it worked very well. (1973: 416)

It may be that only 'natives' possess first order interpretations, and that the anthropologist's is of a second order, but such accounts, carefully constructed, can convey the sense that the writer has 'actually penetrated ... another form of life', has truly 'been there', and validly represents this experience (1988: 4–5).

The three religious expressions which Geertz identified in Java were not, he says, 'constructed types, but terms and divisions the Javanese themselves apply' (1960: 6). Although his fieldwork was based in one town, by drawing on historical and literary sources, he was able to set his research within the wider Indonesian social and political context. Geertz calls anthropologists the 'miniaturists of the social sciences, painting on lilliputian canvases' (1968: 4), yet always oscillating between the particular and the general; 'between looking particularly at particular views and defining globally the attitude that permeates them ... governs', he says, 'the progress of analysis' (1983: 11).

Geertz on Javanese religion

Geertz's analysis of Javanese religion falls broadly within a Weberian framework. The archipelago we now know as Indonesia, of which the island of Java is a part, has experienced at least three cultural incursions; first, what Geertz calls the 'Indic', second, Islam, third, Western culture generally, Dutch imperial culture especially. All met, and mingled with, the island's indigenous culture. What happened as each newcomer arrived was not a displacement of earlier cultures by the latest arrival, but a mingling and a stratification of influence and role. This upsets, to some degree, the neat Western pattern of single loyalties, and somewhat resembles the Chinese and Japanese pattern, where people turn, at different times or even at the same time, to several religious traditions (Buddhism, Confucianism, Daosm, Shintoism) as and when they wish to. Thus, in Japan, the number of people registered as affiliated to religions is 'almost double the population' indicating that 'multiple belonging is common' (Reader, 1994: 169).

First, Geertz identified a general Javanese religio-cultural system, known as *abangan*, which combined elements of the island's original animistic religion with Indic and Islamic beliefs and practices, as each arrived on the island:

> the peasantry absorbed Islamic concepts and practices, so far as they understood them, into the same general Southeast Asian folk religion into which it had previously absorbed Indian ones, locking ghosts, gods, jinns and prophets together into a strikingly contemplative, even philosophical, animism. (1968: 13)

Islam did not come to Indonesia by way of conquest, or invasion, but by way of mendicant Sufi mystics. This style of Islam, 'adaptive, absorbent, pragmatic, and gradualistic' (*ibid.*: 16), an 'Islam of the trance', rather 'than of the book' (p. 65), meshed in well with Hindu, or Indic theosophy, and, also mingled with the existing amalgam of animistic and Indic beliefs, produced *abangan*. However, says Geertz, for different historical, political, even economic and geographical reasons, different 'weight and meanings' have been, and are, given to *abangan's* 'various ingredients' (p. 13) by different social groups.

When greater weight is given to its Islamic elements, the result is *santri*, a purer form of Islam, which at times moves closer towards reformed Islam (which Geertz describes as 'the attempt to re-establish the "plain", "original", "uncorrupted", "progressive" Islam of the days of the prophet and the Rightly Guided Caliphs' (p. 69). He identifies these purer forms of Islam, in the main, with geographic localities, and social groups, where more regular contact with the wider Islamic world occurs – namely, ports and traders. Originally, purer Islam flourished along the coast. With the coming of the Dutch, who dominated the international trade, the Javanese traders were forced inland, 'to forge a domestic marketing system'. Thus, in Modjokotu as elsewhere, it was around the market that 'the social institutions of Islam grew up' (p. 42).

When Indic elements are stressed, the result is *prijaji*. Originally, this particular 'weighting' was popular amongst the traditional ruling class, because it stresses the importance of etiquette and of rank. With the coming of the Dutch, this group lost power, but, moving into the civil service, remained elitist. *Prijaji*, a blend of Muslim, and Indian mysticism, has also absorbed some Western modes of thinking; since its practitioners were amongst those who benefited most from Western education during the colonial period, it has added to its emphasis on inner experience a secular understanding of nationhood. This sometimes creates conflict with the purest of the *santri*, who wish to see Indonesia become an Islamic state. Political parties campaigning for Islamic statehood tend to draw their support from the *santri*, whilst those parties which stress Indonesian, rather tham Islamic identity, are in the main supported by the *prijaji*.

Meanwhile, the majority of Javanese, represented by the rural peasantry, practise what we might call a pure *abangan*. It seems well suited to their day-by-day concerns, health, survival and well being (*slamet*, hence *slametan*, its main ritual – a communal feast). The elitist *prijaji*, traditionally, avoided contact with the peasantry, whilst the *santri's* emphasis on doctrine rather than on ritual, lacked widespread appeal; '*abangans* are fairly indifferent to doctrine but fascinated with ritual detail, while among the *santris* the concern with doctine almost entirely overshadows the already attenuated ritualistic aspects of Islam' (1960: 127).

Thus, what Geertz found in Java was that 'behind the simple statement that Java is more than 90 per cent Moslem' which one can read in some official texts lies concealed a much more complex, and diverse, reality, including 'much variation in ritual, contrast in belief, and conflict in values' (*ibid.*: 7). This diversity, however, he concludes, does not 'deny the underlying religious unity' of the Javanese people, 'or, beyond them of the Indonesian people generally', but brings 'home the reality of the complexity, depth, and richness of their spiritual life' (*ibid.*). In fact, he says, Indonesian society remains, generally, tolerant of this diversity, so that, a type of 'each to their own' ethos has emerged:

Traders and richer peasants are seen, by all groups, as more or less 'naturally' *santris*, civil servants as 'normally' *prijaji*, and poorer peasants and town proletariat as 'typically' *abangan*; and there is really little serious thought in any of the groups that there is much possibility of 'converting' the others. The *santris* may talk much about missionary work (*tableg*) and rail about the heathenism of the non-*santri* groups, but in fact almost all their missionary work is directed inward, toward the *santri* group itself, being designed to improve the docrinal purity of those who are already committed, rather than to gain new adherents. (1960: 374)

My purpose in visiting this aspect of Geertz's work, with its combination of literary, historical and anthropological research, is to illustrate that neither type of research alone could have penetrated as deeply, or as widely, into the reality of Javanese religion, as have both combined. If only official texts (those published by mainstream Muslim organizations) had been consulted, the resulting picture would almost certainly have been much more monochrome. However, through Geertz's work, we are able to see Javanese religion as a rich, interconnecting web of practices and beliefs, differently weighted by different groups, and as a multifaceted and multidimensional, not monolithic, phenomenon. This, we have already noted, runs counter to how Western scholarship has often explained Muslim societies and cultures, that is, 'in terms of the concept of a single, unchanging nature of Islam and what it is to be Muslim' (Hourani, 1991: 57). In contrast, the first generation of students of religion, represented in our survey by Max Müller and Rhys Davids, had not been very interested in contemporary religions, believing that study of scriptures gives access to 'the earliest and ideal' religious traditions, whilst geographic expansion and the passage of time introduced 'beliefs inconsistent with origins' (Harris, 1993: 312). Rhys Davids, though, thought that his efforts at separating the rational and ethical core of Buddhist scriptures from mythological material would contribute towards recovering a pure tradition in his own day.

Geertz's next fieldwork research took place in Morocco, (1964, 1965–66), where he compared Islam's evolution in Indonesia with its evolution in Morocco; Morocco and Indonesia, he writes, 'have participated in the history' of Islamic 'civilization in quite different ways, to quite different degrees, and with quite different results' (1968: 4). What conclusions did he draw?

Geertz on Moroccan and Indonesian Islam

Geertz's research draws out the contrast between the two countries: Indonesia, on the periphery of the Muslim world; Morocco, Arabic-speaking and close to the traditional centres of Islamic civilization. Islam reached Indonesia in the fourteenth century, Morocco in the seventh; Indonesia has an 'extremely productive wet rice' economy, whilst 'pastoralism and agriculture' in the 'climatically irregular, physically ill endowed, and somewhat despoiled environment' of Morocco is economically considerably less 'certain' (1968: 7). Having myself briefly visited both countries, I would add: Morocco, hot, dry and Saharan; Indonesia, hot, humid and green. Indonesia has a mainly settled population, Morocco a mixture of nomadic tribes, rural farmers and urban traders. Economic need has often impelled the 'tribesmen into the cities, if not as conquerors then as refugees ... sometimes ... encircling them and, blocking the trade routes from which they lived, extorting from them' (*ibid.*). Thus, says Geertz, Morocco has bred a vigorously independent, even individualistic, lifestyle; 'a great deal', he says, 'turned on force of character'. This lent itself to a type of Sufi Islam which revolved around the charismatic leadership of saints, and of their (usually hereditary) successors, the *marabouts*. Thus 'what Max Weber called hereditary charisma' was elevated 'over what he called personal charisma' (*ibid.*: 45). Those *marabouts* who claimed descent from the family of the prophet also exercised political power, thus combining spiritual and temporal authority in the classic Islamic model. 'Morocco', says Geertz 'had ... an acute sense of the power of God and the belief that his power appeared in the world in the exploits of forceful men' (1983: 135). Effectively, the *marabouts* replaced the role of tribal shaikhs during the pre-Islamic era. The monarch, too, exercised power because 'he was recognised by the religious adepts around the throne as the member of the ruling family spiritually most fit to hold the office' (1968: 55). To maintain power, he had to function as the chief *marabout* by constantly moving around Morocco's local power centres, demonstrating his *baraka*, or charisma. This mobility also helped to unify the realm. Consequently, Moroccan Islam has stressed unity and uniformity: *shariah* as a unifying legal code and Islamic practices of a rigorously orthodox form 'to impress a seamless orthodoxy on the entire population' (*ibid*.: 16).

In contrast, suggests Geertz, Indonesian Islam (as described above) adopted a very different strategy – 'adaptive, absorbent, pragmatic'. It 'does not even pretend to purity; it pretended to comprehensiveness, not to an intensity but to a largeness of spirit' (*ibid*.). Inner illumination rather than doctrinal conformity, characterizes Indonesian Islam. The individualism of Morroco, too, contrasts with the Indonesian tendency towards the 'radical dissolution of personality'. Both expressions of Islam, however, were responses to the given conditions in which Islam found itself. Morocco needed a unifying force to prevent the disruption of tribal, and rural–urban, clashes; Indonesia's ethos of each to their own (which does not view different systems as rivals, but as complementary) produced an Islam which developed differently amongst different social strata, sometimes purer, sometimes more eclectic. Each 'Islam' reflects the lifestyles of the two countries, thus serving a dual function; they mirror life as people experience it, and 'are guides for action, blueprints for conduct' (*ibid*.: 98). Their respective patterns (or 'symbols' as Geertz tends to call them)

render the world view believable and the ethos justifiable, and ... do so by invoking each in support of the other. The world view [Moroccan individualism or Indonesia's spiritual heirarchy] is believable because the ethos, which grows out of it, is felt to be authoritative; the ethos is justifiable because the world view, upon which it rests, is held to be true (1968: 97).

Islam in both countries has also experienced what Geertz calls a 'scripturalist interlude'; he means the reformist movements which stand for 'credal orthodoxy exactly defined' (*ibid*.: 71) and generally oppose Sufism (especially the role of saints) whether in its Indonesian, or Moroccan form. Islam in each country is also, like religion everywhere, exposed to secularism, and to post-modernity. The reformist influence, itself part of a general response to modernity, 'remains a powerful voice in both countries', but in each, too, the 'classical styles ... are still the axial traditions' (p. 88). What the future holds for these expressions of Islam in this encounter lies beyond the scope of this discussion. Geertz observes:

Predictions in this field ... are pointless. All a student of comparative religion can really do is to lay out the general limits within which the spiritual life of a people has moved, is moving, and, the future never being wholly unlike the present, is likely to go on moving. Just how, within those general limits it will in fact move, God, as they say, only knows. (p. 89)

Geertz's sketches of Islam, 'a supposedly single creed' in 'two quite contrasting civilizations' (p. v), serves to illustrate how socio-historical and political factors influence religion, as well as how fieldwork observation can be complemented by the type of research for which Evans-Pritchard has called. Unscientifically, I wonder whether the very different climates of the two countries has not also influenced their religious ethos – the desert, perhaps, lends itself to individual rigour, the pastoral life to co-operation. The pioneer Muslim social scientist and historiographer, Ibn Khaldun (1332–1406) had it that the nomadic bedouin lifestyle produces 'rude, proud, ambitious' individuals, all 'eager to be leaders', whilst a more sedentary life tends towards a lifestyle of dependency on others (see Ahmed, 1988: 101–6). What, as an anthropologist trained in the United States where Boas' contribution remains fundamental, Geertz did not do was to adjudge any one of the expressions of Islam which he studied any more or less authentically Islamic, than any other. What his work also shows is Islam as a dynamic, not as a static or 'time-warped' tradition. Geertz has frequently revisited both Indonesia and Morocco, and reflects on this experience in his latest book *After the Fact* (1995). Although he expresses some pessimism about the ability to understand, and to translate, across cultures, this book shows how repeated visits to the same places can facilitate diachronic study based on observation and fieldwork as well as on historical research.

Turning now to Richard Gombrich's work in Sri Lanka, we shall see how he had to deal with the views of some who did adjudge what they saw as 'corrupt'.

Richard Gombrich in Sri Lanka

Geertz's work compares and contrasts one religion, Islam, in two different contexts, using historical material to shed light on fieldwork observation, Gombrich's focuses on change and continuity within one religion, Buddhism, in a single context. Citing Evans-Pritchard's invitation to anthropologists to become historians, Gombrich explains why, trained as a philologist, he found himself 'far from home, deep inside the territory of the social sciences, far from Oxford libraries in a village in central Ceylon' (1971: 3). For a total of two years, living in a Sri Lankan village, he researched his doctorate, which, published as *Precept and Practice* (1971), he describes as 'the presentation of a year's fieldwork, the stuff of anthropology'. Gombrich offers this as a 'contribution to the empirical study of religion, and in particular of religious change' (*ibid.*: 1). In it, he combined textual and historical research with anthropological fieldwork. Although 'by education a philologist, far less of a historian, and devoid of anthropological training', his research dealt with the 'problems and conjectural explanations ... of the type which hitherto have interested mainly those trained in the social sciences' (p. 3). The earliest students of religions, also philologists by training, he points out (as we have seen in this survey), thought contemporary religious practice corrupt, and so concentrated on the textual study of the oldest canonical literature. On the other hand, 'the tradition that anthropologists study only what they can observe first hand', suggests Gombrich, produces 'what is called a synchronic study in which the society, including its religion, has its picture taken at one moment and is thus presented as if static' (p. 3). Scholars, whether philologists, historians or anthropologists interested in change, or in continuity, over time (in the diachronic) must study cultures, or religions, through historical sources as well as by fieldwork observation. Thus, if we want to study how a religion may have changed, we need to know 'what the present religion, which we can now see, has changed from' and the best way to do this is to study 'religions based on books', that is, on scriptures. Their textual study may not tell us what the 'mass of adherents' of a religion actually believed when these scriptures were written, 'but they do tell us what their authors believed' (pp. 17–18).

Gombrich chose Buddhism, and Sri Lanka, as his field of study for a very pragmatic reason: he could not study the scriptures of Islam, or of Chinese religion, because he did not know Arabic or Chinese. He might have studied the Hindu scriptures, but 'their interpretation is so obscure that their relevance to what people believe is negligible' (p. 18), whereas his knowledge of Sanskrit, being closely related to Pali, the language of Buddhist scripture, and to modern Sinhalese, would facilitate both his study of Buddhism's canonical literature and his fieldwork observation. Sinhalese Buddhism, too, unlike Burmese and Thai Buddhism, which he might also have researched, has preserved the Theravada (school of the elders) form of Buddhism uninterrupted for possibly as long as 2000 years; Thailand and Burma were Mahayana until 'they adopted Theravada through contact with Ceylon ... in the eleventh and twelfth centuries' (p. 19). Theraveda Buddhism, too, *claims* to preserve the original teaching of the Buddha; unlike Mahayana, it has a 'unitary body of acknowledged scriptures' and so invites this type of study. 'So', said Gombrich, 'Ceylon it was'.

His fieldwork interviews, with *Bhikkhus* (members of the monastic community, often translated 'monks') and with laypeople, were all conducted without interpreters 'although for a few of them bilingual friends were present' (p. 37). He was especially interested in finding out what Sinhalese Buddhists themselves actually believe about such beliefs and practices as 'veneration of the Buddha, attitudes towards the dead, and "prayers" (*prarthana*)' (p. 39) which anthropologists and others, applying Redfield's distinction between great and little traditions, have often branded as 'popular'. This assumes that such beliefs and practices represent departures from the great tradition, and are later accretions to an originally pure Buddhism. Western writers, says Gombrich, such as Sir Charles Eliot (1862–1931) in his *Hinduism and Buddhism* (1921), have commonly depicted Sinhalese Buddhism as syncretistic; an amalgamation of 'local animism, Hinduism and Buddhism ... all inextricably linked together' (p. 46). He also comments on the frequency with which he had been 'told, by books and by people, that Sinhalese village Buddhism was corrupt' (p. 45).

As a result of his research, textual and fieldwork, he reached the very opposite conclusion; that the Buddhism he observed in Kandyan villages was 'surprisingly orthodox', implying that 'religious doctrines and practices ... have changed very little over the last 1500 years', that is, since Buddhism first reached Sri Lanka. He thus argues for continuity, not discontinuity, between the Sinhalese Buddhism of today, and of close to the time when the canonical literature was written. Where anthropologists (he cites Sir Edmund Leach's article 'Pulleyar and the Lord Buddha: An aspect of religious syncretism in Ceylon' (1962)) went wrong was in not checking to see whether what they took to be syncretistic had any scriptural sanction; where textual scholars (such as T.W. Rhys Davids) who condemned the Buddhism they observed as corrupt went wrong was in failing to recognize contemporary practices as legitimate (if unexpected) developments of canonical beliefs. I would add, where both went wrong was in making such value judgements (about pure and corrupt religion) in the first place. Even beliefs and practices which may not be reconcilable with scriptural teaching were, Gombrich argues, firmly established by 1500 CE, evidenced by significant non-canonical texts, therefore the Sinhalese have merely continued what they received, alongside the canonical literature, from their earliest Buddhist teachers.

Gombrich was also interested in the relationship between what he calls the 'cognitive' and the 'affective' levels, between what people believe intellectually, and (as I understand Gombrich) their emotional beliefs. For example, cognitively, Sinhalese Buddhists believe, as the scriptural tradition teaches, that the Buddha is dead, and, in *nibbana*, is unable to assist them in any practical way, either by granting favours or by performing miracles. Affectively, though, they regard him as divine, and as still able to intercede in their lives; thus their prayers to the Buddha, and their worship of Buddha images. Village Buddhists are simply inconsistent:

If pressed they reveal that although the Buddha is dead there is a certain Buddha force (*Budubulaya*), which will exist till at the end of this dispensation, in another 2,500 years, the Buddha's relics (including images) will collect at the Ruvanvalasiya at Anuradhapura and after a last sermon the Buddha will finally disappear.... But the inconsistency is interestingly limited, because this *Budubalaya* does not seem to operate outside the ritual context ... but only in the presence of images; it is virtually a force inherent in the image ... (1971: 131–42)

Yet even this, Gombrich argues, is not necessarily a total departure from the official doctrinal position. At the very least, some ambiguity is suggested by the basic credal statement of refuge, which all Buddhists repeat as a confession of their faith, 'I take refuge in the Buddha, I take refuge in the *dharma* (teaching), I take refuge in the *Sangha* (community)', which 'has a theistic tinge, however it may be interpreted by pundits' (p. 142). Similarly, T.W. Rhys Davids had thought the Buddhism he observed in Ceylon corrupt because Buddhists believed in, and paid tribute to, 'gods'. However, says Gombrich, gods occur in the canonical literature as part of the Buddha's worldview, so belief in them 'is not a novel or syncretistic feature, but has always been the case'. 'As long', he says, as Buddhists treat them 'as a kind of supermen, able to grant favours to suppliants, but still ultimately of limited life and powers ... their beliefs are not syncretistic' (p. 409). However, does not lay preoccupation with acquiring such favours (a better rebirth, or rebirth in one of the heavens) sit uncomfortably with the ultimate Buddhist goal of release from *samsara* (the cycle of existence)? Perhaps, suggests Gombrich, but pragmatically Buddhists have to choose between the goal of *nibbana*, and the ethic, also taught by the Buddha, of compassion and of service to humanity.

This dilemma, or conflict, says Gombrich, 'between self-restraint and love, between selfishness and altruism, between negative and positive goals ... can ... be traced back to the Buddha himself' (p. 320). If only the former were pursued, and achieved, the *dharma* would already have died out (see p. 321). To preserve, and pass on, the *dharma*, the task which the Buddha entrusted to the Sangha, some must continue to be reborn within *Samsara*. The Buddha, too, said that each must find what is religiously appropriate for them at each stage in their journey towards enlightenment, thus the monastic life is not for everyone all the time. Those unable to contemplate enlightenment just now, as it were, 'required something else', and thus 'another system, logically subsumable to' the way of self-restraint, 'but emotionally alternate' to it, came into being 'very early in Buddhist history', certainly before it reached Sri Lanka (p. 326).

Other practices, too, which appear non-canonical (such as monasteries owning property) may also be explained by this need to protect the *dharma*. State support may or may not have been envisaged by the Buddha, but it has certainly helped the *sangha* survive. Gombrich also refers to the doctrine of decline, which was sometimes used to excuse a relaxation of the *Vinaya* rules of conduct. This is the teaching that there will be a gradual decline of the *dharma* towards the end of this aeon. Thus, corrupt or lax practices may actually be a fulfilment of scripture, not a departure from them! By 'postponing meditation and *nirvana* till the time' of the next Buddha, 'people are . . . rendering explicit, on the symbolic level, that they attach at least as much value to the positive' self-sacrificing altruistic service of humanity ideal, as they do 'to the negative ideal' of *nibbana* (p. 323). Gombrich actually argues that what might in fact represent 'the first genuine syncretism in Ceylonese Buddhist history' (p. 56) is the product of the so-called Buddhist revival, which, inspired by Western interest, has attempted to seek 'Buddhism's "purest form as taught by Buddha and his disciples" ' (p. 54). In his later book, *Theravada Buddhism* (1988) Gombrich refers to this as 'Protestant Buddhism', since it developed as a result of the agenda which some Western scholars set for themselves, to depict Buddhism as a 'philosopher's abstraction' (Gombrich: p. 50). This new expression of Buddhism was also much aided by the Theosophical Society (founded in 1875). Central to its ethos, alongside rationality, is an 'emphasis on lay religiosity' encouraged through such bodies as the Young Men's Buddhist Association, established by a Buddhist convert from Roman Catholicism in 1898 (Gombrich, 1988: 187). F. Max Müller, too, encouraged this process. In a letter to Colonel Henry Steele Olcott (1832–1907) of the Theosophical Society, he wrote:

You should endeavour to do for Buddhism what the more enlightened students of Christianity have long been doing . . . you should free your religion from its later excrescences, and bring it back to its earliest, simplest and purest form as taught by Buddha and his immediate disciples (cited in Gombrich, 1971: 54).

His conclusion thus reverses the opinion of the first generation of scholars regarding Sri Lankan Buddhism; representing the Buddhism of the Pali canon, its study might actually take us very close to the religion of a 'Buddhist village nearly 2,500 years ago' (*ibid.*: 56). Only a combination of anthropological fieldwork, with textual scholarship, and history, could sustain this thesis. Fieldwork and textual scholarship singly have both adjudged Sinhalese Buddhism 'corrupt', together they point to a remarkably conservative tradition in which, at least when the cognitive is accompanied by the affective, *precept* and *practice* coalesce. Gombrich, of course, is not saying that no change has occurred, but that the changes which have occurred represent legitimate, not illegitimate, developments of the Buddhist tradition. Thus, the student of religions who turns to fieldwork as well as to historical records and canonical literature, and the anthropologist who uses literary materials alongside fieldwork strategies, are both likely to reap benefits from these departures from the earlier research methods of their respective disciplines. The result will be a richer portrait; it is the job of neither discipline, I believe, to adjudge whether what they see is or is not a corruption of any ideal or classical model. Their job is to ascertain what life, including religious life, is like for those who live it.

In our next chapter, we discuss some critiques of both anthropology and study of religions, and argue that an additional development within each field has brought them even closer, ideologically and methodologically. Both began as 'us' (mainly Europeans) studying 'them'; now, both concern 'us' talking with us about ourselves. Wilfred Cantwell Smith wrote: 'When both the writer, and that about which he writes becomes personal, so does the relationship between them. As we have said, the present position is an encounter. What had been a description is therefore in process of becoming a dialogue' (1959: 47). Previously, scholars had addressed their books to their own circumscribed academic community, now, their books are read by 'others, and especially by that other community which they are about' (*ibid.*: 40). In other words, what began, last century, as an impersonal accumulation of facts, has become a personalized quest for meaning (see Whaling, 1984: 5). Similarly, contemporary anthropologists realize 'that the natives may be inhabiting the same world as the ethnographer and that these natives number increasingly among those who "read and write ethnographies" ' (Shahrani, 1994: 19). Thus, anthropology's task is to contribute to 'the enlargement of the universe of human discourse' (Geertz, 1973: 14).

5 The Go-between Function

During the early phase of the study of religions' development, the scholars maintained a physical, as well as a personal, distance from the subject of their study; the anthropologists reduced the physical distance between themselves and their subjects, but still attempted to maintain an impersonal, or neutral, approach. It was not their job to become involved in the concerns or politics or welfare of their 'tribe', but to dispassionately describe what they saw. The students of religions, ever anxious to stress the scientific status of their discipline, left speculation about religious truth claims, or about any relationship between religions, and ultimate reality, to the theologians. Their task was descriptive, to reconstruct from texts and from classical sources the histories and belief systems of the world's religions. Both the scholars of the religions, and anthropologists, studied 'them', and 'it', 'out there' rather than 'the religious dimension of humankind' (Whaling, 1984b: 25). Their audience, too, was Western academia; it rarely occurred to the early generation of writers that those whom they wrote about might also read their books. In fact, some did. As Gombrich points out, in Sri Lanka modernist (or Protestant) Buddhism was in part the creation of Western scholars. What 'we' write about 'others', then, may influence how 'they' think about 'themselves'.

Anthropology's early subjects were less likely to read anthropological accounts of their cultures or religions, since it was a *sine qua non* that anthropologists worked in pre-literate societies. Their aim, too, was to shed light on Western social, political and cultural institutions by studying those thought to be further down the evolutionary ladder. As we shall see, later in this chapter, this begs the question, 'to what extent did these pioneer anthropologists construct, or invent, the cultures they described?' Only the rigour of data verification techniques used in the field stood between what the anthropologists *actually* saw, and what they *thought* they saw. Perhaps to help to guard against the criticism that their theoretical conclusions could not be justified by the data they had collected, anthropologists concentrated on gathering as much data as possible, and rarely attempted any interpretation at all.

During his time in the Cameroons, Nigel Barley found himself taking refuge in collecting facts: 'The prevalence of factual data in anthropological monographs stems', he says, 'not from some inherent value or interest of the facts but from an attitude of "when in doubt, collect facts" ' (1983: 55). When first contemplating fieldwork, rather irreverently, he remarked how afterwards he would be able to reach into his 'ragbag of ethnographical anecdotes as his teachers had done in their day' whenever 'pressed in debate over some point of theory or metaphysics' (*ibid..* 7–8). Barley's own doctorate was on Anglo-Saxon anthropology – thus, as he told his sceptical examiners (who pointed out his lack of fieldwork experience), 'I travelled in time, not space' (p. 11). His would-be sponsors, too, were uninterested in funding what he said would contribute to theoretical development; they wrote back telling him that they 'were concerned about the completion of the basic ethnography of the area' (p. 14). Such theoretical caution has a good pedigree. Boas, who – as we saw in Chapter 1 – was one of the founding fathers of fieldwork, 'deliberately did little by way of interpretation'; the ethnographer's job was to present facts in 'an undigested form, so that other scholars and later generations could use them' (Kuper, 1994: 547 and see Kuper, 1988: 132–4 for a more detailed discussion of Boas' fieldwork).

The anthropologist's aim was to be an inside 'outsider', interfering as little as possible; after observing, he would take his facts back to his university, leaving the tribe undisturbed. It should be said, though, that many anthropologists have involved themselves in the economic or political concerns of their tribe, often acting as their spokesmen and women; after all, they owed their own academic reputation, even success, to the tribe. Fair play demands that they give something in return. Often, too, enduring friendhips were formed in the course of their fieldwork. Nevertheless, both the study of religions and anthropology regarded themselves as objective, descriptive sciences. However, in this chapter, I argue that the current trend in each is a move towards a much more personal, ethically motivated, engagement with their subjects. Below, we examine the cause and consequence of this shift against the background of some recent criticism of methods and assumptions in both fields of study.

Religion as the faith in people's hearts

Interest in religion as the faith in people's hearts, already identified as a consequence of the phenomenological approach, represents, I believe, the beginning of this shift away from neutrality towards personal involvement, within the study of religions. Wilfred Cantwell Smith has argued that 'no statement about a religion is valid unless it can be acknowledged by that religion's believers' (1959: 42). If this is so, it follows that scholarship about the religions cannot be written for one audience only, but must also address practitioners of the religions; thus

The task of a non-Muslim scholar writing about Islam is that of constructing an exposition that will do justice to the Western academic tradition, by growing directly out of the objective evidence and by being rationally coherent both within itself and with all other knowledge, and at the same time will do justice to the faith in men's hearts by commanding their assent once it is formulated. (*ibid.*: 44)

Neither Max Müller nor Rhys Davids saw any connection between their study of Hindu and Buddhist texts, and the Hinduism and Buddhism of their own time. To move away from historical reconstruction or textual analysis, to actually involve living representatives of the faiths in the process of their study, demands involvement, encounter and dialogue:

When both the writer, and that about which he writes becomes personal, so does the relationship between them. As we have said, the present position is an encounter ... What had been a description is therefore in the process of becoming a dialogue. (*ibid.*: 47)

Far from remaining distant from his or her subjects, the scholar becomes a 'participant – in the multiform history of the only community there is, humanity' (*ibid.*: 55). The implication of this approach to studying religions is that mutual understanding between scholars, and their subjects, will be at least a by-product, if not the main aim, of such scholarship. Smith himself suggests that as 'we' talking together about 'us' replaces 'a we reporting about a they', a sense of mutual responsibility will emerge. All human beings, he comments, do not share the same needs, but all 'in modern times stand under the imperative to understand each other, to help each other, to contribute to the common life, and together to aim at' achieving a 'co-operative ... and acceptable world' (1988: 374).

Arguably, this marks the end of the study of religions as a science, and its birth, not so much as a branch of the humanities, as an exercise in being human. Some scholars still have difficulty accepting the study of religions as a *bona fide* academic exercise. Richard Dawkins (1994), for example, opposes the teaching of public religious education, arguing that 'science is not only empowering, but more uplifting and inspiring than religious ideology'; 'whilst religion is unable to explain the findings of science, science can', he claims 'explain the emergence on this planet of human consciousness – religion included' (Knight and Maisels, 1994: 20). However, as long as people live religiously and, to cite another scholar, far from dying out, 'our existing religious traditions ... appear to be leaping into a period of resurgence' their study, and the quality of relationships between their adherents, will continue to impact on social and political realities (Cox, 1988: 212).

The creation of the 'other' critique

In this part of our survey we investigate the charge that much of what was offered as objective accounts of the 'other' by the early generation of scholars, who claimed neutrality, actually served to enhance the image of European superiority, and consequently the interests of colonialism. The pictures they painted served to fuel the moral argument that conquest and Europeanization of the non-white world was the white man's duty. My argument here is that

Smith's call for encounter and dialogue provides an antidote to such self-serving constructions of 'the other'. Had Sir William Muir, for example, produced his *Life of Mahomet* (1857–8) as part of a process of dialogue and engagement with Muslims, Sir Sayyed Ahmed Khan (1817–98) would not have dubbed his portrait of Muhammad (as a self-seeking opportunist) 'deformed and repulsive' (see Bennett, 1992: 119). What is interesting, too, is that Muir lived and worked amongst Muslims in India for most of his life. Consequently, his work was widely regarded as authoritative, especially by missionaries. One reviewer, commenting on the third edition of *The Life of Mahomet* (1894) called it not only a work of 'high scholarship' but 'the expression of an extensive experience of Muslim life' (*Church Missionary Intelligencer* 1894: 372–5). 'In addition to his well known Arabic scholarship', wrote an earlier reviewer, Muir had 'seen the practical working of Islamism in India' (*The Athenaeum*, July 1874: 16–17). Muir's aim was to produce an accurate biography, based on original sources. He criticized Washington Irving's *Life of Mahomet* (1850); although written as a novel, its author had failed his public by not being rigidly accurate in his use of authorities (see Bennett, 1992: 114). Muir's work is an example of scholarship which aimed at accuracy and at a scientific use of sources, but which could not escape negative *a priori* preconceptions about Islam and Muslims. Although surrounded by Muslims, Muir's sources – like those of other scholars of his day – were primarily literary. The idea that Muslims themselves might contribute to the scientific scholarship of Islam was unthinkable.

Orientalism

The criticism that Western scholars invented others who, always and everywhere, were somehow inferior to themselves, was briefly discussed in Chapter 2. The writer who has done most to expose this hidden agenda is Edward Sa'id in *Orientalism* (1978), *Culture and Imperialism* (1993) and other works. Sa'id, a Harvard and Princeton graduate, was born in Jerusalem (1935), attended an English language school in Cairo and has taught English Literature at Columbia University, New York, since 1963. His thesis is that the West's scholarship of the non-Western world was developed as a type of device, or tool, for

dealing with the Orient – dealing with it by making statements about it, by settling in it, ruling over it; in short, Orientalism is a Western style for dominating, restructuring and having authority over the Orient. (1978: 37)

Implicit in this process was the tendency to generalize; Orientals, for example, were much the same: liars, lazy, suspicious, and generally incapable of rational or of logical thought. The European lived in one world, the Oriental in another (*ibid.*: 44). Various institutions were then created by the West to perpetuate both its domination of the Orient, and its all too convenient and self-serving view of what the Orient was like. Trading companies, learned societies, missionary agencies, colonial offices, all played their part in what Sa'id describes as 'an increasingly profitable dialectic of information and control' (*ibid.*: 36). Put bluntly, 'subject races did not have it in them to know what was good for them' (*ibid.*); the European did, and could govern them better than they could govern themselves. The scholars provided the 'knowledge' they needed. Whilst some scholars were more or less in the pay of colonial governments, others unconsciously lent credibility to the view of universal European superiority. Ethnocentric assumptions assumed that the norm, or standard, was the European; whatever appeared different, strange, exotic, or even debased, was adjudged inferior, be it cultural, moral or religious.

Ethnocentrism, anthropology and the construction of the other

Ethnocentrism refers to the 'tendency to judge or interpret other cultures according to the criteria of one's own' (Seymour-Smith: 97). Anthropology has long been alerted to this possibility, and the whole development of its empirical tradition described in Chapter 2 was designed to minimize misinterpretation. Boas' view of cultural relativity also discouraged anthropologists from making value judgements about other peoples' cultures. In practice, however, without some *a priori* assumptions, no anthropologist could even begin to decode, or decipher, another culture. Assuming that most cultures have taboos, for example, they may have identified some taboos which were not really taboo at all. In other words, convinced that taboos must exist, in their eagerness to identify some they may have labelled as taboo perfectly acceptable, or perhaps anomalous, behaviour. Even Evans-Pritchard, whose lifelong concern was to faithfully translate the experiences of the cultures he studied into those of his own, and whose fieldwork research was meticulously conducted, denied 'that witches exist, even though there is no way within Zande thought that such existence could be disproved' (Beidelman, 1968: 177).

Feminists point out how the Western view of gender has often been imposed on data, perhaps unconsciously. They ask, 'To what extent is the male dominance enshrined in the ethnographic record itself the product of male dominance, and corresponding reporting bias, in the anthropological profession itself' (Lewis, 1992: 364). For example, in Western thought, 'man' has been associated with 'culture' (or with technology), 'woman' with 'nature' (Moore, 1988: 14). However, the culture–nature distinction is not a value-free, unmediated category, thus 'we must also be aware that other societies might not even perceive nature and culture as distinct and opposed categories' (Moore: 19). Anthropologists may have pre-assigned women to a natural (childbearing and rearing) role, men to technological, culture-producing roles (they cannot bear children, therefore they compensate by creating technology). Western notions of personhood, or of individuals as free social agents, too, have influenced how anthropologists interpret social interaction, leading to misrepresentation of cultures where the distinction between people and community is more fluid. It is equally possible that masculinity and femininity may themselves be fluid concepts. We have already referred to Margaret Mead's pioneering work on gender. As long ago as 1950, she was asking, 'Do real differences exist, in addition to the obvious anatomical and physical ones – but just as biologically based' and, 'Will such differences run through all of men's and all of women's behaviour?' (1950: 8).

Mead, as we noted earlier, concluded that gender roles are culturally, not biologically, determined. Henrietta Moore, who teaches social anthropology at the London School of Economics, throughout her *Feminism and Anthropology* (1988) also represents gender as a social and symbolic construct. She uses a great deal of anthropological data to support her viewpoint. Of course, it would be surprising if everyone agreed! Derek Freeman (1983), who conducted his fieldwork in Oceania, where Mead had gone before him, argues that her account of Samoan life was misleading, and inaccurate. Mead's work, he says, 'was in error' in its 'description of the nature of adolescence in Samoa' (1983: 268) – Samoans were just as sexually repressed as teenagers elsewhere. Mead, he says, was so anxious to prove the 'antibiological orientation of the Boasian paradigm' (1983: 295) that she allowed herself to be duped by her informants. The truth, he suggests, lies somewhere between biological and cultural determinism, thus 'biological determinism' was the 'thesis to which cultural determinism was the antithesis' whilst what is required is a 'synthesis in which there will be, in the study of human behaviour, recognition of the radical importance of the genetic and the exogenetic', and of their interaction (1983: 302). However, others uphold Mead's conclusions, and reject Freeman's. No doubt debate will continue!

Moore also explores the possibility that the 'male subordination of women' might be a universal truth, or fact. Feminist anthropology, says Moore, rejects this, arguing that just as there are no single 'universal or unitary sociological category of woman', or of man (as Moore herself concludes, which Freeman and others question), so there are no universal conditions of sameness, including the universal subordination, and oppression, of women by men (Moore: 189).

Anthropological studies demonstrate that women do exercise power. However, when this is differently exercised from men's power, Western analysts have tended to devalue its currency. This follows the Western juxtaposition (alongside the nature–culture polarity) between private and public spheres, which assumes that unless women exercise power in the public domain, we cannot see them 'as effective social agents in their own right' (Moore: 39). Yet can we justify this viewpoint? Moore asks, 'is it enough to say that' women 'have power within a specifically female domain, or must we argue that they have power in those areas of social life which have been so often presented as the public, political domain of men?' (*ibid.*: 39). The general Western perception of Muslim women, already referred to above, as 'heavily veiled, secluded wives, whose lives consist of little more than their homes, their children, and the other women of the harem' is, say El-Solh and Mabro, 'of limited relevance to understanding the lives of the majority of contemporary Muslim women' (1994: 4). Their volume *Muslim Women's Choices: Religious Belief and Social Reality* contains a range of ethnographic sketches depicting Muslim women 'consciously as well as unconsciously negotiating their gender role within the situational context of their lives'. Also, both seclusion and veiling originally developed as cultural, rather than as religiously sanctioned, conventions, although they later acquired legal status (see *ibid.*: 8–9). Patricia Caplan's study of Muslim women in Tanzania demonstrates how women operate, and maintain, their own income stream, and negotiate with their husbands over its disposal (1984). This conforms with Islamic law, which grants women the right to keep their own earnings, and places full responsibility for maintaining the household on men. Fatima Mernissi's *The Forgotten Queens of Islam* (1993), too, 'uncovers a hidden history of' Muslim 'women who held the reins of power, but whose lives and stories, achievements and failures, have largely been forgotten' (back cover). This book – albeit history, not anthropology – counters the arguments of some Muslim men that, 'since no woman had ever governed a Muslim state between 622 and 1988, Benazir Bhutto could not ... do so either' (p. 1).

Marxist anthropologist Eleanor Leacock's work on small-scale societies argues that the public–private dichotomy makes very little sense in such contexts. These two spheres are rarely rigidly differentiated, and women often 'make a substantial economic contribution' for which they are valued; their status is not dependent on their role as childbearers and rearers. Amongst the Iroquois, women's ability to control food supply gives them effective power 'to veto declarations of war, and to intervene to bring about peace' (Leacock, 1978: 253; Moore: 31–2). Similarly, Annette Weiner's work amongst Trobriand women suggests that:

Whether women are publicly valued or privately secluded, whether they control politics, a range of economic commodities, or merely magical spells, they function within that society not as objects but as individuals with some measure of control. (Weiner, 1976: 228)

Malinowski, she says, relied overmuch on men to find out about 'women's business', and so 'failed to appreciate the importance of women in the maintenance of collective life' (Sass, 1993: 16). Work amongst Aborigines in Australia has also shown that 'neither women nor men in very simple societies celebrate women as nurturers or women's capacity to give life' (Collier and Risoldo, 1981: 275). In some societies, all the 'processes of life-giving', including 'child-birth ... are social concerns of society as a whole, and are not confined to women or the domestic domain alone' (Moore, 1988: 28). Nor is it uncommon for children to be reared by somebody other than their biological mother; 'Biological mother-hood', says Cheater, 'does not necessarily entail social motherhood' (1986: 177). In the Cameroons, Nigel Barley says that Dowayo men and women live quite independent lives, 'she grows her food, he his'. 'Women always', he writes, 'expect to receive reward for sexual services even within marriage ... there is always a strong sense of keeping accounts even between husband and wife' (1983: 77), which suggests an egalitarian arrangement, not subordination; 'They give as good as they take, and stick up for themselves with a will' (*ibid.*: 76). In other words, feminist anthropology says: women's actual experiences cannot be understood solely with reference to gender, or to a preconceived notion of 'sameness' but needs to be discussed and analysed with reference also to class, culture, religion and history.

Feminist anthropologists, however, whilst criticizing male colleagues for 'listening only to official male ideology and discourses', and thereby (like Malinowski) 'misconstruing gender-roles' (Lewis: 364) do not argue that only women can understand, or study, women. On the one hand, women anthropologists can gain access to women which may well be denied men, on the other 'the privileging of the female ethnographer, as Shapiro points out, not only casts doubt on the ability of women to study men, but ultimately casts doubt on the whole project and purpose of anthropology' (Moore: 5).

An example of misconstruing from the Indian context

Just as Western scholars have assumed a public–private dichotomy, and a rigid individual–community distinction, so they have tended to assume a matter–spirit dualism. Not all cultures, however, distinguish rigidly between these. In India, when Western scholars and observers encountered the Tantric tradition, in which sexuality and sexual practices are incorporated within ritual and worship, their response was moral outrage. One early observer, Brian Hodgson, (1800–94) who 'lived in Kathmandu from 1820 to 1844 ... spoke of Saktism as "lust, mummery, and black magic" ' (cited in Payne, 1933: 75). Hodgson's entry in the *Dictionary of National Biography* describes him as 'one of the pioneers of scientific ethnography' (XXII: 856). E.W. Hopkins, author of *The Religions of India* (1896) used such words as 'obscenity', 'bestiality', 'pious profligacy', and wrote 'a description of the different rites would be to replicate an account of indecencies of which the least vile is too esoteric to sketch faithfully' (cited in Payne: 1). Payne comments, 'language almost equally violent is to be found in the pages of William Ward, the Abbé Dubois, H.H. Wilson, Monier-Williams, Barth, William Crooke', thus naming some of the most distinguished Orientalist scholars. William Ward (1764–1823), a Baptist missionary and Orientalist scholar, was largely responsible, according to eminent Indian historian R.C. Majumdar, for creating the myth that the Hindus were 'a sort of moral monster' (see Majumdar, 1951–69). A later Baptist scholar, E.A. Payne (1902–80), Lecturer in comparative religion at Oxford 1940–51, however, turned to a sympathetic study of Tantric thought and practice, convinced that the bias of earlier writers had prevented their seeing its genuine piety, as well as its nobler philosophical and spiritual aspects. His *The Saktas: An Introductory and Comparative Study* (1933) is a much more balanced and sober treatment which, albeit not the result of direct encounter, begins to penetrate into a thought world different from the author's by questioning his own *a priori* assumptions. Payne still speaks about 'blots' and 'blemishes', but he also identifies what lies at the heart of practices which others had condemned, namely the Tantric rejection of a matter–spirit divide. He wrote:

The connubial relations between Devi and her husband were held to typify the mystical union of the eternal principles, matter and spirit, which produces the world. The self-existent being is regarded as single, solitary, impersonal, quiescent, inactive. Once it becomes conscious and personal it is duplex and acts through an associated female principle, which is conceived as possessing a higher degree of activity and personality. Sakti is the instrumental cause, Prakriti the material cause, and Siva the efficient cause of the world. (1933: 77–8)

In the ritual known as the *kulaprakiya*, culminating in sexual intercourse, the merging of opposites is achieved. The rite involves eating, or handling, impure substances (eating meat, blood, drinking alcohol), and transgresses normative moral codes (such as sex outside marriage; sex with lower caste women) as an active denial of opposites. In other words, by embracing what is unclean you deny that there is, ultimately, any dualism at all; ideas such as subject–object, pure–impure, male–female all uphold duality. What is really real is beyond duality. This non-dualism draws on the Vedantic philosophy of the *Upanishads* (a body of Hindu scripture). Buddhist Tantra, similarly, declares that the whole of life is 'one and beautiful', since everything is Buddha-nature. Payne, whilst commenting, 'obviously such rites are an encouragement to immorality, and cannot be tolerated by those of a healthy developed moral sense', could still consider 'their intentions in the best possible light' (1933: 16). Towards the end of his book, he observes that, at its best, what Tantric practice represents is what 'in both East and West . . . is called "Sacramentalism", and . . . seeks to make all acts holy, to bring the divine near through the common things' (1933: 137). Western dissociation of sex with religion confused Tantric eroticism with immorality; instead, the *kulaprakiya* may celebrate the ultimate holiness of matter as well as of spirit, since they are, in essence, the same.

Other consequences follow, not irrelevant to the focus of this chapter; for example, women 'in Tantric traditions . . . have been regarded as channels of esoteric power and knowledge' (Flood: 1994: 87) and have been valued as such. R.C. Zaehner (1913–74), Oxford's Spalding Professor, argued in *Our Savage God* (1974) that monistic traditions, such as Tantra, which 'uphold the union of opposites . . . tend towards unethical behaviour'. Zaehner was a scholar in the mould of Max Müller and Rhys Davids – a scholar of the classical texts. However, he failed to support his arguments with empirical evidence. He drew a parallel between 'a passage in the Kularnvava Tantra which describes an ecstatic orgy' and 'the behaviour of the "family", a twentieth century quasi-religious group led by Charles Manson, a multiple murderer ... arguing that such behaviour is a consequence of belief in a transcendent state of being beyond good or evil' (*ibid.*: 88). In the case cited, Manson may well have used this belief to justify his action, but there is little if any evidence to support the view that Tantric practitioners are any more, or less, moral, than anybody else in their day-to-day lives. Flood writes:

Caste restrictions on sex and impurity are suspended during the left-hand rites, but these only serve to underline the difference during everyday worldly transactions. The high-caste Brahman in a left-hand ritual would not mix with the low-caste woman outside of the ritual context (p. 90).

In other words, Tantric transgression of normative codes are limited to the ritual context, when their purpose is explicitly soteriological. In this context 'liberation' (*mukti*, here understood as the cessation of the appearance of duality) is not seen as incompatible with pleasure, joy or sexuality (p. 92). I would argue that Zaehner (who, incidentally, was a devout Roman Catholic, as well as an ethical rationalist) failed to bracket out his *a priori* assumption that religion and sexuality do not mix. Similarly, another scholar, William St-Clair Tisdall (1859–1928), writing in 1901, remarked that common decency restrained him from explaining to his readers the 'true meaning of the *linga* and the *yoni*' – the phallic symbol representing Shiva, and the female sexual organ representing Sakti (Tisdall: 128). On the other hand, a colleague has met Hindus in South India for whom the *linga* and *yoni* are images of the formlessness of God, who believe that their sexual interpretation is a Western construct.

Towards a solution in the study of religions

Turning now to an example from Islamic studies, we have already referred to what has been called the 'essentialist' view, which regarded Islam, and Muslims, as much the same everywhere. Some scholars of Islam, though, were perhaps guilty of another charge; alongside the view that Islam was always and everywhere the same, the opposite view also emerged: that the Muslim world was disunited, and not, as Islam itself claims, politically united. This view reduced the threat which a united, strong Islam might otherwise have posed. However, whether depicted as the same everywhere or as many Islams, Muslims were left puzzling how they could reconcile the popular Western view of Islam, informed directly or indirectly by Orientalist scholarship, with their own self-perception. One might, in passing, wonder how Tantric devotees reacted to the calumny written about their tradition! With reference to Islam, little has changed; anthropologist and Cambridge academic, Akbar Ahmed (1993) describes today's media representation of Islam in its relation to the West as:

Muslims are fanatic; that Christians have been tolerant; that Muslim civilization is worthless; that Muslims spread Islam with sword in one hand, Qur'an in the other; and that Muslim women are mistreated and subjugated. (1993: 9)

He finds little resonance between this picture, and the Islam he knows and loves.

It may not be very surprising to find all of these images presented as fact in nineteenth-century works; it is more surprising to see that some of these 'us and them' images were reproduced this century. Sir Hamilton Gibb (1895–1971), for example, Oxford's Professor of Arabic, whom Sa'id calls 'a dynastic figure within British (and later American) Orientalism' (1978: 275) speaks about the aversion of the Arab mind 'from the thought-processes of rationalism ... The rejection of rationalist modes of thought', he continues, 'is inseparable from them' and 'has its roots ... in the atomism and discreteness of the Arab imagination' (cited in *ibid*.: 106). Gibb, says Sa'id, defined Islam as static; any knowledge passed on to Europe during the period of scholarly excellence in Spain was merely that which it had 'originally derived from the West' (1978: 280). 'Law', says Gibb, was elevated above all other discourses, taking 'the place of the discarded sciences' (1949; 1978 edn: 7) and this Law is inflexible (see *ibid*.: 72). Thus, in responding to the challenges of modernity, Islam has no choice; if it is to remain true to itself, it has to resist change. Sa'id writes:

in his two important works of the forties, *Modern Trends in Islam*, and *Mohammedanism: An Historical Survey* ... Gibb is at great pains to discuss the present crises in Islam, opposing its inherent, essential being to modern attempts at modifying it. (1978: 280)

We are close here to Lord Cromer's famous dictum, 'Islam reformed is Islam no longer' (Cromer was for twenty-five years Consul-General of Egypt), and to Muir's 'Islam ... is powerless to adapt ... to varying time and place' (1899: 598). Gibb, like Muir, was by no means unfamiliar with Muslims; he was one of the first Western scholars to visit the Muslim world regularly, 'until World War 1 he spent a sizeable period every winter in Cairo, and was a member of the Egyptian Academy' (Smith, 1959: 46n). In fact, in Smith's estimate, Gibb represents the beginning of the movement towards recognizing Islam as 'the faith of living persons', and his 'greatness as a scholar lies in' incorporating this 'awareness ... into the Western academic tradition' (*ibid.*). Similarly, Albert Hourani remarks how Gibb was careful to avoid expressing personal opinions about his subject, believed that firsthand knowledge of Muslim society was a necessary tool, and that he was interested in Islam within its social context, rather than as a scholarly abstraction. His pessimistic view about the possibility of reform may have been because he knew that attempts at reinterpretation would meet opposition from traditionalists. 'Not for the first time, the *ijma* of the people is opposed', he wrote, 'to the *ijma* of the learned' (Hourani, 1991: 72–3). Nevertheless, he did not deny anyone the 'right to reinterpret their documents and symbols ... in accordance with their own convictions'. Arguably, then, Gibb began to break the mould, but did not completely succeed. Perhaps this was because, in the end, he claimed a scholarly authority which sometimes overrode the believers' authority. An example of this lies in his defence of the title of his classic *Mohammedanism: An Historical Survey* (1949). He knew that no Muslim calls him or herself 'a Mohammedan', but argued that what really distinguishes Muslims from followers of other religions is not their belief in God, but in the prophethood of Muhammad. 'Mohammad was not an apostle, one amongst many', but the final Prophet, and 'no one ... who does not hold this belief ... is entitled to call himself a Muslim' (1978: 2). Therefore, he chose the term 'Mohammedanism' over and above 'Islam'. This, says Sa'id, depends on a 'logic deliberately outside Islam' (1978: 280). Similarly, his equation between Law and the totality of Islam does an injustice to Muslim achievements in architecture, philosophy, poetry, let alone to its theological discourse.

Until very recently, Gibb's *Mohammedanism* remained the standard introductory text on Islam for most undergraduate courses. Indeed, I think my copy was the first textbook on Islam I ever owned! What has replaced it, in the view of at least one eminent reviewer, is John L. Esposito's *Islam: The Straight Path*. (1988; revised 1991; see Morgan: 1994). Significantly, Akbar Ahmed regards Esposito as one of a new generation of Western scholars whose work is

scholarly and fair; their aim is sympathetic scholarship, they have a need to know and understand; their methodology is impeccable; in the main they allow respondents to speak for themselves. It is in this that they differ from the Orientalist. They allow the native voice, through its literature and scholars, to be heard. When they interject or interpret they do so with sensitivity. There is little evidence of racial or cultural superiority. (1992: 183–4)

Ahmed describes *Islam: The Straight Path* as 'scholarship in the highest tradition'. In 'its humanity' it reflects, he says, 'something of what academics at their best are capable of achieving' (p. 185). Its 'succinct and up-to-date survey' of Islam's development resonates well with how Muslims understand their own story; as 'a struggle to define and adhere to their Islamic way of life'. This is, he says, 'the straight path' of the title (p. 184). In listening to Muslim voices, in presenting an account of Islam capable of 'commanding their assent', Esposito stands as one human alongside others within the same, not supposedly different, worlds. Fulfilling all the criteria of Smith's 'personal encounter', his books may well contribute to better political understanding, and co-operation, between the Muslim and non-Muslim worlds, as he himself argues:

As some dream of the creation of a New World order, and many millions in north Africa, the Middle East, Central Asia, and southern and Southeast Asia aspire to greater political liberalization and democratization, the continued vitality of Islam and the Islamic movements need not be a threat but a challenge. (1992: 215)

Esposito, who now teaches at Georgetown University, Washington DC, where he directs the Center for Muslim–Christian Understanding, says that his understanding of Islam has been informed by seeing and experiencing 'Islam as a "lived" religion in classes, seminars, and conversations, and in working and living with Muslim friends both' in the United States and overseas (1988: x). This ethical concern, to represent others as they perceive themselves, by questioning and confronting the assumptions of Orientalism, may move us beyond that mindset towards a genuine interreligious discourse and understanding. This corresponds to what has been called the 'interpretive approach' to social science, which 'resonates [with] or feels right to those who are being studied', although in my model the polarity between researcher and researched would to a large degree be removed (Neuman, 1994: 75). This is the modern student of religions' task. As Sa'id says, Orientalism's failure was as much a human as an intellectual failure, for 'in having to take up a position of irreducible opposition to a region of the world it considered alien to its own', it 'failed to identify with human experience, failed also to see it as human experience' (1978: 328).

Anthropology and the Orientalist critique

In *Orientalism*, Sa'id appeared to exempt anthropology from his critique, even praising the work of Clifford Geertz, whose 'interest in Islam is discrete and concrete enough to be animated by the specific societies and problems he studies and not by the rituals, preconceptions, and doctrines of Orientalism' (1978: 326). Later, though, Sa'id seems 'to have revised his views on the matter' (Shahrani, 1994: 19). However, it is possible to argue that although anthropologists did, at times, attempt to sell their services to colonial governments, they may also have been less guilty of collusion than were scholars in other disciplines. In fact, they often found themselves at odds with government interests, wanting to preserve their 'tribe from outside contacts', to 'keep them as museum exhibits in splendid isolation from trade, government, and Christianity' (Kuper, 1983: 114). Their going native was regarded as letting the side down; whilst 'it is probably sheer romanticism to suppose that' they are 'ever really accepted as a member of a native tribe', 'anthropologists do participate in native life much more closely than do other categories of Europeans ... They must ... live in a native village and not in the nearest European settlement'. They 'share in the work and play of the people and attend their ceremonies'. It would, for example, 'be difficult for Europeans occupying positions of high authority, or closely identified with a particular Church, to attend beer drinks or magic ceremonies with the same freedom as the anthropologist does' (Kuper, 1983: 114, citing A.I. Richards). Colonial governments were often embarrassed by 'poor whites' who gave the natives the impression that not all members of the ruling race were quite so superior! During my years in Bangladesh, a curious left-over from colonial days was still available to us missionaries – a 50 per cent reduction on a first class riverboat ticket (train travel being very limited, boat is the main means of transport). The authorities did not want missionaries travelling second class!

On the whole, anthropological research was privately, not publicly, funded. Governments rarely saw much practical benefit accruing from their work. Evans-Pritchard comments, 'Professor Seligman once told me that in all the years he had worked in the Sudan ... he was never once asked his advice' by government representatives (1946: 97). However, Evans-Pritchard's own fieldwork amongst the Nuer in the 1930s was instigated by colonial officers, who told him that this tribe was being troublesome. Later, he researched the Sufi Sanusi order whilst serving as a political officer with the British Army during World War Two. He was mentioned in despatches. Some government grants, too, were available for anthropological work. At issue here is less anthropological collusion with colonial domination than its self-serving construction of the cultures studied. As Kuper points out, Marxists, nationalists, and others all find in primitive society evidence which conveniently supports their ideological *a priori* beliefs; for example 'that all societies were based on either blood or soil', so 'descent and territoriality' is intrinsically and inescapably linked with 'ideas of race and citizenship' (1988: 240).

This fits Michel Foucault's view that the social sciences 'objectify' their subjects. He argues that each discipline, effectively, exercises a *disciplinary* function. Fascinated by mental illness, by sexual eroticism and homosexuality, Foucault (1926–84), from 1970 Professor of the History and System of Thought at the College of France, was particularly interested in the normality–deviancy distinction, which, he believed, is a social construct. Once those in power have dubbed certain behaviour deviant, ('power', he says 'produces knowledge') disciplinary measures are applied to those who choose deviancy rather than normality. He explored these themes in his *Madness and Civilization* (1961) (based on his doctoral work), *The Archeology of Knowledge* (1972), *The Birth of the Clinic* (1973), *History of Sexuality* (1976) and *Discipline and Punishment: The Birth of the Prison* (1979), and other works.

He is famous for his use of the panoptic metaphor, borrowed from Jeremy Bentham (1748–1832) which posits a 'radical separation' between the observed and the observer, as if the social scientist views his, or her, subjects from an observation tower and, themselves 'invisible ... peer through slits at the prisoners displayed before them like specimens'. Thus, the powerless – the deviant, insane, alien, poor, were exposed whilst the power lies 'in the relentless, invisible gaze which studies them' (Sass: 13; Foucault, 1979, pt 3 chap. 3). Furthermore, says Foucault, all discourse, whether historical, psychological or anthropological, is produced by a process of choosing one method of selecting, or of classifying, data over other methods. What the writer leaves out is lost to the reader. In this view, anthropological monographs tell us more about the anthropologist, 'and his cultural assumptions than about the society under investigation' (*ibid.*: 17). Indeed, in Foucault's view, all knowledge is actually discourse; there is no such thing as abstract truth, no transcendent reality, there is only what people construe. Thus, right and wrong, normality and abnormality are not fixed polarities, but are subject to change. Modern definitions of sanity, insanity, sick, healthy, normal, abnormal are, he argues, the products of the eighteenth and nineteenth centuries, when popular movements of dissent made it necessary for those in power to invent mechanisms to control these movements. This, he says, was a characteristic of the age of invention; prisons, clinics, the whole apparatus of law enforcement were all invented to effect this control;

Generally speaking, all the authorities exercising individual control function according to a double mode (mad/sane, dangerous/harmless, normal/abnormal) and that of coercive assignment, of differential distribution; how he is to be recognised; how constant surveillance is to be exercised over him ... (Foucault, 1979: 199)

Foucault's thought is thus profoundly anti-positivist, indeed anti-empirical. This is why, for him 'forms and categories of cultural life' were all discourse (White: 82). The modalities of sickness/ health, normality/abnormality, and so on, do not correspond to some universal norm, but are the inventions of whatever discourse prevails at the time in the centres of power. Nothing, as it were, links ideas and external reality. The modalities, too, are

in turn less a product of an autonomous exchange between hypothesis and observation, or theory and practice, than the basis of whatever theory and practice prevailed in a given period. (White: 90)

Foucault rejected any notion of 'sameness' in favour of a world of infinite difference: 'all discourse opens upon a silence in which only "things" exist in their irreducible Difference, resisting every impulse to find a Sameness uniting them in any order whatever' (*ibid.*: 86). He did, however, believe in experience, and experienced for himself some of the behaviours dubbed perverse by the objectifiers of the subjective. If, as Foucault's post-modernism suggests, everything is subjective, and all values personal, then the anthropological enterprise becomes somewhat redundant.

Can we only know ourselves?

This question, 'Can we ever really know, or understand, the other in their own terms, or only ourselves in ours?' has caused something resembling an epistemological hypochondria within anthropology. Anthropology, like scholarship of the world's religions, may have been guilty of defining and constructing the 'other', not always, perhaps, to enhance Western superiority, or even to support ideological presuppositions so much as to sell its own product as 'of interest'. Malinowski talked about the anthropologist as impressario; after all, 'each piece of fieldwork aims at achieving a "scoop" which will redound to the anthroplogist's credit, and the more interesting and exciting the raw data the better' (Lewis: 26). This can lead to a god-like feeling of ownership: 'Malinowski wrote in his diary of his "feeling of ownership" over the Trobrianders: "It is I who will describe them or create them" ' (cited in Sass: 16). Certainly, the assumption that the natives 'understand themselves less well than does the anthropologist' underlies some of these pioneer anthropological texts (*ibid.*: 16). Evans-Pritchard once said that the anthropologist 'discovers in a native society what no native can explain to him and what no layman ... can conceive – its basic structure ... a set of abstractions ... fundamentally a construct of the anthropologist himself' (The Marett Lecture, 1950).

Reflexivity and discourse

Three main responses can be identified to the question, 'Can a member of one society ever achieve an objective understanding of another?' First, some writers express outright scepticism. The best that an anthropological account can do is to render a second order interpretation of what the anthropologist has observed; the anthropologist reads the society like a primary text, but in recording data produces a secondary text. In this view, only the natives themselves possess first order accounts. One solution is the nativist – that only natives should study, talk, and write, about themselves. The problem with this solution is its extreme pessimism about human nature, all but claiming that cultural differences preclude the possibility of genuine two-way communication between different peoples. This approach can, in fact, reinforce old racist ideas of inalienable separateness, and has been used by some Afrikaaners in South Africa to justify their view that black and white cannot and should not mix, socially, maritally, or even co-habit the same institutions. Applied to the religions, it implies that since only members of a religion can really understand it, only members of a tradition should teach about it. This would make the subject unacceptable in most universities, where equal opportunity policies are enforced. Kuper identifies another danger; that nativist anthropology can become '*Volkskunde*, the romantic celebration of an ethnic identity by nationalist scholars' – a no more accurate a construct than that of a foreign anthropologist (1994: 545).

The postmodernist view, which Foucault represents, resembles the nativist in as much as it claims that any text means what it means for the individual reader; no authoritative interpretations of the type about which Geertz writes are possible. I personally find the 'it takes one to know one' solution much too gloomy; if it takes one to know one, then the whole anthropological enterprise 'would be an aberration' (Shapiro, 1981: 125). Similarly, the study of religions becomes redundant; it also undermines the possibility of global co-operation, of global peace, perhaps even of anyone ever understanding anybody else! In fact, postmodernism is pervaded by a 'sense of meaninglessness and pessimism, belief that the world will never improve' (Neuman: 74). The second response to the 'it takes one to know one' view has been to turn ethnography into autobiography. If anthropological accounts do tell us more about the reseacher than about the researched, then the best that the anthropologist working amongst 'others' can do is to study themselves in relation to these others. Such accounts take us into the fieldworker's experience of cultural dislocation, but tell us, intentionally, very little about the culture being studied. This type of account has inspired the joke (for which Marshall Sahlins claims authorship) in which the native pleads with the ethnographer, 'Can't we talk about me for a change!' (Kuper, 1994: 542). Such writing probably does make a valuable contribution to our understanding of the psychology of being a stranger in a strange land, but dismally fails to further the anthropological enterprise. It really simply reverses the nativist response – if I can only talk about myself, not about others, autobiography becomes the only discourse I am capable of writing.

The third response, which I prefer, resembles Kuper's 'cosmo-politan anthropology'; combining features of the nativist and of the autobiographical approaches it avoids, I believe, the pitfalls of both. Just as the first generation of scholars of the religions wrote for 'us' about 'them', so did the first anthropologists. Indeed, it was unlikely that any of the natives read any of the anthropological writing about themselves. However rigorous an anthropologist's use of triangulation techniques to check the veracity and reliability of his, or her, data, few gave their 'informants' (a term which actually makes the whole operation sound somewhat sinister; they are now more commonly called 'consultants') any voice in what was finally published. The account was his, not theirs. The issue of common ownership of the account was not on the agenda. Ethics, in today's global village, may itself demand such a voice but an equally strong argument in favour of a collaborative approach is that a more holistic picture may emerge as a result of insider–outsider collaboration.

The situation has also changed because, in today's world, 'they' are also reading what 'we' write about them, and some are unhappy with what they read. For example, Keelung Hong, in his 'Experiences of being a "native" observing anthropology' (1994) criticizes anthropologists working in Taiwan for 'looking at us to try to see "traditional Chinese culture" '. They were not really interested in Taiwanese culture at all (1994: 7). 'Negative assessment' of a foreign anthropologist's work, says Lewis, can be 'devastating'. On the other hand, he comments how gratified he feels when Somali anthropologists (he did fieldwork in Somalia) confirm his 'studies of their culture and society'. Positive native response, he suggests, is 'perhaps the most impressive endorsement of the fidelity of the foreign fieldworker's reportage' (1992: 368). Whilst, as we noted above, Annette Weiner's work (she is now Professor of Anthropology at New York) suggests that Malinowski may not always have been quite as omniscient as he felt, the 'general accuracy of his pioneering accounts' of Trobriand life have, for example, been confirmed by 'native "auto-anthropologists" ' (Lewis: 368).

At the very least, the cosmopolitan approach says, instead of turning all anthropology over to insiders as the solution, a critical engagement between insiders and outsiders can still justify non-native anthropology. In my view, though, the cosmopolitan approach goes further. It says, there is a more valuable role for outsiders to play; they can actually help others understand themselves. In other words, none of us fully understand ourselves and, even if we grant that outsiders can never gain the full picture, it is possible for outsiders to see, or to recognize something about ourselves which we don't see, because we take it for granted. In today's world, says Diana L. Eck, Smith's successor at Harvard, 'Whether we like it or not, all of us bear witness to each other'

(1993: 213). Indeed, certain insiders may have a vested interest in ensuring that their account (an elite view, for example) has precedence over others' (that of the poor, women, laity, political prisoners, and so on). Outsiders, by consulting people from different backgrounds, may succeed in constructing a more holistic overview.

Anthropology should become, I believe, a shared, collaborative, or cosmopolitan venture. Instead of the foreign anthropologist creating, and publishing, and therefore owning the account, it should be produced by negotiation and consultation. Previously, even when beneficial consequences did accrue to tribes as the result of an anthropologist voicing their concerns, the process was intrinsically disempowering:

> By casting those we study as a non-political audience, as an audience with no access to the information creating machinery ... we reproduce the belief and the objective conditions for its persistence, that the powerless are politically docile and uninterested. (MacDonald and Norris, 1981: 16)

In contrast, a more democratic and also empowering model of working is now widely practised within small scale, often institutionally based, participant observer type research. Such research, often carried out within the researcher's own institution, uses case study strategies and aims, like anthropology, to gain a complete and rounded view of the phenomena studied. Usually, such research also aims to achieve specific goals in terms of improving a service, standards or professional practice. In this process, certain data may be threatening to some individuals concerned, suggesting incompetency, others may make comments about colleagues which they would prefer not to be made public. If an outside researcher thinks that some of these damaging comments fall within the right to know category, a dilemma will emerge between 'two conflicting values – the pursuit of truth through scientific procedures and the maintenance of respect for the individuals whose lives are being lived, focally or peripherally, in the context of one's research paper' (Smith, 1980: 192). The most viable solution to this ethical impasse, I suggest, lies in a democratic, participatory approach to research. Helen Simons describes such an approach in her chapter, 'Ethics of case study in educational research and evaluation' (1989). Such a democratic approach gives consultants maximum say in the reporting process by introducing 'the notion of a collective responsibility ... for accurate and fair reporting' (1989: 127). The 'let me tell you about you' becomes 'let's learn, together, more about ourselves and about each other'.

Reflexivity, reflecting on one's own role, and *a priori* assumptions, remains vital. However, in this democratic process outsider interpretations, possibly with their particular and unique insights, are brought into creative discourse with insiders' interpretations, until an account emerges which moves all parties forward in terms of their self-understanding, as well as in their understanding of the other. We thus have Geertz's opinion:

To see ourselves as others' see us can be eye opening. To see others as sharing a nature with ourselves is the merest decency. But it is from the far more difficult achievement of seeing ourselves amongst others, as a local example of the forms human life has locally taken, a case among cases, a world among worlds, that the largeness of mind, without which objectivity is self-congratulation and tolerance a sham, comes. If interpretive anthropology has any general office in the world it is to keep reteaching this fugitive truth. (1983: 16)

All partners in the process will have to come clean about their *a priori* values, about their 'discourses', to use Foucault's phrase. I think Foucault is right to question whether there are any universal norms out there waiting to be discovered, but wrong to be so pessimistic about the possibility of discourse *between* people achieving an agreed, common perspective. I accept that meanings and knowledge are constructed, but believe human beings capable of collaborative construction. Thus, anthropology is not a positivist science, but a conversation, in which people are honest and open about their starting points. The functionalist, believing that cultures express shared social identity, will have an *a priori* bias towards seeing or construing harmony, or consensus. The conflict, or Marxist, *a priori* will tend to construe a variety of interest groups; for example, controlled and controllers, powerful and powerless. By constantly bringing these, and other, perspectives into debate and dialogue, a shared, more accurate, holistic picture can, I believe, be painted.

Such a picture does not deny difference, or assert sameness. Rather, it aims at facilitating conversation about what it means to be human across 'societal lines – of ethnicity, religion, class, gender, language, race' (Geertz, 1988: 147). It will not attempt to create a universal culture, but to 'enlarge the possibility of intelligible difference between people quite different from one another ... yet contained in one world, where, tumbled as they are into endless connection, it is increasingly difficult to get out of each other's way' (*ibid.*). This represents, in fact, what at its best anthropology has always struggled to establish: 'that "cultural difference" is not about the peculiarities and oddities of "other cultures" ' compared with one's own, 'but rather about recognizing cultural uniqueness, while at the same time seeking out the similarities in human cultural life' (Moore: 9). Kuper's call for a cosmopolitan anthropology similarly sees anthropology as conversation, 'implicating ethnographers, informants and the ancestral voices they invoke' but his audience is more limited than mine, 'we should once again address social scientists, and aspire to contribute a comparative dimension to the enlightenment project of a science of human variation in time and space' (1994: 55). I agree with Kuper's aim, to forward the human enterprise, but follow Angela Cheater's view that 'anthropology has proved too useful to be left just to anthropologists' or even just to social scientists (1986: ix). Cheater, who teaches anthropology in Zimbabwe, wrote her *Social Anthropology: An Alternative Introduction* (1986) for 'anyone wanting an approachable and stimulating introduction to the subject'. My audience, like hers, would be anyone who is interested in understanding more about being human. Thus, the anthropologist may serve as a go-between 'for the people they study and the people they write for', which, for cosmopolitan anthropology, is everyone.

Full circle

In a sense, anthropology has come full circle; it began with a fascination for other peoples, other cultures, other places. As trade, travel, exploration and conquest widened Europe's horizons, the world became an even more interesting and diverse place. Anthropologists studied others as much to learn more about themselves as to learn about the other; however, they designed, executed and owned the process of enquiry. Heirs of the positivists, they thought that observation and empiricism alone could produce an accurate, value-free understanding of other peoples' meanings. Later, awareness of *a priori* preconceptions, of cultural relativity, of the problematic of arguing for any universal norms, resulted in epistemological hypochondria. This at best turned anthropological discourse into good literature, at worst, into introspection. Perhaps one could only know oneself. My argument, that cosmopolitan anthropology can lead to shared knowledge about each other, brings us back to anthropology's starting point – a quest for self-knowledge through the medium of studying other peoples. What cosmopolitan anthropology leaves out is the studying of others as if they were objects. All are subjects together.

Incidentally, I am not arguing that every published account of anthropological (or of interreligious) research must have multiple authors. Nor am I arguing that all involved in the research process must have an explicit say in how the final account is rendered. What I am advocating is more openness and democracy during the actual process of research. What is finally published, or submitted to a university, may still be the ultimate responsibility of a single researcher, in which his or her perceptions are brought into conversation with others' perceptions. However, what will judge whether this account fulfils the 'go-between' function, or not, will not be the award of a degree, or publication, but the response, positive or negative, of one's research partners. Does it, or does it not, command their assent?

Before we conclude this chapter, we need to note again developments within the study of religions. Clearly, there is convergence between the idea of discourse between scholars, and practitioners (so that the account rendered can 'do justice to the faith in people's hearts by commanding their assent once it is written') and what I mean by cosmopolitan anthropology. However, cosmopolitan anthropology goes one step further: if outsiders can help insiders know themselves better, and vice versa, then we are talking about progress in our mutual understandings. Can this apply equally to the study of religions?

Towards a world theology

The problematic in speaking about new, or changed, understanding of ourselves and of the other, from the religious point of view, is that it encroaches onto the remit of theology. The job of the scientific scholar of religions is to study what traditions say, and have said, about themselves, not to act as an agent of changing what they say, or believe. The job of theology, within each tradition, is to critique and interpret that tradition for each new era; some traditions view themselves as already definitively defined, and oppose change, others view themselves as in process. Some theologians see themselves as guardians of continuity, others as agents for change. The study of religions, it can be argued, should hold no opinion about the relative value of either change or of continuity. However, if a rigid distinction is to be maintained between theology, and the study of religions, there is a danger that anthropology will leave it behind as a mechanism for furthering human understanding of humanity.

There is, though, at least one other possibility: that the study of religions reduces its distance from theology, and that theology moves from a confessional location within the traditions, to an autonomous location outside. This is perhaps what Heiler meant when he said, as previously quoted, 'Religion is about a final reality ... any study of religion is in the last analysis theology'. *De jure,* where theology is taught in secular or state funded colleges and universities it is non-confessional; *de facto,* whilst no faith commitment is presupposed of teachers or of students, most of what is taught in such contexts is mono-confessional, that is, Christian. Any exposure to theologies other than Christian will be through a study of religions strand. Yet a theology open to concepts, ideas, truth claims, from all religious traditions has been advocated by several distinguished scholars. In his *Towards a World Theology* (1981), Wilfred Cantwell Smith called for theology which would 'interpret intellectually the cosmic significance of human life generically, not just for one's own group specifically' (1981: 187). Smith calls this 'colloquy', which he prefers to 'dialogue'; 'partly for its multilateral connotations but chiefly to suggest a side by side confronting of the world's problems rather than a face to face confronting of each other' (*ibid.*: 193). It would involve 'cross-cultural teams of scholars', and would also need 'to generate new terminologies', which, comments Edward J. Hughes, 'presupposes an acceptance that one's religious culture is but one of many paths to the Divine' (1986: 183). Smith is well aware that, for Christians, what he advocates is a radical idea, implying that all religions are equally valid and that all can contribute to a better understanding of human life, an understanding unachievable by any one alone (see *ibid.*: 77). For Smith, Christianity is the Christian experience of God, as uniquely mediated for them, Islam is the way for Muslims, uniquely mediated for them, and so on. Smith thus rejects what is usually called 'exclusivism', the view that only your own tradition is valid, that others are at best inadequate, at worst false, in favour of 'pluralism'. Rejecting the concept of 'ultimate revelations', he argues for a worldwide religious community of 'non-ultimate revelations' in which 'the revelation in Christ is only one' (Hughes: 191). 'From this standpoint', Hughes explains, 'Christ may be confessionally witnessed to as a personal ultimate, but this does not entail an absolute ontological claim' (*ibid.*).

Faith as a universal concern

John Hick, who wrote the preface to Hughes' volume on Smith, has long advocated a similar pluralist theology. Both Hick and Smith regard human religiosity, primarily, as differently experienced, differently articulated human responses to the Ultimate. Their rejection of ultimate revelations enables them to view all religions as dynamic, as in process: 'To be a Muslim means to participate in the Islamic process, as the context of one's religious life. To be a Buddhist means to participate in the Buddhist process' (Smith, 1981: 31). Smith justifies this claim historically, indeed empirically. All religions have, even if they claim to be definitively defined by a primary revelation, existed cumulatively, not statically. Neither the Christian canon, nor creeds, existed in the first century. Mahayana Buddhism developed at a later point in time than the Theravada. Islamic metaphysics and philosophy didn't exist at the time of the Prophet. Religion, for Smith, exists primarily within people; thus, there are Christians rather than Christianity, Muslims rather than

Islam. Islam becomes what people experience, and say about their experience. Although Smith does surmise that there may be no such reality as Islam, or as Christianity, only what this or that Muslim, or Christian, believes, I would not want to go too far down this road. I do not share postmodernist pessimism about human ability to share anything; a religion may, I think, be what this group, or that group, takes it to be.

Most people, too, are conscious of personal growth, of developing or – in the language of Carl Rogers – of 'becoming persons' (see Rogers: 1961). Religiously, most locate themselves somewhere along a path. Commonly, the religious life is viewed as a journey, or pilgrimage. Few religious individuals think that they have completed the journey. Muslims are thus all in the process of becoming better Muslims, Christians in the process of becoming better Christians. Indeed, most religions make provision for the ongoing faith nurture of adults. Influenced by Smith, psychologist James W. Fowler has explored the theme of faith development in the context of human development, or maturation, in his classic *Stages of Faith* (1981). For him, as for Smith, faith is a universal human concern for ultimate truth. It may not be religious. It may be a person's way of learning, of making sense of life, of construing meaning. More verb than noun (and hence active, not passive) it is a dynamic system of images, values and commitments which guides one's life. Traditions and scriptures serve less as 'repositories of truth' than as 'guides for the construction of contemporary ways of seeing and believing'. Received documents 'become for present members of the faith community invitations and stimuli for contemporary experiments with truth' (Fowler: 295). Or, as Smith writes, 'Any scripture – Gita, Bible, a Buddhist sutra, or whatever – and any verse or term within it, means what it in fact means, and has meant, to those for whom it has been meaningful' (1993: 89).

Thus, if we allow that there is room for individual, personal development of believers within each tradition, and for new interpretions of faith, it is also logical to assert that people of one tradition can learn from those of another. Fowler sees this capacity as a characteristic of adulthood, of being 'a self actualised person', or a 'fully functioning human being'. This final stage of faith, and of human development, has, he says, a universal orientation. Such people as Martin Luther King, Jr, Mahatma Gandhi, Mother Teresa, exemplify this stage; universal principles enable them to transcend the particular in the cause of universal peace, justice, or humaneness, often against the grain of prevailing attitudes. This universal orientation transcends their personal ego, enabling the recognition and acceptance of others' value and worth. Diana Eck says of Gandhi, for example, that he 'considered himself a follower of Jesus but ... did not respect the dogmatism he saw in much of the Christian tradition' (1993: 206). If we do not feel our beliefs, our sense of personal completeness, threatened by what others believe, awareness of their faith may actually deepen ours. However, we shall still participate in the process from within our existing traditions, as did Gandhi. Martin Luther King, Jr (1929–68) was, in his turn, influenced by Gandhi but remained profoundly Christian. As Hick says, 'that *these* people are experiencing the Real in this way is not incompatible with *those* people experiencing the Real in that way' (1994: 22).

The influential therapist and educationalist, Carl Rogers, writes similarly about 'the person of tomorrow' who will have as heroes such people as Gandhi, Martin Luther King, Teilhard de Chardin. Eager 'to be of help to others', they will seek 'new forms of closeness, of harmony, of intimacy, of shared purpose' with others and be 'keenly aware that the one certainty of life is change – that they are always in process, always changing' (Rogers, 1980: 350–2). In a moving and personal article 'Growing old – or older and growing' (1980) Rogers, aged 75, speaks about feeling 'more open to new ideas', 'to new experiences, new risks. Increasingly', he says, he discovers that to be alive is to change; 'the process of change is life. I realize that if I were stable and steady and static, I would be a living death' (1980: 16). I perhaps should add that I first encountered Rogerian theory in 1977 whilst on placement in a psychiatric hospital chaplaincy; I have admired, and used, his writing ever since. Diana Eck (cited above), Smith's former student and his successor at Harvard, has written about how her own spirituality has been enhanced by her exposure to Hinduism, and by her friendship with Hindus (see *Encountering God* (1993)). This is an excellent example of an academic student of religions who has not hesitated to become personally involved in her subject, humankind's experience of being religious. Refering to Gandhi, she calls for a 'wider sense of "we"' (1993: 200–31). Smith has suggested that an outsider can sometimes 'break new ground in stating the meaning of a faith in, say, modern terms more successfully than a believer' (1959: 43).

The theological enterprise and the religions

The scholarly task, for Smith (which Eck fully endorses, and pursues in her work) is for 'we-all' to participate together in 'the disciplined self-consciousness of man's variegated and developing religious life' (1959: 55); a 'we-all' talking together about 'us'. Or, as he put it elsewhere, 'Our vision and our loyalties, as well as our aircraft, must circle the globe' (1965: 92). Eck writes of how, having written 'an interpretive study of the city of Banaras', she has 'participated, as a Christian, in a small way, in the history of the Hindu tradition'. Similarly, her 'Hindu friends and teachers', she says, 'have participated in the history of the Christian tradition through their influence on' her and on her thinking (1993: 212). Christian theology this century has also been much influenced by the writing of Martin Buber (1878–1965), a Jew. On the other hand, 'while we Jews don't read Buber as much as you do, we do read Tillich and Harvey Cox, earnestly and the day has long passed when we write only for ourselves' (Smith, 1981: 143). Thus, 'we-all' will contribute to each others' development. Hans Küng, Professor of Ecumenical Theology at Tübingen, and one of the most prolific contemporary German theologians (censured by the Vatican in 1969 for questioning papal infallibility), in his ambitious *Christianity and the World Religions* (1984) has similarly called for 'mutual critical enlightenment, stimulation, penetration and enrichment' among the religions (1984: xx). His theology tends towards the position usually called 'inclusivist', rather than towards the pluralism of Hick or Smith. Christ, for Küng, is the 'crucial standard' that judges all religious life, including the Christian (for example, see 1984: 129). Increasingly, theologians are arguing that theological reflection can no longer, validly, ignore the issue of religious plurality. As early as 1953, Paul Tillich (1886–1965) argued that 'a Christian theology which is not able to enter a creative diaolgue with the theological thought of other world religions misses a world-historical occasion, and remains provincial' (1953: 3: 6). It was contact and friendship with Mircea Eliade that helped to convince Tillich that this was the right direction for Christian theology to travel. He, like Smith and Fowler, took faith to be a universal human concern.

Here, I may appear to be side-tracking too much into a theological debate in a book about anthropology and the academic study of religions. However, my argument is that this very debate, about the parameters of the theological task, is crucial to the future of the study of religions. As theologians are increasingly turning to dialogue and encounter with other religious traditions, they are also turning to a deeper study of these traditions as part of the dialogue process. What role might this leave for the professional student of religions? Possibly, a theologian who must also master languages and texts within his or her own tradition may never become as skilled in their handling of other peoples', and may need to turn to the specialist for advice. However, at least part of the student of religions' agenda, learning about faiths through encounter, discovering what people themselves believe, rather than what the official texts say, is already very much part of the theologian's task.

For example, Hans Küng's *Christianity and the World Religions*, even if produced with the help of a large research team, exhibits a factual knowledge of the religions beyond the reach of earlier generations of theologians. More significantly, it manages to capture something of the ethos of the traditions discussed. Another excellent example of this learning about others from others, and about oneself in the process, is Harvey Cox's *Many Mansions* (1988). This book invites its readers to 'journey with' Cox 'through some of the discoveries and disappointments that ... marked' his 'attempts to cultivate the conversation with people of other faiths while trying to nurture the vital sources of the faith that motivates the conversation' (1988: 19). This is a participation in the process of religious life of the type for which Smith has called. Cox has long valued what he calls 'testimony', or the 'personal voice'; 'after all', he says, 'it is never the religions themselves that converse but individual people who embody those religions' (1988: 5). Arguably, then, the process has already begun. Undoubtedly, some students of religions will not wish to participate in this process. For some, it calls for too much personal involvement; it implies that one needs to have a faith to study faiths. I would argue that personal faith is not a prerequisite; only recognition that all people participate in a universal process of becoming better, more rounded human persons, in which their understanding of self in relation to others, and of others in relation to themselves, is open to change and reinterpretation. This perhaps adapts Waardenburg's 'faith as as scholarly category' to 'faith as a human experience'.

Finally, Smith and Küng both call for collaboration between the religions towards achieving a better world order; 'there will be no orderly human coexistence in this world, no resolution of all the problems of peace, justice, and preservation of the created world unless the religions make a decisive contribution, each from its own spiritual resources' (Küng, 1984: xii). A statement on global ethics, drafted by Küng, was endorsed by many delegates at the 1993 centenary meeting commemorating the 1893 World Parliament of Religions. This statement has been widely published (for example, in *World Faiths Encounter*: 6:63–64). The four Catholic theologians who wrote *Death or Dialogue? From the Age of Monologue to the Age of Dialogue*, too, argue that unless we learn about 'others as they really are, and not as we have projected them in our monologues' the human race will be unable to avoid ecological disaster and planetary destruction (see Swidler, *et al*: 1990). Yet can professional students of religions properly regard promoting such collaboration as part of their academic task? In fact, as long ago as the 1958 Congress of the International Association for the History of Religions, Heiler presented a paper on 'The history of religions as a way to unity of religions' in which he argued that if (as he believed) academic study was bringing religious unity to light, then:

Whoever recognizes ... unity must take it seriously by tolerance in word and deed. Thus scientific insight into this unity calls for a practical realization in friendly exchange and in common ethical endeavour, 'fellowship' and 'co-operation'. (1960: 19)

Even earlier, in 1921, Heiler's teacher, Rudolf Otto had founded (as we noted in Chapter 1) an Inter-Religious League to encourage co-operation of the 'entire cultural civilization to master evil through mutual effort and a mutual aim, through reciprocal responsibility and a well planned interchange of purpose' (cited in Sharpe, 1988: 257). However, given that some scholars think such aims outside the remit of an academic enterprise, those who wish to become proactively engaged in promoting interreligious co-operation towards improving social conditions, or achieving world peace, might have to do so in their private capacities. Inevitably, though, this very process of collaboration will itself generate data and ideas for study; and if scholars are not present, they will lack direct access to this new material. On the other hand, if participant observation is a legitimate method of academic enquiry, scholars have no excuse not to become personally involved. Probably, if the scholars of religions stay aloof, anthropologists (quickly followed by the theologians) will take their place. My colleague, Peggy Morgan, has explored some of these issues in a recent article, asking whether participation by academics in interfaith meetings 'in any way tinges the academic agenda with a kind of para-theology', and 'Does the agenda of interfaith work potentially cast a shadow over the shape of the study of religion?' (1995: 157). Her conclusion tends towards my own, that 'to be present at occasions of inter-religious meeting is often to see a stage in the mutation of religions which results from their encounter', which, she says, 'is certainly a fitting subject for scholarly reflection' (*ibid.*: 163). If not present, academics will lack access to this subject.

Résumé

I am not arguing that every academic, or professional, scholar of the religions should participate in some collaborative programme. I do, however, hope that some will. Whilst on the one hand, to have excluded reference to this trend would have left this survey incomplete, on the other, I believe that fulfilment of the 'go-between' function will itself present scholars with sufficiently demanding an academic challenge. I will argue, though, in our last chapter in favour of what we might call a 'critical paradigm'. This aims at unveiling myths and stereotypes so that the 'truth may set people free', to reveal 'true conditions' and to help people 'see the way to a better world' (Neuman: 75). Also, in arguing for methodological convergence between anthropology and the study of religions, I am not suggesting that every student of religions should employ an anthropological methodology, or that every anthropologist should also study religions. There are many other areas of the anthropological agenda in which anthropologists can, and should, specialize. Similarly, the study of religions' agenda includes work on classical texts and languages which require their own specialist training and commitment. Not everyone can do everything. Therefore, my suggestion is that some students of religions will find it profitable to employ, and gain competencies in, anthropological research strategies, and vice versa, some anthropologists will also want to work with primary religious texts, and with written historical records. Both disciplines, I believe, will continue to need their separate institutions, but increasingly some scholars will find themselves *de facto*, if not *de jure*, members of both establishments. What I have said in this chapter also raises the question, 'Should the study of religions be subsumed within the theological enterprise, or vice versa?' As more and more theologians turn to the study of religions, will the distinction between the fields remain valid?

Perhaps the best formula is the one already used in many North American universities; the study of religion (in the singular) within schools, or faculties, of religion. This might well solve the present somewhat untidy position where the study of the many religions is often located within theological faculties implicitly rooted in a single tradition. This is why Smith has suggested that a new term might be needed to designate the new enterprise (theology being overly Christian, study of religions too impersonal). Peggy Morgan, commenting on a draft of this chapter, argued that the study of religions is broader than theology, since 'the faith seeking understanding enterprise of any tradition' (their theological dimension) forms part of its subject matter.

In our final chapter we explore how, by operating in the ethical, relational 'go-between' mode for which I have argued above, anthropology and the study of religions can continue to perform valuable functions, not only in the accumulation of knowledge, but also in helping solve some of the practical problems which threaten our world and our societies today. As examples of good practice, I shall identify some successful efforts at bridging the 'we–them' divide. Finally, I shall suggest some strategies which readers of this book might use to research and produce their own projects, dissertations or theses. These will not be of the large-scale, world-changing genre. Rather, they will aim at encouraging increased understanding between people of different faith traditions and at contributing something distinctive towards scholarship. They will combine anthropology (or ethnography understood as anthropological praxis) with some textual or historical scholarship. My thesis here is that a combination of textual and fieldwork research is more likely to produce a unique study than historical, archival or textual work alone; every student likes to achieve a degree of originality in their work.

6 Our Disciplines: Good Practice for Today

Some examples

In noting the work of John L. Esposito, amongst others, we have already identified an example of the 'go-between function' within the academic study of religions. By listening to Muslim voices, Esposito has produced accounts of Islam which fulfil Wilfred Cantwell Smith's dictum that anything we 'say about Islam as a living faith is valid only in so far as Muslims can say "Amen" to it' (1959: 43). In writing about Muslims as fellow human beings, rather than as a 'they', and as a 'they out there', Esposito has also treated Islam as, essentially, a 'faith in people's hearts', not as a scholarly abstraction. I have several times cited the work of Muslim academic, Akbar Ahmed, including his appreciative comments on Esposito. Ahmed, an anthropologist who also writes about Islam, and about the relationship between the Muslim and non-Muslim worlds, represents another example of our go-between function. In his recent writing (1988, 1992, 1993), he has set himself the task of addressing two audiences, a Western one, and the Muslim world. He offers Western readers keys to unlock an understanding of Muslim society liberated from its media stereotype. He also invites fellow Muslims to confront their stereotypes of the West, to develop a discourse with the West capable of creating a dialogue between Muslim and non-Muslim responses to such 'contemporary problems as those of population, refugees, poverty, drugs, pollution, famine ... within this complex world of ours' (1988: 216). 'Dialogue, harmony, communication and debate' are, he says, key issues in the engagement between Islam and the West (Hawkey,

1995: 16). Whilst critical of media coverage of events in the Islamic world, of the 'blacking out ... of good, decent Muslim citizens and the high profile projection of the extremists', he also praises the 'magnanimity and chivalry' of colleagues at Selwyn College, Cambridge when, during his induction as its first Muslim Fellow, references to the Trinity were dropped from the ceremony, and his glass was filled with juice 'every time the port was passed round the high table after the formal dinner which accompanies the ceremony' (1992: 176). Ahmed, who acknowledges 'the comments and stimulation' of non-Muslim as well as of Muslim scholars during the formulation of his writing, is able to move at ease within Muslim and non-Muslim society. One reviewer of Ahmed's television series *Living Islam* (1993), though, does point out an interesting difference between Ahmed's role whilst filming within the Islamic world, and outside it, 'In Britain, Ahmed wore European clothes and was projected as scholarly mediator, whereas in the Islamic world he wore a Pakistani suit and was projected as culture mediator' (El-Guindi, 1995: 25). Ahmed's role is mediatory in both contexts but, suggests the reviewer, whilst 'casting the expert scholar as a native, or insider' allows 'the viewer a privileged entry into the inside' it simultaneously 'may deny the expert authority, and herein lies a problem' (*ibid*.: 24). We may note, too, that the Israeli Embassy in London called the series 'the work of a fundamentalist', whilst 'from Kalim Siddiqui's Muslim Institute came the cry that [it] was part of a Zionist/Anglo/American conspiracy'. This proves Ahmed's point: that 'it can be very uncomfortable, perhaps even dangerous, to stand in the middle' (Hawkey: 16).

However, whilst Esposito and Ahmed write from out of the experience of encounter, and elicit an 'Amen' from the appropriate source, neither actually represent collaborative scholarship as such. Perhaps one of the best examples of this emanates from the City of Bradford, where Muslims and non-Muslims worked together to produce *The Satanic Verses: Bradford Responds* (1992). This book explores some of the issues involved in the Salman Rushdie affair, the controversy surrounding the novel *The Satanic Verses* by author Salman Rushdie, published in 1988. The project was co-ordinated by David G. Bowen, who edited the book; however, he was advised by a committee whose membership included Muslims, Christians and Jews. The authors

acknowledge the complexity of the issues and propose no easy answers to demanding and perplexing questions, but ... clarify the values that underlie their beliefs. Together they provide an arena in which emotional investment in religious beliefs is explored and in which uncritical acceptance of freedom of expression is examined. As such the book allows the two roads to come together and the investments to be shared. (1992: iii)

In other words, a conversation about different ways of being religiously human was achieved through a process of discussion, dialogue and encounter. The publication was preceded by a series of seminars. Another example is *The Emptying God* (1990) edited by John B. Cobb and Christopher Ives, in which practising Jews, Christians and Buddhists discuss their respective understanding of particular themes.

Another example of Muslim–non-Muslim collaboration is the book *Meeting Muslims* (1992). Bringing together the work of six Muslims and six Christians, this publication aims to promote meaningful encounter between Muslims in Britain and members of the wider community. It is primarily intended for a non-Muslim audience, but the fact that the project was jointly financed by the Muslim College, Ealing, and contains contributions by prominent members of the Muslim community, will guarantee a Muslim as well as a non-Muslim readership. Dr Zaki Badawi, Principal of the Muslim College and Bishop Kenneth Cragg, author of *The Call of the Minaret* (1956) and of numerous books on Christian–Muslim encounter, each wrote a Foreword. Another publication, again primarily intended for a non-Muslim audience but written with a view to eliciting Muslim approval, is *Issues in Christian–Muslim Relations: Some Ecumenical Considerations* (1991) published by the World Council of Churches. 'We ... can no longer', says the document, 'speak as if Muslims are not listening; everything we say and do must be in the knowledge that they are partners, whether directly or indirectly' (1992: 1). It drew on a series of regional conferences between Christians and Muslims, including eminent scholars, and was drafted at a meeting in Cartigny, Switzerland (May 1990), where Muslims were fully involved in the discussion.

Further consultation followed before a final draft was produced for committee approval. I was a member both of the Cartigny colloquy, and of the smaller drafting group (October 1990). The published version also took note of some additional comments offered during the committee process. It aims to provide an agenda for common action, as well as for future theological dialogue, between Muslims and Christians. More recently, building on the above initiative, the World Council of Churches has published *Religion, Law and Society: A Christian–Muslim Discussion,* (1995) edited by Tarek Mitri. The essays, by Christians and Muslims, are based on papers presented and discussed at a series of consultations, and address such issues as human rights, secularization, Islamic revival, pluralism and the position of minorities.

So far, our examples have illustrated the go-between function within the wider area of the study of religions. I have mainly chosen publications which address the Muslim–non-Muslim relationship because involvement in this area has dominated my working life. I shall now return to anthropology.

Clifford Geertz, whose contribution has featured prominently throughout our survey, is a notable example of an anthropologist whose work has elicited approval from Muslims. Akbar Ahmed writes that, amongst other non-Muslim anthropologists, Geertz has produced 'some of the finest material in Islamic anthropology'. His work provides 'the most meaningful analytic methods of studying Muslim society' (1988: 215–16). Akbar also speaks approvingly of Ernest Gellner's *Muslim Society* (1981). Another example from anthropology is the volume *Cultural Politics* (1995) by Glenn Jordan and Chris Weedon. This study of 'culture, subjectivity and power', which includes fieldwork in the Tiger Bay area of Cardiff, asks 'Whose history is it?' (Chapter 5 is essentially dialogue between the researcher and local 'voices'). Jordan and Weedon explore the power–knowledge dynamic with reference to gender, class and race, which relates to our earlier discussion about how anthropological constructions of other peoples' cultures have often served the observer's interests, rather than those of the observed. In an important paragraph, they point out that 'if people from the community and people who share its interests, do not collect, preserve, publish and exhibit Tiger Bay's past, someone else will and we can be sure gauging it from the past 150 years, that what they produce will be more colourful, romantic and negative stereotypes' (1995: 171).

Communities such as Tiger Bay, with multiracial, multicultural populations, contain many untold stories; stories of cultural adjustments, of dislocation, of interracial tension, as well as of cross-racial harmony. What is it like to leave one's homeland, to travel to a foreign country, to live and work in an alien environment, to begin to make a habitable home within that environment? How do these experiences affect people's sense of identity, their loyalties to homelands old and new? How are mixed loyalties, or competing loyalties, reconciled – during cricket matches between Pakistan and MCC, or during conflict between the United Kingdom and one's country of origin? What changes in religious faith and practice, if any, follow from this process of migration and transplantation? These, and other, research questions demand exploration – whilst the people who can answer them are still alive. Of course, their demise will leave us with a new generation, born and brought up in Britain (or in the United States, Canada, etc.) with its own unique set of experiences to explore and research, thus adding to our understanding of what it means to be socially and religiously human. Sajdah Currah's contribution to *Meeting Muslims* offers insight into this second-generation experience.

Jordan and Weedon's reminder, that if 'the people concerned, and those who share their interests', do not 'tell their stories', others will, introduces us to one possible idea for future research: the recording of people's stories. In a modest way, I was involved in helping members of the Bangladeshi community tell its story through my friend Yousuf Choudhury's *The Roots and Tales of the Bangladeshi Settlers* (1993). Much of this book's story, especially about the early days of Bangladeshi settlement, when men lived together in lodgings with white landladies, might easily have been lost had Choudhury's project not attracted the support of interested outsiders. By assisting his project, outsiders enabled the publication of his 'courageous ... unique, insider's view of his own migrant people' (Bennett, 1993: vii–viii). Others, less committed to telling it as it is, with a different agenda (such as fuelling racist attitides) may have painted a different picture. Thus, Jordan and Weedon's work effectively calls for a critical approach, rather than for a value-free approach, to anthropological reconstruction. I am not suggesting that we should impose our values, or preconceptions, on the data. An outsider's job, in enabling people to tell their story, is to assist their articulation of what they have experienced, so that the result will command their assent. However, a critical approach deliberately confronts any myths and stereotypes of which we are aware, and which, if left unchallenged, will disable other people from hearing the true story. Jordan and Weedon stress the importance of community publishing, or film production, to enable people to tell their stories as they wish them to be told.

This suggests that anthropology and the study of religions operating in the go-between mode, have valuable functions to play in our increasingly pluralist world. Unless we retreat into religious, or cultural, or national isolation, we needs must find ways of living harmoniously alongside others, whose cultures, religions, skin-colours, are different from ours. By enabling us to confront our own assumptions, including our values, and to listen to others' experiences, our two disciplines may enable a constructive exchange of diverse ideas and experiences of what it means to be human. Briefly, the Western preoccupation with technology, for example, may benefit from conversation with those for whom living in harmony with the natural world is more important. Or, Muslim suspicion that capitalism breeds social inequality may engage creatively with the West's elevation of the market place above all other cultural institutions. Many more examples can be added. However, before offering some concluding remarks about this survey, I want to suggest some practical ideas for future research; what follows might be suitable for final year undergraduate, or for graduate, dissertation work.

Ideas for future research

These ideas indicate some general areas. What I have in mind is a combination of textual, or archival, and ethnographic work (taken here to mean 'doing anthropology'). One possibility: reconstructing a story to which you have, or can gain, access, either as an insider, or as an interested outsider. This could be the story of a local mosque, of a residents' association, of a church, or of a local neighbourhood. Begin by exploring existing published material. This might be an institution's own publicity, articles in the local press, or general background information about 'Islam in Britain', or about 'Hindu temples in Britain'. You will need to check relevant journals for appropriate entries. This research should provide historical background, a framework into which you can incorporate data gathered by conversation, interview and observation – the ethnographical component. In gathering this data, you may need to focus on a limited, or specific issue; for example, what differences do people perceive between life here and in their land of origin; or, what particular challenges do they encounter, and why? Or, do women perceive any difference between their experience here, and back in Pakistan, in the Caribbean, or wherever? Or, have people rediscovered anything within their traditions as a result of migration? Your background research on, say, Pakistani migration to Britain may reveal when, and why, migration started. Does this match the story told by your consultants?

A variation on this theme: interview a selection of, say, Sikh women about their self-perceptions – as Sikh women in Britain. This would begin with an examination of gender within the Sikh scripture, in order to create a conversation between the canonical tradition and contemporary experiences. Some might claim that this type of textual work cannot properly be pursued without knowledge of the scriptural language. If one was primarily working on the classical text, I would agree. However, for the purposes of comparing and contrasting this material with your ethnographical data, translations will prove quite adequate. You will also need to see what has already been written about gender and Sikhism. What will be original about such a project is unlikely to be your discussion of the classical tradition; others will have studied that at greater length than you, indeed existing literature will probably cover most of the material already. Rather, your ethnographical material will, by definition, be unique; what you will have recorded will be the experience of *those* women. Others may, will, tell a different story. This does not detract from, or question, the value or validity of *their* experience. In setting this data alongside your discussion of the canonical tradition, too, you are not making a value judgement about either; you are simply drawing out similarities and differences as interesting facts. If you want to pursue a collaborative, or cosmopolitan, approach, then agree your account with your consultants. What do they think about your rendering of the classical tradition? Include this in your final account.

To conduct this type of project effectively, and validly, you will need to use a manual on interview and fieldwork research strategies. One we use in supervising Masters' research at Westminster College, from which I have cited in this book, is W. Lawrence Neuman's *Social Research Methods* (1994). This discusses relevant theories and strategies but, although written for 'upper level undergraduates or beginning graduates' probably contains far more information than you will easily digest. More digestible, covering such important issues as 'recording and organising data', 'insider accounts', and 'analysis' is Hammersley's and Atkinson's *Ethnography* (2nd ed., 1995) 'a must text for theory and methods courses'. This book is also sound on the issue of reflexivity. Very useful, and readable, is Judith Bell's *Doing Your Research Project* (1993), which I recommend as a very useful primer. It has excellent checklists to help you prepare interview schedules, draft questionnaires, or observe. However, what follows by way of handy hints may provide a useful set of general guidelines.

Your research project

Begin by identifying your topic, or research question, within your own interests, professional or personal context – if this is possible. Make your own assumptions, values, preconceptions, explicit in your introduction. Later, using reflexivity you can tell the reader how your presuppositions have been challenged, changed, or modified, by your research. You may begin with a general issue or question, and focus down onto a more narrowly defined topic, or question, during the research process. Next, decide what broad research strategy you are going to adopt – for example, are you attempting a case study, or an evaluation of a project, or initiative? Are you an insider, or an outsider? Identify how you will gather your information, by observation, by interview, by questionnaire.

These are called research instruments, or tools, and, like any artisan, you must choose the right tool for the job. You will need to justify your use of a research instrument. You will also need to say something about how you went about selecting your sample, remembering that ethnographers are always interested in a wide range of perceptions. You will want to paint a multidimensional, not a monodimensional, picture, creating dialogue and conversation between different viewpoints. This is where you will need to be aware of the issues of reliability and validity, and make certain that you have triangulated.

Next, review whatever literature is available, either to shed light on the political, historical or social background, or to see what similar research has shown. Your main source of information here may be newspapers, rather than books. Also, show some familiarity with the literature on methodology. You will now be ready to move into the substantive presentation of your data – using thick description, if possible. Use quotations to add authenticity to your account, to help convince the reader that you saw what you saw and heard what heard. Your aim, usually, is to make sense of your subject – of what happens in a mosque, for example, of what it 'means' to those who worship, socialize, or meet there. You may, correctly, be less concerned with analysing what you see than with expressing it in language accessible to outsiders. This is very much what the go-between function involves.

The manuals often talk about analytical frameworks. Such a framework may be appropriate, especially if your research represents an evaluation. Your framework could be supplied by the project's own aims and objectives; success or failure can be judged against what a project, organization, or initiative, sets out to achieve. Given the concerns of this book, though, you are more likely to present, say, the 'official' view, alongside a 'popular' view, or views, and to attempt to create a dialogue between these, asking how do those involved interpret what they do?

Throughout your account, you will wish to reflect on your own presence – to engage in reflexivity – about which much has been said in this book. Here, a research diary can be very useful – both to keep a record of your own perceptions, and to record data. Usefully, remember that the research account can tell two stories – that of the project, initiative, community, or phenomenon under scrutiny, and of the research process itself. Ensure, for example, that any focusing down is made explicit. Finally, your conclusions should always be cautious. Discuss problems ('I could not interview everyone I wanted to because ...'). Show awareness of any limitations and shortcomings. Do not claim too much for a small scale project.

Conclusion

The purpose of this search, of course, was not to find the sacred but to discuss different understandings of this elusive dimension of human life, and some strategies for exploring it. We have encountered many theories of how human belief in the sacred may have evolved. Some of these theories regard the sacred as 'really real', others as a psychological, or social, construct. Whilst we cannot properly adjudicate between these different theories, what we have also noted is that humankind shows little intent of abandoning belief in things sacred. On the contrary, in today's world, there is a proliferation of ways of being religious. Many people are looking to new, or to alternative religious traditions, or to nature, or to a universal cosmic consciousness, for life's meaning and purpose. What we may conclude, I suggest, from this survey is this: as long as people construe, and follow, different religious paths (and as long as a plurality of cultures continue to flourish) our two disciplines will have their subject matters. This may run somewhat counter to the view of some that the study of religions (and religion itself; see Dawkins, 1994) is outmoded, and anthropology redundant, in today's cosmopolitan world. What our survey has shown, too, is that our disciplines should be rooted in human relationships, in conversation; and should not be based on observation from afar, or on textual study alone. Both, ultimately, have to do with what it means to be equally human, but racially, religiously, or culturally, different.

References

Ahmed, Akbar (1988) *Discovering Islam: Making Sense of Muslim History and Society*, London, Routledge.

Ahmed, Akbar (1992) *Postmodernism and Islam: Predicament and Promise*, London, Routledge.

Ahmed, Akbar (1993) *Living Islam: From Samarkand to Stornoway*, London, BBC.

Ahmed, Leila (1992) *Women and Gender in Islam: Historical Roots of a Modern Debate*, New Haven, Yale University Press.

Armstrong, Karen (1993) *A History of God*, London, Mandarin.

Banu, Razia Akter, U.A.B. (1992) *Islam in Bangladesh*, Leiden, E.J. Brill.

Baring, Evelyn, Lord Cromer (1908) *Modern Egyptians*, London, Macmillan.

Barker, Eileen (1989) *New Religious Movements: An Introduction*, London, HMSO.

Barley, Nigel (1983) *The Innocent Anthropologist: Notes from a Mud Hut*, Harmondsworth, Penguin.

Bate, John Drew (1884) Report, in *92nd Report of the Baptist Missionary Society*, London, BMS, p.7.

Beidelman, T.O. (1968) 'Evans-Pritchard', in David L. Sills (ed.) *International Encyclopedia of the Social Sciences, New York*, The Free Press, pp. 176–80.

Bell, Judith (ed. 1993) *Doing Your Research Project: A Guide for First Time Researchers in Education and Social Science*, Buckingham, Open University Press.

Bennett, Clinton (1992) *Victorian Images of Islam*, London, Grey Seal.

Bennett, Clinton (1993) 'Foreword', in Yousuf Choudhury *The Roots and Tales of the Bangladeshi Settlers*, Birmingham, Sylheti Social History Group, pp. vii–viii.

Bennett, Clinton (1994a) 'Islam', in Jean Holm with John Bowker (eds) *Sacred Place*, London, Pinter, pp. 88–114.

Bennett, Clinton (1994b) 'Islam', in Jean Holm with John Bowker (eds) *Rites of Passage*, London, Pinter, pp. 90–112.

Bennett, Clinton (1994c) 'Impressions of Bangladeshi Islam', in *Meeting Muslims*, Leicester, Christians Aware, pp. 37–43.

Bennett, Clinton (1994d) 'Islam', in Jean Holm with John Bowker (eds) *Making Moral Decisions*, London, Pinter, pp. 95–122.

Bennett, Clinton (1995) 'New spiritualities: Islam and Muhammad Iqbal', paper presented at 'Modern spiritualities: An international debate' Conference March 1995, to be published in L. Brown, Hoffmann, Joseph R. and Farr, Bernard C. (eds) *Modern Spiritualities*, New York, Prometheus Books.

Benthall, Jonathan (1995) 'Missionaries and human rights', *Anthropology Today*, vol.11, no.1, pp. 1–3.

Berlin, Isaiah (1956) *The Age of Enlightenment*, New York, Mentor.

Boas, Franz (1938; ed. 1963) *The Mind of Primitive Man*, New York, The Free Press.

Bottomore, T.B. and Rubel, Maximilian (1963) *Karl Marx: Selected Writings in Sociology and Philosophy*, London, C.A. Watts & Co.

Bowen, David G. (ed.) (1992) *The Satanic Verses: Bradford Responds*, Bradford, Bradford and Ilkley Community College.

Bowker, John (1983) *Worlds of Faith: Religious Belief and Practice in Britain Today*, London, BBC.

Braybrooke, Marcus (1992) *Pilgrimage of Hope: One Hundred Years of Global Interfaith Dialogue*, London, SCM.

Caplan, Patricia (1994) 'Cognitive descent, Islamic law and women's property on the East African coast', in Rene Hirschon (ed.) *Women and Property, Women as Property*, London, Croom Helm, pp. 23–43.

Capps, Walter H. (1995) *Religious Studies: The Making of a Discipline*, Minneapolis, Fortress Press.

Cheater, Angela (1986) *Social Anthropology: An Alternative Introduction*, London, Routledge.

Choudhury, Yousuf (1993) *The Roots and Tales of the Bangladeshi Settlers*, Birmingham, Sylheti Social History Group.

Church Missionary Intelligencer (1894) Review of William Muir's *Life of Mahomet*, vol. xlv, pp. 372–5.

Cobb, John B. and Ives, Christopher (eds) (1990) *The Emptying God: A Buddhist-Jewish-Christian Conversation*, Maryknoll, New York, Orbis.

Cole, Owen with Morgan, Peggy (1984) *Six Religions in the Twentieth Century*, London, Hulton.

Collier, Jane and Risoldo, Michelle (1981) 'Politics and gender in simple societies', in S. Ortner and H. Whitehead (eds) *Sexual Meanings*, Cambridge, CUP, pp. 275–329.

Cox, Harvey (1988) *Many Mansions: A Christian's Encounter with Other Faiths*, London, Collins.

Cox, James L. (1992) *Expressing the Sacred: An Introduction to the Phenomenology of Religion*, Harare, University of Zimbabwe.

Cracknell, Kenneth (1995) *Justice, Courtesy and Love: Theologians and Missionaries Encountering World Religions, 1846–1914*, London, Epworth.

Cragg, Kenneth (1956; rev. 1986) *The Call of the Minaret*, London, Collins.

Cross, F.L. and Livingstone, E.A. (eds) (1983) *The Oxford Dictionary of the Christian Church*, Oxford, OUP.

Cunliffe-Jones, Hubert (1970) *Christian Theology Since 1600*, London, Duckworth.

Currah, Sajdah (1994) 'Muslim, Young, Pakistani, Female ... and in Britain', in *Meeting Muslims*, Leicester, Christians Aware, pp. 52–3.

Darwin, Charles (1858) *On the Origin of Species*, London, John Murray.

Davids, Thomas W. Rhys (1878; 1894) *Buddhism*, London, SPCK.

Davids, Thomas W. Rhys (1880) *Buddhist Birth Stories*, London, Pali Text Society.

Davids, Thomas W. Rhys (1899a) *Dialogues of the Buddha*, London, Pali Text Society.

Davids, Thomas W. Rhys (1899b) *Digha Nikaya*, London, Pali Text Society.

Davidson, Basil (1987) *The Story of Africa*, London, Mitchell Beazley.

Dawkins, Richard (1994) 'God in a test-tube', *The Guardian*, August 8.

De Lange, Nicholas (1986) *Judaism*, Oxford, OUP.

Dictionary of National Biography (from 1921), Oxford, OUP.

Douglas, Mary (1966; 1991 edn) *Purity and Danger: An Analysis of the Concepts of Pollution and Taboo*, London, Routledge.

Douglas, Mary (1970) *Natural Symbols*, Harmondsworth, Penguin.

Douglas, Mary (1975) *Implicit Meanings*, London, Routledge.

Douglas, Mary (1987) *How Institutions Think*, London, Routledge.

Douglas, Mary (1992) *Risk and Blame: Essays in Cultural Theory*, London, Routledge.

Douglas, Mary (1993) *In the Wilderness: Doctrine of Defilement in the Book of Numbers*, Sheffield, JSOT Press.

Drury, Nevill (1989) *The Elements of Shamanism*, Shaftesbury, Element Books.

Durkheim, Emile (1912; trans. 1915) *The Elementary Forms of the Religious Life*, London, George Allen and Unwin.

Durkheim, Emile and Mauss, Marcel (1903; trans. 1963) *Primitive Classification*, Chicago, University Press.

Eck, Diana L. (1993) *Encountering God: A Spiritual Journey from Bozeman to Banaras*, Boston, Beacon.

El-Guindi, Fadwa (1995) 'Voice of Islam, experience of Muslims: The television series' *Anthropology Today*, vol. 11, no. 1, pp. 24–6.

Eliade, Mircea (1958) *Patterns in Comparative Religion*, London, Sheed and Ward.

Eliade, Mircea (1959) *The Sacred and the Profane*, New York, Harcourt, Brace.

Eliade, Mircea (1969) *The Quest: History and Meaning in Religion*, Chicago, University Press.

Eliade, Mircea (ed.) (1987) *The Encyclopedia of Religion*, New York, Macmillan.

Eliot, Sir Charles (1921) *Hinduism and Buddhism*, London, Arnold.

El-Solh, Camillia Fawzi and Mabro, Judy (1994) *Muslim Women's Choices: Religious Belief and Social Reality*, Oxford, Berg.

Esposito, John L. (1988; 1991 edn) *Islam: The Straight Path*, Oxford, OUP.

Esposito, John L. (1992) *The Islamic Threat: Myth or Reality?*, Oxford, OUP.

Evans-Pritchard, E.E. (1946) 'Applied anthropology', in *Africa: Journal of the International African Institute*, vol. 16, pp. 8–15.

Evans-Pritchard, E.E. (1961) *Anthropology and History*, Manchester, MUP.

Evans-Pritchard, E.E. (1965) *Theories of Primitive Religion*, Oxford, OUP.

Feuerbach, Ludwig A. (1841) *The Essence of Christianity*, New York, Harper.

Flood, Gavin (1994) 'Hinduism', in Jean Holm with John Bowker (eds), *Making Moral Decisions*, London, Pinter, pp. 66–94.

Foucault, Michel (1961; 1990) *Madness and Civilization*, London, Routledge.

Foucault, Michel (1972) *The Archeology of Knowledge*, London, Tavistock Books.

Foucault, Michel (1973) *The Birth of the Clinic*, London, Allen Lane.

Foucault, Michel (1976; trans. 1978) *History of Sexuality*, vol. 1, London, Allen Lane.

Foucault, Michel (1979) *Discipline and Punish: The Birth of the Prison*, London, Allen Lane.

Fowler, Don D. and Hardesty, Donald L. (1994) *Others Knowing Others: Perspectives on Ethnographic Careers*, Washington, Smithsonian.

Fowler, James W. (1981) *Stages of Faith: The Psychology of Human Development and the Quest for Meaning*, New York, Harper and Row.

Fraser, Robert (1994) 'Introduction', in *The Golden Bough*, London, OUP, pp. x–xlix.

Frazer, James George (1926) *The Worship of Nature*. Edinburgh, Gifford Lectures.

Frazer, James George (new abridged edn 1994) *The Golden Bough*, London, OUP.

Freeman, Derek (1983) *Margaret Mead and Samoa: The Making and Unmasking of an Anthropological Myth*, Cambridge, Harvard University Press.

Freud, Sigmund (1913, trans. 1938) *Totem and Taboo: Resemblances between the Psychic Lives of Savages and Neurotics*, London, George Routledge & Sons.

Geertz, Clifford (1960) *The Religion of Java*, New York, The Free Press.

Geertz, Clifford (1968) *Islam Observed: Religious Development in Morocco and Indonesia*, Chicago, The University Press.

Geertz, Clifford (1973) *The Interpretation of Cultures*, New York, Basic Books.

Geertz, Clifford (1983) *Local Knowledge*, New York, Basic Books.

Geertz, Clifford, (1988) *Works and Lives: The Anthropologist as Author*, Stanford, Stanford University Press.

Geertz, Clifford (1995) *After the Fact: Two Countries, Four Decades, One Anthropologist*, Cambridge, Harvard University Press.

Gellner, Ernest (1981) *Muslim Societies*, Cambridge, CUP.

Gibb, Hamilton (1949; 3rd edn 1978) *Mohammedanism: An Historical Survey*, Oxford, OUP.

Gilsenan, Michael (1990) *Recognising Islam: Religion and Society in the Modern Middle East*, London, Tauris.

Gombrich, Richard (1971) *Precept and Practice: Traditional Buddhism in the Rural Highlands of Ceylon*, Oxford, OUP.

Gombrich, Richard (1988) *Thervada Buddhism*, London, Routledge.

Haddon, Alfred C. (1934) *History of Anthropology*, London, Watts & Co.

Hammersley, Martyn and Atkinson, Paul (1995 edn) *Ethnography: Principles in Practice*, London, Routledge.

Harris, Elizabeth (1993) *Crises, Competition and Conversion: The British Encounter with Buddhism in Nineteenth-Century Sri Lanka*, (unpublished PhD thesis), Postgraduate Institute of Pali and Buddhist Studies, Sri Lanka.

Hawkey, Ian (1995) 'Ambassador for Islam', *CAM: The University of Cambridge Alumni Magazine 1995*, pp. 16–17.

Heiler, Joseph (1959) 'The history of religions as a preparation for the co-operation of religions' in M. Eliade and Joseph Kitagawa (eds) *The History of Religions: Essays on Methodology*, Chicago, University of Chicago Press, pp. 132–60.

Heiler, Joseph (1960) 'The history of religions as a way to unity of religions', in *Proceedings of the XIth International Congress for the History of Religions, Tokyo and Kyoto*, ISHR, pp. 7–22.

Herskovits, Melville J. (1963) 'Foreword', in Boas, F. *The Mind of Primitive Man*, New York, The Free Press, pp. 5–12.

Hick, John (1994) 'Christianity among the religions of the world', *Discernment*, NS vol. 1, no. 3, pp. 11–24.

Hinnells, John (ed.) (1984) *A Handbook of Living Religions*, Harmondsworth, Penguin.

Hinnells, John (ed.) (1984) *The Penguin Dictionary of Religions*, Harmondsworth, Penguin.

Hobbes, Thomas (1651; 1914 edn) *Leviathan*, pt 1, London, J.M. Dent & Sons.

Hocking, William Ernest (ed.) (1932) *Re-thinking Missions*, New York, Harper.

Holm, Jean with Bowker, John (n.d.) Editors' instructions to contributors in Themes in Religious Studies Series.

Holm, Jean with Bowker, John (1994) *Picturing God*, London, Pinter.

Hong, Keelung (1994) 'Experiences of being a "native" while observing anthropology', *RAIN*, vol. 10, no. 3, pp. 6–9.

Hopkins, E.W. (1896) *The Religions of India*, London, Arnold.

Hourani, Albert (1991) *Islam in European Thought*, Cambridge, CUP.

Hughes, Edward J. (1986) *Wilfred Cantwell Smith: A Theology for the World*, London, SCM.

Hughes, H.J. (1958) *Consciousness and Society*, New York, Random House.

James, E.O. (1968) *Christianity and Other Religions*, London, Hodder & Stoughton.

Johnson, Anne Janette (1992) 'Clifford Geertz', in (ed.) James G. Lesniak *Contemporary Authors*, New Revised Series, vol. 36, Michigan, Gale Research, pp. 148–50.

Jordan, Glenn and Weedon, Chris (1995) *Cultural Politics: Class, Gender, Race and the Postmodern World*, Oxford, Basil Blackwell.

Kaur-Singh, Kanwaljit (1994) 'Sikhism', in Jean Holm with John Bowker (eds) *Women in Religion*, London, Pinter, pp. 141–57.

Kitagawa, Joseph (1959) 'The history of religions in America', in M. Eliade and J. Kitagawa, *The History of Religions: Essays in Methodology*, Chicago, University Press, pp. 1–30.

Kitagawa, Joseph (1987) 'Mircea Eliade', in M. Eliade (ed.) *Encyclopaedia of Religion*, vol. 5, pp. 85–90.

Knight, Chris and Maisels, Charles (1994) 'An instinct for revolution', *RAIN*, vol. 10, no. 6, pp. 22–22.

Knott, Kim (1994) 'Arti in a Leeds temple', in Wolffe, John (ed.) *The Growth of Religious Diversity*, London, Hodder and Stoughton, pp. 79–84.

Kraemer, Hendrik (1938) *The Christian Message in a Non-Christian World*, London, Edinburgh House.

Kraemer, Hendrik (1956) *Religion and the Christian Faith*, London, Lutterworth.

Küng, Hans (1984) *Christianity and the World Religions*, London, SCM.

Kuper, Adam (1973; rev. 1987) *Anthropology and Anthropologists: The Modern British School*, London, Routledge.

Kuper, Adam (1988) *The Invention of Primitive Society: Transformations of an Illusion*, London, Routledge.

Kuper, Adam (1994) 'Culture, identity and the project of a cosmopolitan anthropology', *Man*, NS vol. 29, no. 3, pp. 537–54.

Lang, Andrew (1898) *The Making of Religion*, London, Longmans & Co.

Lang, Andrew (1901) *Magic and Religion*, London, Longmans & Co.

Latham, Robert Gordon (1854) *Natural History of the Varieties of Man*, London, Orr's Circle of the Sciences.

Latourette, Kenneth Scott (rev. edn 1975) *A History of Christianity* (2 vols), New York, Harper and Row.

Leach, Edmund R. (1958) 'Magical hair', *MAN*, vol. 88, pp. 147–64.

Leach, Edmund R. (1962) 'Pulleyar and the Lord Buddha: An aspect of religious syncretism in Ceylon', *Psychoanalysis and the Psychoanalytic Review*, vol. 49, no. 2, pp. 80–102.

Leach, Edmund R. (1970) *Levi-Strauss*, London, Fontana.

Leach, Edmund R. (1988) *Social Anthropology*, London, Fontana.

Leacock, Eleanor (1978) 'Women's status in egalitarian societies', *Current Anthropology*, vol. 19, no. 2, pp. 247–75.

Leeuw, G. van der (1933, trans. 1938) *Religion in Essence and Manifestation*, New York, Harper and Row.

Leeuw, G. van der (1954) 'Confession Scientifique', *NUMEN*, vol. 1, Leiden, E.J. Brill, pp. 8–15..

Lessa, William A. and Vogt, Evon Z. (1965) *A Reader in Comparative Religion: An Anthropological Approach*, New York, Harper and Row.

Levi-Strauss, Claude (1945) *The Elementary Structures of Kinship*, London, Eyre & Spottiswoode.

Levi-Strauss, Claude (1955) *Tristes Tropiques*, Harmondsworth, Penguin.

Levi-Stauss, Claude (1959, trans. 1963) *Structural Anthropology* (vol. 1), Harmondsworth, Penguin.

Levi-Strauss, Claude (1966) *Savage Mind*, London, Weidenfeld & Nicolson.

Lewis, I.M. (2nd edn 1992) *Social Anthropology in Perspective*, Cambridge, CUP.

Lewis, Philip (1994) *Islamic Britain: Religion, Politics and Identity among British Muslims*, London, I.B. Tauris.

Lindholm, Cherry and Lindholm, Charles (1993) 'Life behind the veil', in P. Whitten and D.E.K. Hunter (eds) *Anthropology: Contemporary Perspectives*, New York, Harper Collins College Publishers, pp. 231–4.

Ling, Trevor (1968) *A History of Religions East and West*, London, Macmillan.

Lipner, Julius (1983) 'Theology and religious studies', *Theology*, no. 86, pp. 193–201.

MacDonald, B. and Norris, M. (1981) *Looking Up for a Change: Political Horizons in Policy Evaluation*, Norwich, Centre for Applied Research in Education.

Majumdar, R.C. (1951–69) *History and Culture of the Indian People*, Bombay, Bharitiya Vidya Bhavan.

Malinowski, Bronislaw (1938) *Methods of Study of Culture in Africa*, London, International African Institute.

Malinowski, Bronislaw (1944) *A Scientific Theory of Culture and Other Essays*, Chapel Hill, University of North Carolina Press.

Malinowski, Bronislaw (1948) *Magic, Science and Religion and Other Essays*, New York, Doubleday Anchor.

Malinowski, Bronislaw (1967) *A Diary in the Strict Sense of the Word*, London, Routledge.

Margoliouth, William (1911) *Mohammedanism*, London, William & Norgate.

Marriott, McKim (1977) 'Hindu transactions, diversity without dualism', in Kapferer, Brian (ed.) *Transactions and Meaning*, Philadelphia, Institute for the Study of Human Issues.

Mead, Margaret (1928) *Coming of Age in Samoa*, New York, Morrow.

Mead, Margaret (1935) *Sex and Temperament in Three Primitive Societies*, London, George Routledge & Sons.

Mead, Margaret (1950) *Male and Female*, London, Victor Gollancz.

Mernissi, Fatima (1987) *Women and Islam: An Historical and Theological Enquiry*, Oxford, Basil Blackwell.

Mernissi, Fatima (1993) *The Forgotten Queens of Islam*, Cambridge, Polity.

Mitri, Tarek (ed.) (1995) *Religion, Law and Society: A Christian–Muslim Discussion*, Geneva, World Council of Churches and Kamen, Kok Pharos Publications.

Moore, Henrietta L. (1988) *Feminism and Anthropology*, Cambridge, Polity.

Morgan, D.O. (1994) Review of J. Esposito's 'Islam: The Straight Path', *Journal of the Royal Asiatic Society*, 3rd series, vol. 4, part 3, p. 406.

Morgan, Peggy (1995) 'The study of religions and interfaith encounter', in *NUMEN*, vol. 42, Leiden, E.J. Brill, pp. 156–71.

Morris, Brian (1987) *Anthropological Studies in Religion: An Introductory Text*, Cambridge, CUP.

Muir, William (1894) *Life of Mahomet* (abridged), London, Smith, Elder & Co.

Muir, William (1891; 3rd edn 1899) *The Caliphate: Its Rise, Decline and Fall*, London, Smith, Elder & Co.

Muir, William (1858–60) *Life of Mahomet* (3 vols), London, Smith, Elder & Co.

Müller, F. Max (1860) *A History of Ancient Sanskrit*, London, Longmans & Co.

Müller, F. Max (1867–75; rev. edn 1894) *Chips from a German Workshop*, London, Longmans & Co.

Müller, F. Max (1870) *Lectures on the Science of Religion*, London, Longmans & Co.

Müller, F. Max (1873; 1882) *Introduction to the Science of Religion*, London, Longmans & Co.

Müller, F. Max (1892) *Anthropological Religion*, London, Longmans & Co.

Müller, F. Max (1902) *Life and Letters*, G.A. Muller (ed.) London, Longmans & Co.

Neuman, Lawrence W. (1994) *Social Research Methods: Qualitative and Quantitative Approaches*, Boston, Allyn and Bacon.

Neusner, Jacob (1979) *Stranger at Home: The Task of Religious Studies*, Tempe, Arizona University.

Nicholson, Reynold A. (1914; 1975 edn) *The Mystics of Islam*, London, George Bell; Routledge.

Ottenberg, Stephen (1994) 'Changes over time in an African culture and in an anthropologist', in D.D. Fowler and D.L. Hardesty, (eds) *Others Knowing Others*, Washington, Smithsonian, pp. 91–118.

Otto, Rudolf (1917) *The Idea of the Holy*, trans. Harvey, John W. (1923), Harmondsworth, Penguin (1959).

Pace, David (1983) *Claude Levi-Strauss: The Bearer of Ashes*, London, Ark.

Parkin, Frank (1992) *Durkheim*, Oxford, OUP.

Parrinder, Geoffrey (1964) *The World's Living Religions*, London, Pan Piper.

Parrinder, Geoffrey (1965, 1995) *Jesus in the Qur'an*. Oxford, Oneworld.

Payne, Ernest A. (1933) *The Saktas: An Introductory and Comparative Study*, London, OUP.

Pickering, W.S.F. (ed.) (1992) 'Anthropology and missionaries', *Journal of the Society of Anthropologists of Oxford*, vol. xxiii, no. 2.

Radcliffe-Brown, Alfred Reginald (1952) *Structure and Function in Primitive Society*, London, Cohen & West.

Reader, Ian (1994) 'Japanese religions', in Jean Holm with John Bowker (eds) *Rites of Passage*, London, Pinter, pp. 169–83.

Rogers, Carl (1961) *On Becoming a Person*, London, Constable.

Rogers, Carl (1980) *A Way of Being*, Boston, Houghton Miffin & Co.

Rogers, Carl (1980) 'Growing old – or older and growing', in *Journal of Humanistic Psychology*, vol. 20, no. 4, pp. 5–16.

Ross, Walter W. (1992) 'Clifford Geertz' (interview) in James W. Lesniak (ed.) *Contemporary Authors*, New Revised Series, vol. 36, Michigan, Gale Research, pp.150–54.

Ruthven, Malise (1990) *A Satanic Affair*, London, Chatto and Windus.

Sa'id, Edward (1978) *Orientalism*, Harmondsworth, Penguin.

Sass, Louis A. (1993) 'Anthropology's native problems', in P. Whitten and D.E.K. Hunter (eds) *Anthropology: Contemporary Perspectives*, New York, Harper Collins College Publishers, pp. 9–17.

Schleiermacher, Friedrich (1799, trans. 1958) *On Religion, Speeches to its Cultured Despisers*, New York, Harper and Row.

Seymour-Smith, Charlotte (1986) *Macmillan Dictionary of Anthropology*, London, Macmillan.

Shahrani, M. Nazif (1994) 'Honored guest and marginal man: long-term field research and predicaments of a native anthropologist', in D.D. Fowler and D.L. Hardesty (eds) *Others Knowing Others: Perspectives on Ethnographic Careers*, Washington, Smithsonian Institution Press, pp. 15–67.

Shapiro, Judith (1981) 'Anthropology and the study of gender' in E. Langland and W. Grove (eds) *A Feminist Perspective in the Academy*, Chicago, University Press, pp. 110–29.

Sharpe, Eric J. (1983) *Understanding Religion*, London, Duckworth.

Sharpe, Eric J. (2nd edn 1986) *Comparative Religion: A History*, London, Duckworth.

Shourie, Arun (1994) *Missionaries in India: Continuities, Changes, Dilemmas*, New Delhi, ASA Publications.

Sills, David L. (ed.) (1968) *International Encyclopedia of the Social Sciences*, New York, The Free Press.

Simons, Helen (1989) 'Ethics of case study in educational research and evaluation', in R.G. Burgess (ed.) *The Ethics of Educational Research*, London, Falmer, pp. 114–38.

Smart, Ninian (1983) *Worldviews*, New York, Scribner.

Smart, Ninian, (1984) 'The scientific study of religions in its plurality', Frank Whaling (ed.) *Contemporary Approaches to the Study of Religions*, vol. 1, The Hague, Mouton, pp. 365–78.

Smith, L. M. (1980) 'Some not so random thoughts on doing fieldwork', in H. Simons (ed.) *Towards a Science of the Singular*, Norwich, Centre for Applied Research in Education.

Smith, Wilfred Cantwell (1943) *Modern Islam in India: A Social Analysis*, Lahore, Minerva.

Smith, Wilfred Cantwell (1950) *The Comparative Study of Religion: An Inaugural Lecture*, Montreal, McGill University.

Smith, Wilfred Cantwell (1957) *Islam in Modern History*, New York, Mentor.

Smith, Wilfred Cantwell (1959) 'Comparative religion: Whither and why?' in M. Eliade and Joseph Kitagawa (eds) *The History of Religions: Essays on Methodology*, Chicago, University of Chicago Press.

Smith, Wilfred Cantwell, (1963) *The Meaning and End of Religion: A New Approach to the Religious Traditions of Mankind*, New York, Macmillan.

Smith, Wilfred Cantwell (1967) *Questions of Religious Truth*, New York, Scribner.

Smith, Wilfred Cantwell, (1981) *Towards a World Theology*, Philadelphia, Westminster Press.

Smith, Wilfred Cantwell (1988) 'Mission, dialogue and God's will for us', *International Review of Mission*, vol. lxxviii, no. 307, pp. 360–74.

Smith, Wilfred Cantwell (1993) *What Is Scripture?*, London, SCM.

Smith, William Robertson (1885) *Kinship and Marriage in Early Arabia*, Cambridge, CUP.

Smith, William Robertson (1889; 1927 edn) *The Religion of the Semites*, London, A & G Black.

Spencer, Herbert (1851; 1954 edn) *Social Statistics*, London, Routledge.

Spencer, Herbert (1855) *The Principles of Psychology*, New York, Appleton.

Spencer, Herbert (1877) *The Principles of Sociology*, New York, Appleton.

Sperber, Dan (1979) 'Claude Levi-Strauss', in John Sturrock (ed.) *Structuralism and Since*, Oxford, OUP, pp. 19–51.

Steiner, George (1966) 'A conversation with Claude Levi-Strauss' *Encounter*, vol. xxvi, no. 4, pp. 32–8.

Swider, L., Cobb, J.B., Knitter, P., Hellwig, M.K. (1990) *Death or Dialogue? From the Age of Monologue to the Age of Dialogue*, London, SCM.

Tambiah, Stanley J. (1990) *Magic, Science, Religion and the Scope of Rationality*, Cambridge, CUP.

Tillich, Paul (1953) *Systematic Theology*, London, Nisbett.

Tisdall, William St-Claire (1901) *India: Its History, Darkness and Dawn*, London, Student Volunteer Missionary Society.

Tisdall, William St-Clair (1909) *Comparative Religion*, London, Longmans & Co.

Trompf, Garry (1990) *In Search of Origins*, New Delhi, Sterling.

Tylor, E.B. (1861) *Anahuc, or Mexico and the Mexicans, Ancient and Modern*, London, Longmans & Co.

Tylor, E.B. (1865) *Researches into the Early History of Mankind*, London, John Murray.

Tylor, E.B. (1871) *Primitive Culture* (2 vols), London, John Murray.

Vrijhof, Pieter H. and Waardenburg, Jacques (ed.) (1979) *Official and Popular Religion: Analysis of a Theme for Religious Studies*, The Hague, Mouton.

Waardenburg, Jacques (1973) *Classical Approaches to the Study of Religion*, (2 volumes), The Hague, Mouton.

Waardenburg, Jacques (1978) *Reflections on the Study of Religion*, The Hague, Mouton.

Wach, Joachim (1944) *Sociology of Religion*, London, Kegan Paul, Trench, Trubner and Co.

Watson, James L. (ed.) (1977) *Between Two Cultures: Migrants and Minorities in Britain*, Oxford, Basil Blackwell.

Weightman, Simon (1984) 'Hinduism', in John Hinnells (ed.) *A Handbook of Living Religions*, Harmondsworth, Penguin, pp. 191–236.

Weiner, Annette (1976) *Women of Value, Men of Renown*, Austin, University of Texas Press.

Werblowsky, R.J.Z. (1959) 'The comparative study of religions: A review essay' in *Judaism*, vol. 8.

Whaling, Frank (1984a) *Contemporary Approaches to the Study of Religions: The Humanities* (vol.1), Berlin, Mouton.

Whaling, Frank (ed.) (1984b) *The World's Religious Traditions*, Edinburgh, T&T Clark.

Whaling, Frank (1986) *Christian Theology and World Religions: A Global Approach*, London, Marshall, Morgan and Scott.

White, Haydon (1979) 'Michel Foucault', in John Sturrock (ed.) *Structuralism and Since*, Oxford, OUP, pp. 81–115.

Whitten, Phillip and Hunter, David (eds) (1993) *Anthropology: Contemporary Perspectives*, New York, Harper Collins College Publishers.

Willis, Roy (1975) Review of Adam Kuper's *Anthropology and Anthropologists*, *MAN*, vol. 10, no. 3, September 1975, pp. 490–91.

Wollfe, John (ed.) (1994) *The Growth of Religious Diversity: Britain from 1945 – A Reader*, London, Hodder and Stoughton.

Wood, Heather (1980) *Third-class Ticket*, Harmondsworth, Penguin.

Wood, John G. (1868; 1870) *Natural History of Man*, London, G. Routledge and Sons.

World Council of Churches (1990 edn) *Guidelines on Dialogue*, Geneva, WCC.

World Council of Churches (1992) *Issues in Christian–Muslims Relations: Some Ecumenical Considerations*, Geneva, WCC.

Zaehner, R.C. (1974) *Our Savage God*, London, Collins.

Zakaria, Rafiq (1988) *The Struggle within Islam: The Conflict between Religion and Politics*, Harmondsworth, Penguin.

Index